Legacy of the

Sacred Harp

A singer takes her turn in the center to lead a song at the William J. Reynolds Sacred Harp Singing Convention at Southwestern Baptist Theological Seminary in Fort Worth in January, 2006. (Photo by Joshua Martin.)

Legacy of the
Sacred Harp

Chloe Webb

TCU Press
Fort Worth, Texas

Library of Congress Cataloging-in-Publication Data

Webb, Chloe, 1937-
Legacy of the sacred harp / Chloe Webb. -- 1st ed.
p. cm.
Includes bibliographical references and index.
ISBN 978-0-87565-416-4 (pbk. : alk. paper)
1. Dumas family. 2. Webb, Chloe, 1937---Family.
3. Webb, Chloe, 1937---Travel--Southern States. I. Title.
CS71.D8813 2010
975'.04092--dc22
[B]
2010004051

TCU Press
P. O. Box 298300
Fort Worth, Texas 76129
817.257.7822
http://www.prs.tcu.edu
To order books: 800.826.8911

Designed by Vicki Whistler

Cover: Natalie Davis and Corissa Sweatt lead a song at the 2006 National
Sacred Harp Singing Convention in Birmingham, Alabama.
Music notation in background:
"New Britain" ("Amazing Grace") #45 in
The Sacred Harp, 1869 edition,
credited to Baptist Harmony, p.123

for all grandchildren

CONTENTS

PREFACE

—■—

Grandma could easily have left her old Sacred Harp songbook to any of her other grandchildren. I've wondered if she even gave a thought to what might become of the book, or if in her heart she knew what a treasure it would become to me. One might say it just happened; she just handed the tattered book to the nearest outstretched hands.

At first, I knew nothing about the ancient-looking music with strangely shaped notes. It seemed only a coincidence that I picked up a *Texas Highways* magazine that told about the long tradition of Sacred Harp singing. The "sacred harp" is not a harp at all, but the human voice. The name, *The Sacred Harp*, was chosen for a collection of hymn-like songs that has been in continual usage since its first publication in 1844. *The Sacred Harp* continued the American innovation of assigning identifying shapes to music note heads, making their position on the music staff more recognizable to singers—even illiterate singers—to sound out, or sight read, a tune.

The music is often called *fasola* or *solfège* music because of the syllables given to each note in an octave of music: Fa-So-La, Fa-So-La-Mi-Fa (which most of us know as: Do-Re-Mi-Fa-So-La-Ti-Do). The fasola system uses only four syllables and four shapes. Fa is a triangle; So, a circle; La, a square; and Mi, a diamond.

I later learned that fasola music is even older than the shape-notes that originated in New England in the early nineteenth century. However, I have not set out to define and encompass the music; rather, *Legacy of the Sacred Harp* is a family memoir through four hundred years of generations linked by the music. Fasola is the thread that binds their stories together.

I undertook this manuscript because I had an unexpected opportunity to delve deeper into intriguing family stories. I suspect most of us would like to know more about our connections to the past before all the experiences are forever lost. Perhaps we hope to find connections that will root us more firmly and help us better understand ourselves and others. I eventually found an unfathomable connectedness and a wider breadth of understanding that has helped me come to terms with the controversial issues one finds when exposing the roots of a family tree.

The steps in a genealogical search have been greatly simplified now that such a wealth of information is available on the Internet. Nevertheless, personal background can often be learned only by going to the place where ancestors lived. I was fortunate to have the opportunity to do so. Yet the information I learned in most cases would have been typical for anyone who lived in that time and place; these are anyone's ancestors. They journeyed through time and history, not always as leaders, but ever as participants, as were the ancestors of us all.

Perhaps your own ancestors tie into this cast of thousands at some point. Indeed, there is a suggestion of a loose thread in the early days of Jamestown that might, if the truth were known, reveal that any particular reader shares this bloodline.

The genealogy of my Dumas family had already been completed by the main author, John H. Wilson, with the enlisted assistance of Dr. John E. Manahan and Yvette Longstaff. Since then, Dr. Manahan's credibility had been irrevocably damaged in the Grand Duchess Anastasia scandal, when Anna Anderson convinced Dr. Manahan that she was the long lost daughter of Russian Tsar Nicholas II; Anna's claims were later proved false through DNA testing. Despite this disgrace, I found nothing to dispute Dr. Manahan's research regarding the Dumas genealogy.

The pursuit to retrace my family's journey began simply, with no formulated plan. I merely wanted to know more about what had happened in their time on Earth. Peeling away layer by layer, as in an archaeological excavation, the journey took me back in time four hundred years to the pivotal actions of an ancestor in the early days of the Jamestown settlement.

My search led from boxes of keepsakes and personal interviews—which I recorded on tape, like a reporter—to courthouses and their dusty annexes throughout the South, to innumerable libraries and archives, to small country churches and big city churches, to cemeteries, to cotton fields, to deserted Indian villages, and ultimately, to an authentic archaeological dig at the original fort in Jamestown, Virginia. It was at the church in the fort that an ancestor, Sir George Yeardley, as governor of the Virginia Colony, established in 1619 the first elected-representative government in the New World. Within thirty days of this historic event, this same man accepted a cargo of twenty starving Africans from a Dutch trading ship situated in Jamestown harbor and unwittingly set in motion the events that would lead to slavery in the English-speaking New World.

Though my journey began with a simple curiosity, I came to understand that I had become the living link with information to share; I'd been entrusted with their hard-earned lessons. When I learned that Yeardley's first legislature based the monetary standard on tobacco instead of gold, the contemporary irony of his actions long ago struck me to the heart; my own mother was dying of lung cancer. It became my mission to pass on to future generations such milestones that shaped once their lifestyles and now shape ours.

The search to know my family took me through emotional valleys so dark I could not see, but could only hear groans and cries of human misery. Even then, remembered Sacred Harp phrases reached out to soothe and console me. Marker messages left by others who had passed that way before urged me onward and pointed me to safety. I found connectedness in a bond with other singers, some who have now passed on, but whose spirits remain with me. The connectedness—this giving, sharing, caring for other humans—goes beyond the years, beyond death itself.

The music forms its own language that can be universally understood. Voices through the centuries revealed personal stories that were not for me alone. Unexplainable happenings have been described by realists as mere coincidences, and I've tried to downplay them as such, but I have become so emotionally attuned to the spiritual realm that I think a new word should be coined for surprising gifts that appear without asking. Regardless, whether from coincidence or a gift of providence, I've received an extraordinary blessing that is meant to be shared.

Because this is a memoir, I have not included footnotes one would find in an academic work. In order to assist any reader seeking further information regarding a subject I've discussed, I've included a bibliography organized in alphabetical order.

Legacy of the Sacred Harp describes the path of one family line, beginning with the most recent relations back through the past four hundred years. In looking back, we can appreciate how far we've come. Through my quest to know the generations of ancestors who have passed the music to me, I've discovered that their spirits still speak to us. Their stories are told in our shared music. Their Sacred Harp songs contain the fullness of their lives and their faith—their living legacy to me and to all of us.

The group of singers with whom I now sing every month includes a number of children, who are also active participants. A young woman, who grew up singing Sacred Harp, as did her parents and grandparents before her, brings her three-year-old daughter. The little girl steps confidently into the center of the square and leads with enthusiasm, throwing her head back for emphasis, like her mother does. In the beginning, the appeal for the children might be the rhythm or the strong beat, or perhaps it's the unaccustomed dignity of being accepted as equals with adults. Still, they are absorbing the inherent beauty and truth of the music and its poetry. Unknowingly, their souls are nourished with inner strength to draw upon when storms of life blow over them. The music continues.

ACKNOWLEDGMENTS

—■—

For their help with *Legacy of the Sacred Harp*, I am indebted to the following people and sources:

The genealogy book, *Dumas Families of Union Parish, Louisiana*, by John H. Wilson, Carine Dumas Nolan, and Lorena Craighead Dumas, which was published in 1979 by the Dumas Family Reunion. John H. Wilson's research, plus that of professional genealogists Dr. John E. Manahan and Yvette Longstaff, contributed needed information to publications by other branches of the family tree and furnished me with the names, dates, and places of my early family history.

Carine Dumas Nolan provided almost daily guidance and support during my research, and after her death, Carine's youngest sister, Melba Dumas Brashier, generously continued to share special knowledge of the family.

Four long lost, but now found, cousins—Mabel Crenshaw Goehe, Martha Dumas Abel, Faye Dumas Kimbrell, and Jo Rice—simplified the complex list of family members by agreeing to speak through one important composite character, the resulting cousin Barbara.

My immediate family kept me focused and motivated through the investigative process: my husband, Douglas Webb, who insisted that I continue on this historical path as far as it could lead me; my mother, Hettie Stradley, who overcame her hesitancies of disturbing long-buried issues and became entranced, like myself, with each new discovery; my son, Michael Arden, who devotedly provided technical support through numerous computer disasters; my brother, John Stradley, who grew steadily more involved with the unfolding story of a family Bible listed in an ancestor's estate and presented me with a similar, rare Geneva translation of the Bible, published in 1599.

My friend and fellow church choir soprano, Dr. Kay Norton, associate professor of music history at Arizona State University and author of a defining book on pre-Sacred Harp music, *Baptist Offspring, Southern Midwife, Jesse Mercer's Cluster of Spiritual Songs (1810): A Study in American Hymnody*, provided precision-focused insights and unfailing academic guidance. Kay Norton's mentor, C. Ray Brewster, author of *The Cluster of Jesse Mercer*, also shared his special knowledge with me.

I relied extensively on the scholarship and writings of Kiri Miller in her books *The Chattahoochee Musical Conventions, 1852-2002* and *Traveling Home, Sacred Harp Singings and American Pluralism*; on David W. Music's *I Will Sing the Wondrous Story, A History of Baptist Hymnody in North America*; and on Warren Steel's postings on www.Fasola.org and in email correspondence. Ian West directed me to superb websites for information in the United Kingdom, such as www.NationalArchives.gov.uk, where I obtained a copy of an ancestor's will dated 3 February 1625/6.

Innumerable singers generously shared their personal knowledge about Sacred Harp music: John Plunkett, a Sacred Harp scholar; Don Clark; Buell Cobb; Richard DeLong; Amanda Denson; Harry Eskew; Mike Hinton; Hugh McGraw; Richard Mauldin; David Music; Gaylon Powell; Donald Ross; and Robert Vaughn.

Joe Dan Boyd shared his research of Sacred Harp music in the black community and allowed me to use photographs from his book, *Judge Jackson and the Colored Sacred Harp*, published by Alabama Folklife Association.

Jason Runnels of Southwestern Baptist Theological Seminary gave able assistance with historically important music and rare books.

Margaret (Maggie) Leonard, a Tucson singer, read an early version of this manuscript, and her questions and comments helped clarify the story.

Esther Huckaby, long-time teacher at Texas Christian University and my dear friend, gave freely of her knowledge and heart while opening doors that were beyond my field of vision.

The Sacred Harp Publishing Company, publisher of *The Sacred Harp* 1991 edition, deserves special thanks for the music notation referenced in this text.

Judy Alter, then-director of TCU Press, saw promise in the manuscript I submitted, and the skillful expertise of the editorial and production staff, Susan Petty, Sarah Dombrowsky, and Melinda Esco, has brought the promise to fulfillment.

An unnamed reader, who read the manuscript twice, gave generous advice and encouragement that I greatly appreciate.

Finally, I am most grateful to my grandmother, Terry Louisa Dumas Nolan, who gave me her worn Sacred Harp songbook that began the long journey of *Legacy of the Sacred Harp* that has become for me, as it was for her, a joyful expression of life on an unending path.

CHRONOLOGY

—■—

Family Timeline

1844
JAMES FRANKLIN DUMAS born in Georgia;
ca. 1875 married Margaret Dacus in Louisiana

1817
JEREMIAH DUMAS born in Georgia;
September 13, 1839 married Irena Adams in Georgia

1783
BENJAMIN FRANKLIN DUMAS born in North Carolina;
ca.1805 married Martha Ussery in North Carolina

1756
BENJAMIN (III) DUMAS born in North Carolina;
ca.1780 married Susannah Hutchins(on)

1730
DAVID DUMAS born in Virginia;
ca.1750 married Sarah Moorman in Virginia

1705
BENJAMIN (I) DUMAS born in Virginia;
ca.1730 married Frances Clark in Virginia

c. 1680
UNITY SMITH DUMAS born in Virginia;
ca. 1702 married Jerome Dumas, a Huguenot refugee, in Virginia

c. 1660
MARY WHITE SMITH born in Virginia;
married George Smith in Virginia

c. 1640
MARY CROSHAW WHITE born in Virginia;
married Henry White in Virginia

1619
ELIZABETH YEARDLEY CROSHAW born in Virginia;
married Joseph Croshaw, son of Captain Raleigh Croshaw, in Virginia

1588
LADY TEMPERANCE FLOWERDEW YEARDLEY born in England,
1618 married Sir George Yeardley, governor of Virginia Colony,
in London

PART ONE

———————————————■———————————————

THE CIVIL WAR GENERATIONS

Union Primitive Baptist Church was organized in 1837 in Monroe
County, Georgia. Benjamin Franklin Dumas (1783-1852) donated
five acres of land for the church. His son, Edmund Dumas,
a shape note music composer, was the pastor.

THE CIVIL WAR GENERATIONS

1844
JAMES FRANKLIN DUMAS born in Georgia;
moved as a small child to Louisiana with his parents;
ca. 1875 married Margaret Dacus in Louisiana
Children: Ida, Martha, Jennie, Terry Louisa, Jeremiah, Nettie,
William Augustus, Julia, Maggie (Frankie)

1817
JEREMIAH DUMAS born in Georgia;
September 13, 1839 married Irena Adams in Georgia;
ca. 1847 they moved their family to Louisiana
Children: William Adam, Benjamin Covington, Sidney Moses,
James Franklin, John Thomas, Monroe, Jeremiah, Stacia

1783
BENJAMIN FRANKLIN DUMAS born in North Carolina;
ca.1805 married Martha Ussery in North Carolina; by 1817
they had moved their family to Georgia
Children: Edmund, Uriah, Thomas, Sarah, Frances,
Susan Elizabeth, Jeremiah, Aaron David, Eugene Nehemiah,
Moses, Nancy, Benjamin Covington.

CHAPTER 1

The Sacred Harp

IN a dentist's waiting room, I turned through pages of the August 1987 issue of *Texas Highways* and a photograph caught my eye. Aged hands held a book of music with oddly shaped notes. The article's headline read, "Sacred Harp, a Tradition Lives." The unusual music looked curiously familiar and the out-of-date print of the book's title page called to mind a music book Grandma had given me. This much-used book, *The Sacred Harp*, had belonged to her father, and earlier, to her grandfather, whose brother, Edmund Dumas, had written a number of its songs. The passed-down book was so worn that most of the cover was missing, the pages were yellowed, and the frayed binding threads were rotten. But I could never have thrown it away. I thought perhaps I could find Grandma's copy of *The Sacred Harp* in a collection of sheet music and songbooks at my home.

I realized with surprise that Grandma had been dead over a decade now, yet I felt her presence as near as the person in the next chair. I could hear the familiar timbre of her singing voice; she'd said her father and grandfather played the fiddle, but she just sang. Oh, how Grandma loved to sing.

On one summer afternoon during our family's annual visit to Louisiana, I sat next to Grandma in the glider on the porch, helping her shell peas. Suddenly, she burst out loudly, "I'll sing halle-lu-jah, and you'll sing halle-lu-jah, and we'll all sing halle-lu-jah, when we arrive at home!" Her foot tapped a lively beat, and, when a hand was occasionally free, she gestured her arm to the rhythm in an emphatic up-down motion.

"Chloe Ann, you're a good little singer. You ought to stay and go with me to one of our singing schools. All we do is sing, all day long—except to eat, which is almost as important. Everybody brings a dish for dinner on the ground. It never fails that it's a real feast. We'll try to talk your folks into letting you stay on a while longer when they go back to Texas. The next one's going to be at Rocky Branch Church up by Antioch. It'll be a real rafter-shaker."

It was easy to see that Grandma loved those folksy, hymn-like tunes, but I was skeptical; I'd never heard anyone sing like she did. There seemed to be no melody. I didn't want to hurt her feelings, but I was convinced Grandma couldn't carry a tune and those singing schools weren't doing her any good whatsoever. Still, I was thrilled to have her Sacred Harp songbook because anything Grandma loved was precious to me as well.

A page in the book held a glimpse into the budding romance of my grandparents. I pictured the young Burch Nolan taking Grandma's book at a singing and penciling his words to her above the song "Fillmore" #434 in *The Sacred Harp*. From the hurried look of his writing, she'd struggled playfully to get it back, but she must have been pleased for she never erased his bold message: "Miss Terry Dumas is my girl." Terry Louisa (pronounced Lou-eye-za) was his girl the rest of their lives.

A page in the Sacred Harp songbook that my grandmother bequeathed to me holds a glimpse into the budding romance of my grandparents. I picture the young Burch Nolan taking her book at a singing and penciling his words to her above one of the songs, "Miss Terry Dumas is my girl."

I'd made only slight attempts to play the music on the piano, because the strange three-line staff was unlike any music I'd ever seen. It was written with two lines of treble clef and one of bass, with note heads in a variety of shapes, not the familiar round notes. I concluded that the music was written exclusively for fiddle players. The magazine article, however, explained that Sacred Harp had nothing to do with any musical instrument. It was to be sung *a cappella*, for the *sacred harp* is the human voice.

The writer continued that Sacred Harp singing, called fasola or solfège music, originated in Elizabethan England and was brought to America by early colonists. Although they had no room on their ships for any but the smallest musical instruments, the colonists could always sing. The syllables Fa, So, La, and Mi together formed a simplified method to write down both new and well-known folk tunes. Churchmen later used this method to teach their uneducated parishioners to read music easily. An American innovation allowed for even easier music sight reading; recognizable shapes—triangles, circles, squares, or diamonds—were assigned to all music note heads, visually indicating the corresponding syllables—Fa, So, La, or Mi.

The magazine article told of the upcoming 119th Annual East Texas Sacred Harp Singing Convention to be held in Henderson, only a couple of hours from our family home in Dallas. The writer advised that the music was not performance music but instead could be better described as participatory. A long-time singer said he'd travel a hundred miles to sing the music, but he wouldn't cross the road to listen to it. "Uncle" Tom Denson, a Depression-era singing school master, cautioned readers, "If some of you folks don't like this Sacred Harp music, you'd better get out, 'cause if you stay here, it's going to get aholt of you and you can't get away."

My husband, Doug, had an early tee time at the golf course that particular Saturday, and Elise, the last child still at home, had nothing planned until evening, so early Saturday morning my daughter and I headed for Henderson down Interstate 20. At the end of the pleasant drive we reached the outskirts of the small town and, after asking directions three times, located the community center. A single space remained vacant near a tree at the edge of the large graveled parking area. As I stepped from the car, I heard a sound like nothing I'd ever heard.

I quickly glanced at Elise, and she rolled her eyes. "Weird."

The music had an eerie quality with a compellingly primal appeal, somewhere between bluegrass and a Gregorian chant. As we entered, a thunderous rolling chorus of voices reverberated off the hard surfaces of the large hall and washed our bodies with rhythmic vibrations, like being baptized in sound. Although it was new to me, it seemed I'd known the music before I was even born. We sat in two folding chairs near the door and settled to soak in the experience.

An elderly woman offered me a book marked "Loaner." The seating was arranged in four singing sections facing the center, forming a tight square with a hollow core. The singers sang not for an audience, but to each other. At the end of each song, a name was called for a new leader: "William Brown, who will be followed by John Doe." William then stepped to the center of the square, immediately raised his arm to give the downbeat, and got the song started. Then it was everyone for himself. One singer pitched the key, like the first violin playing the A at the symphony. However, this was not the standard A found on a pitch pipe, but a relative A that accommodated the vocal range of the singers.

The meaning of participatory music was readily apparent. With the exception of a few on the sidelines, each of the approximately three hundred people present sang loudly and enthusiastically. It was equally evident that auditions were not required. I struggled to understand the words until I realized that, on beginning a new song, they weren't singing words at all, but the syllables, Fa, So, or La. The four sections of voices weren't even singing the same syllables at the same time as they followed the music, yet the names of the strange shapes came easily to their tongues.

Only men sat in the bass section, women in the alto section, and both sang in the tenor and treble sections. Even small children were called to the center of the square; a child only five years old led one song with an assurance that rivaled the adults. Most of the singers were white, but a round of affectionate applause followed an aged black man as he hobbled, leaning heavily on a cane, to the center to lead. I later learned that he was Dewey Williams, who had been featured in a Bill Moyers PBS special about the universal appeal of the hymn "Amazing Grace."

"New Britain" ("Amazing Grace") # 45t in *The Sacred Harp*, 1869 revision. "New Britain" is on the same page and position in the 1991 revision.

I was unable to determine who was singing any particular line. In conventional choral music, the top line, typically soprano, ordinarily has the melody; here, there was no soprano. The top line was called treble, but the trebles didn't have the melody. I spotted a couple of vacant chairs in the section nearest us and indicated to Elise to move at the song break. After we took our seats in the tenor section, following the third line down, the singers began a number titled, "New Britain." "So-Fa La-Fa-La, So-Fa-La-So," they sang, and I recognized the tune of "Amazing Grace."

"We finally found the melody," I whispered.

My whisper carried farther than intended and, at the song's end, the woman seated next to Elise leaned forward to say, "Actually, no one section has the melody all the time. All the parts together are needed to form the complete sound. That's why we face the center. The center is where the sound converges. It's the very heart of the music. We change leaders when we change songs so everyone can have a chance to stand in the center and hear the full sound in its entirety."

It's like Mozart's description of opera, I realized—what God must hear when we make our individual and simultaneous petitions. I then understood why Grandma's songs had no obvious tunes; she sang only one part of the whole while hearing the other parts of a great choir in her head.

A mid-morning break was called to catch a breath and sip of water. The woman next to Elise leaned forward again, her book in hand, to give a few pointers for reading the shape-note tunes. "Fa is a triangle-shaped note, like a flag. Sol, or So, is round, like the sun. La is a square. Think of two adjoining *Ls*." She positioned her thumbs and forefingers into two right-angled *Ls*, forming a square. "The diamond shape is for Mi, which isn't used often. Think, 'diamonds are for me.'"

She explained that the syllables Fa, So, and La are repeated in ascending order and Mi becomes the seventh note in the full octave—Fa-So-La, Fa-So-La-Mi-Fa. "To play an octave on the piano, a pianist knows exactly how far to reach eight notes from the bottom Fa to the top Fa. In the same way, you'll learn to know the interval between the first two Fas—four notes up the scale, or a fourth interval. The same is true for the intervals between the two Sos and between the two Las. An easy way to remember how a fourth interval sounds is to think of a song like, 'The Eyes of Texas' or 'Here Comes the Bride.' The repetition of syllables might sound confusing at first, but you'll become accustomed to hearing the fourth intervals. That is extremely significant; because it will then become a marvelous tool to help you sight read any kind of music."

At lunchtime, singers greeted us from all sides, insisting that we join them, because socializing over food is almost as important to a Sacred Harp convention as the music. I took only small portions from the bountiful table, and yet my plate was brimming before I was halfway to the end.

I purchased a copy of the songbook the group was using and met Hugh McGraw, head of Sacred Harp Publishing Company, publisher of the latest edition. I showed Grandma's tune book to him, and he gingerly turned the pages. "I see these early editions from time to time," he said. "The old books tended to drop out of usage when newer versions with the latest compositions became available, but you could have used your family heirloom for many of the songs we sang this morning."

He explained that the front part of the book has remained basically the same since the first one in 1844, which had three lines for three-part singing. A fourth line for an alto part was added after *The Sacred Harp* was originally published. "This old book has obviously been to many a Sacred Harp singing. These occasions haven't changed much at all since the first one came out— other than the vehicle that brought 'em there, that is. They might have come in covered wagons; or more often, the wagon was uncovered, their version of a convertible with the top down."

Elise chose to sit in the rear of the hall when the singing resumed after lunch. "I'll follow along in the loaner book. Don't forget we're going to leave at the break. You promised."

"I'll keep my eye on the time." I wished I'd let her stay home. Her interest level was the same as my own at her age. But now, I didn't want the singing to end.

On our return drive to Dallas, Elise said she'd located some of the songs written in the nineteenth century by our relative Edmund Dumas. "The words are strange," she concluded. "I guess you could call them 'churchy.' One of his songs wouldn't go over today, even in church. No way. It says the wife is supposed to obey. I know I'll never agree to let some guy tell me what I can or can't do."

"I think it was a given back then. There was a pretty definite pecking order in families."

"Did Grandma have to obey?"

"I'm sure the phrase was in their marriage vows. But women have usually found their own power."

"The words of the song said the husband is commanded to love his wife, but it didn't say she had to love him," Elise said, sarcastically. "She just belonged to him, I guess, like a slave, who had to obey. But does he really love her if it's an order? What kind of relationship is that? I think everything should be fifty-fifty."

"Grandma used to say it had to be ninety-ten on both sides."

Elise paused. "I wonder what the songwriter's wife thought about it. Do you know anything about him? Personal, I mean, how he treated her?"

"Personal? Good grief, no. That was back before the Civil War."

"Well, under some of the songs there are bio notes about the composers," she said. "Maybe we could find out more… It says he lived in Monroe County, Georgia."

"Yes, Grandma's family was from Georgia. Her father was born there. Mother's cousin, Carine Dumas Nolan, might know something; she wrote the genealogy book about the family. We have a copy of her book at home and we can see what it says about him…but I'll warn you that, for the most part, it's just the facts and not much more. It has about as much plot as the dictionary."

"How did she find out about all that old stuff?"

"She worked with a relative from another branch of the family tree who'd written an earlier version. They contacted the best genealogists they could find and traced our ancestors to where they lived in France and England."

Carine, my mother's younger first cousin, was a member of the Colonial Dames and the Daughters of the American Revolution, organizations with requirements that every generation must be documented. She was also the family member who organized family reunions regularly. The reunion had been important to Grandma, yet I had never gone. Mother still spoke of wanting to drive to Louisiana for the annual event, though she could no longer see to drive that far. I thought of her now-persistent cough and guiltily reminded myself to spend time with her before it was too late.

Elise, reminiscing on her own memories of visiting Grandma, stated, "She must have been a natural-born comedian. Granny told me about the time her daddy was rushing to town and asked Grandma to sew a missing button on his pants, and she sewed on a great big red one."

"Oh, Grandpa enjoyed pulling a good prank, too. They could afford a good laugh even in the hard times, and times were plenty hard back in the Depression. The whole family worked in the field together—all of 'em, right along with the hands. The children worked, too."

"Yeah, Granny told me when she was a little girl, she had to hoe and pick cotton," Elise said, laughing. "One time, she made an excuse that she wasn't a good hoe-er, and her mama said there's no such thing as a good whore."

Grandma's language could be rather earthy, but she always managed to work in a moral.

"Did she ever tell you about Uncle Elzy?" I asked. "She made it clear he was on Grandpa's side of the family. Behind his back, she called him B. Elzy Bubba. He'd led a scandalous life, but he got his comeuppance when he died. While the mourners were on the way to the graveyard, the wagon caught fire and they had to pull the casket out to keep it from going up in flames. Grandma said the Devil was in a hurry to claim his due."

David Burch Nolan—"Grandpa," 1881-1944.

Terry Louisa Dumas Nolan, "Grandma," 1881-1975.

David Burch Nolan and Terry Louisa Dumas were married in Union Parish, Louisiana, on January 18, 1906.

"Was that real," Elise asked, "or was it another story she just made up?"

"Pulling the coffin from the fire was real. I can't say about Uncle Elzy's soul."

The highway was going through a small town, and we passed a school yard. "If the kids had to work in the fields," Elise said, "when did they go to school?"

"They didn't work in the fields all the time. But the harvest wouldn't wait. Everyone on all the farms had an indispensable job. School was closed for the duration. Everything revolved around getting the crops in. Grandma started making preparations back in the summer with home-canned food they grew on the farm. When harvest was over, they celebrated with a big all-day singing and a pot luck feast called dinner-on-the-ground."

"Did you ever get to help Grandma with the canning?"

I glared at her, because I wasn't that old. By the time I came along, Grandma no longer needed as much food stored on a day-to-day basis, and the kitchen was off-limits to children when she was canning, anyway. I didn't object because the canning device with gauges like huge eyes looked like an unearthly robot as it rattled and hissed ferociously.

"When I was older, we sometimes made mayonnaise (pronounced my-o-naise) with egg yolks fresh from the hen house. Grandma gave instructions for precision timing, explaining that only two people who see things heart to heart can make good mayonnaise together."

Elise was quiet for a moment, and then asked, "Did Grandma and Grandpa make good mayonnaise together? Or did she simply obey?"

"Let's say that Grandma was never one to keep her opinions to herself. I didn't get to know Grandpa very well because he died of a heart attack in the early 1940s when I was a small child. Grandma was a widow for a long, long time. That's how I remember her, yet her widowhood was also part of her marital relationship. Her devotion went beyond death."

After Grandpa died, their oldest son built Grandma a house near his own, across from the cemetery where Grandpa was buried. I walked with her across the road once to tend flowers and pull up new weeds while we visited Grandpa. She showed me an earth-hugging plant called "Shame-faced Mary" whose tiny leaves closed together when touched. Blackberry vines grew along the fence, and, using her apron as a basket, we picked enough berries to make a cobbler. She taught me through ordinary acts that a cemetery could be a pleasant garden spot, a peaceful and consoling retreat. The simple serenity of the place, its seasonal vegetation showing the ebb and flow of life's renewal, pushed aside any suggestion of sadness.

There was only silence for a moment. I glanced to see Elise drifting off to sleep.

I remembered one of my last visits with Grandma. She walked with me, stooped, but holding onto my arm across the road "to visit with Burch awhile." She knew his spirit was not in the grave, but her life took direction from their marital intimacy and its consequences; she missed the physical man, but she would never part with his spiritual presence in her life. She said he was waiting for her.

After thirty years of widowhood, her life span was ultimately defined in the joint headstone's final entry, "Terry Louisa Dumas Nolan, October 3, 1881—January 14, 1975."

Your name is there, Grandma, but it can't tell us who you were, or who you still are to me and all who loved you. The beginning and ending dates—holding a pearl of time—tell nothing about you or your life, nothing about what you loved, and nothing about what you believed in or how fervently. Those dates say nothing about your strong faith and your trust in wherever God might lead you. They tell nothing about a lifetime of struggle nor acknowledge any triumphs. They say nothing about how you squeezed every drop of living from life—a hard life, but a life of joy and hope.

Oh, Grandma, I now understand that death does nothing to alter love, nothing at all. You are still Grandma and our love is not diminished; I feel you near, waiting for me.

Give joy or grief, give ease or pain, take life or friends away,
But let me find them all again, in that eternal day.
And I'll sing hallelujah, and you'll sing hallelujah,
And we'll all sing hallelujah, when we arrive at home.

"Hallelujah" #146 in *The Sacred Harp*
Words, Charles Wesley, 1759; music, William Walker, 1835

CHAPTER 2

Grandma's Louisiana

IN the months after I first heard Sacred Harp music, I learned of additional singings in or near the Dallas area. Although I knew I'd never be as accomplished as life-long Sacred Harp singers, I was fascinated with the shape-note music. Part of the appeal was that music proficiency was not a requirement; with a complete lack of self-consciousness, they sang for the simple joy of singing.

Gradually, I learned that within the widespread network of Sacred Harp singers there were pockets of singing enthusiasts in Henderson, Austin, and beyond Texas; most singers came from the same parts of the South where Grandma's Dumas family lived when the notes Fa, So, La, and Mi first took their identifying shapes. Those families, like Grandma's grandparents, brought the music with them as they moved westward.

The Powells, a singing family in the Austin area, had ancestors who had lived and sung Sacred Harp in Union Parish, Louisiana, where my mother was born; it is possible our ancestors sang together at the local singings that drew huge crowds. At a singing near Austin in McMahan, Texas, I learned that my composer ancestor, Edmund Dumas, had performed the marriage ceremony for the great-grandparents of Don Clark, a visiting singer from Alabama. Sacred Harp singers are tied by many unknown links.

Within my own family, the links were severed within the last couple of generations. In 1935, when the country was in the depths of the Depression, my mother lived with an aunt in Monroe, Louisiana, during college. After graduation, she was told of a teaching position opening up in Texas, but after arriving she found there would be no new teaching job. Instead she found my father and came to live in the range country of the Texas Panhandle, far from the land of Sacred Harp singings.

My parents, like most of their early twentieth-century generation, became more sophisticated and wanted to put country ways and old-sounding music behind them. Our church sought to project a smoother, more polished image in offering our best to God. However, my parents still loved many

Carine Dumas Nolan (1917-1996) compiled our
family genealogy, *Dumas Families of Union Parish,
Louisiana.*

styles of music and made deep sacrifices to provide me years of piano and
voice lessons at the Musical Arts Conservatory in Amarillo. I dreamed of
becoming an opera star and once sang the role of Musetta in *La Bohème.*
I received a voice scholarship to college and, although I instead pursued a
career in architecture, my love for music never ceased.

Now nothing could have appealed to me more than the power, spirituality,
and sweet communion of Sacred Harp music, and I regretfully recalled
Grandma's coaxing to stay awhile in Louisiana and sing with her. I wanted to
learn about Grandma's Dumas family and the old songbook. Studying Carine
Dumas Nolan's genealogy book, I found little more than names, birth dates,
and death dates. Surely she knew more.

When I dialed her Louisiana phone number, Carine's melodic voice
greeted me. I told her my name and reminded her of our relationship.
Carine's father, my great-uncle Jerry, was Grandma's brother and the most

recent Jeremiah Dumas in a long line dating all the way back to the first Jeremiah Dumas who arrived in Jamestown in 1700.

"Oh, of course," (pronounced co-us) she responded. "You are Hettie Jane's daughter, out in Texas." I pictured her spontaneous smile that made her eyes sparkle and her eyelids crinkle at the edges and the sharp contrast of her bright pink lipstick against perfect teeth, white as a toothpaste ad. Ever the genteel southern lady, she loved gardening but wore gloves and a wide-brimmed hat to protect her fair skin.

I told her of the worn Sacred Harp songbook Grandma had given me, how she in turn had received it from her grandfather, and of my interest in learning everything possible about that grandfather, Jeremiah Dumas, who brought the book and its music from Georgia.

There was a throaty laugh. "Well, shu-gah, I'll tell you everything I know, but it comes with a lot of caveats."

"I cannot accept that. I've been reading your book again. You seem to know everything about the family. How on earth did you ever compile all that minutiae of names and dates and places without losing your mind?"

Following a brief pause, her voice took a serious tone. "Truth is, that book is what saved my mind. When Ronnie—our only child—died so suddenly as a young adult, I was desperate for something absorbing and demanding to hold reality together. At times, it seemed I'd lost it all, living in another age."

Carine sighed audibly, but her voice brightened. "Then, finally, all the puzzle pieces began to take shape and I could see a broader picture, the order of it all. Organizing that book was what helped me to see that, after life is gone, we are permanently connected in what is more immense and important than life itself."

Those sounded like words straight out of *The Sacred Harp*, the essence of why the abundance of songs dealing with death are comforting, hopeful, and even joyous instead of mournful. But I wondered how, in the midst of grief, Carine managed to sort through age after age of repetitious names.

"They reminded me of the series of begats in the Bible, tracing the lineage of Jesus from David, and I was distracted, wanting to know the details of each person listed," I said.

Carine answered, "I had to get rid of distractions. Anywhere you look, folks are always getting in a snit about something. These were all ordinary people, so we know they made a grand mess of everything, the same as we do. I just made it a rule to ignore problems they hadn't been able to solve in a complete lifetime."

I contended, "But a life can't be defined by a span of beginning and ending dates. I want to know why they did the things they did, what mattered most to them. If we could only take a trip back in time and talk to them in person about their world."

"Maybe that's exactly what you should do, like I did. I stepped back in time. I have two big boxes of research material you're welcome to pore over any time you want. Come on over to see me, and I'll get you started. My guestroom is waiting, anytime you want to come."

Elise was now no longer at home, and Doug had an upcoming business trip; there was no reason *not* to go. Carine, who'd been recently widowed, was a link to Grandma that should not be lost. Her boxes of photos and clippings might tell me about the people who brought the Sacred Harp songbook from Georgia.

I imagined stepping through time and following the umbilical cord to my grandmother's life as far back as I could go, from daughter to mother to grandmother and beyond, to learn forgotten links. Though they wielded powerful influence, little is known of the lives of ordinary women. There was a deep sadness in Grandma's voice when she told me her mother had died of typhoid fever. Tucked in a Bible I'd used as a teenager, I located the obituary clipping Grandma had given me long ago. Grandma had written the notice herself:

Death Angel visited the home of Mr. and Mrs. William A. Dumas and took from us our darling Mama, Mrs. Margaret Dumas. She was born August 17, 1860, being 56 years, 4 months, 28 days of age at her death. She leaves behind a mother 93 years of age and nine children. She was down with typhoid fever for seven weeks before she died on January 15, 1916. All the medical skill of doctors and all that loving hands could do for her was of no avail for God in His Wisdom had claimed her for His kingdom. It's so hard to live without Mama, but we all know she's resting in the arms of Jesus, and some sweet day we shall meet her beyond the dark river. We must not bow our heads in grief, but look up and continue to live, so when God sees fit to call us home, we'll clasp our Mama in our arms.

We shall meet but we shall miss her. There will be one vacant chair.
We shall linger to embrace her when we breathe our evening prayer.
When a year ago we gathered, joy was in her mild blue eyes.
But now a golden cord is severed, and happiness in ruin lies.
At our fireside sad and lonely, oft' will our bosom swell
At remembrance of the stories our dear Mama used to tell.
True, they tell us wreaths of glory evermore will grace her brow,

But it poorly soothes the anguish sweeping o'er our heartstrings now.
Sleep today, O dear Mama, in your cold and narrow bed,
Dirges from the pines and cypress mingle with the tears we shed.
She will wake in fairer lands where the angel voices sing.
There the floweret shall expand. There shall Love perfection bring.
Mama has reached the Golden Shore through the river cold and deep,
Angels bore her safely o'er. Mama's gone to sleep.

A loving daughter, T.L.N.

When I arrived at Carine's house in Farmerville, Louisiana, the landscaped grounds were in summer's full glory and the air was heavy with jasmine and gardenia. Day–lilies, with faces seeking the sun, lined a path down the sloping lawn to the terrace on the creek.

Great-uncle Jerry and Grandma, the fourth and fifth of nine children, were close all their lives. Coming of age shortly after the turn of the twentieth century, Grandma said their generation had lived in the most exciting time in existence, that man had acquired more knowledge in her lifetime than in all recorded time before. Once-incredible ideas became reality through amazing inventions, and her childhood fantasy of flying came true with her first airplane flight. They were born in a rural farming area in north Louisiana but, even in such a remote location, they recognized that technology was re-shaping the world and it would never be the same again.

"Did great-uncle Jerry describe their life to you as a golden era?"

"You obviously heard only the bright side," Carine said, running her fingers through short, white curls. "Life wasn't made of everyday excitement. My father and your grandmother grew up poor. They were poor, I grant you, but they were good people. After their daddy died, they had a terrible struggle just getting by. He died when he was needed most, leaving behind a thirty-two-year-old widow expecting their ninth child. His oldest brother, Uncle William, took on the burden of providing for the family along with his own."

I remembered that Grandma told me she'd looked on her uncle William as her father. I asked, "Didn't he have a wooden leg?"

"That's right; he lost his leg in the Civil War. William and his family lived on the farm next door, and he tried to raise crops to take care of them all. Poor old fellow, I don't know how he did it, crippled as he was."

Carine's usually cheerful expression became solemn. "My daddy didn't talk much about those days. He said it's a wonder they didn't starve to death. 'We might nigh did, honey, we might nigh did.' Those were his exact words.

He said they lived on nothing more than hope and prayer and the grace of God."

I thought of the serious nature of the words of Sacred Harp songs. Sorrow and death were part of their everyday life; still they kept on singing, even through the hard times. The familiar songs they'd brought with them served as guideposts, and it helped to know that someone had passed that way before.

"Life was hard for everybody and our family was mighty thankful for the land they owned," Carine said. "Your great-grandfather and his six brothers—William was the oldest—had each inherited a farm. I can show you the old home place; it's just a little piece out of town. The land I still own here in Union Parish was part of it."

The farms had originally been part of a large parcel of over five hundred acres bought after their father, Jeremiah Dumas, came from Georgia, and it was divided into seven eighty-acre farms for his seven sons.

"Families of those days seem unusually large to us, but to a farmer, a lot of sons meant a lot of needed help. The first four boys were born in Georgia. When Irena and Jeremiah—he's the one who brought your songbook— moved west, their older boys were hardly more than toddlers. Another baby was born soon after they arrived."

"Grandma told me the old songbook came all the way from Georgia on a wagon train," I said.

"That's right. It was a long train of wagons. Many of them were Irena's family, the Adamses. They stopped once for months—long enough to grow food to continue—before they finally settled in Louisiana."

Carine said that few family members were in agreement about whether the wagon train families came first to Louisiana or Arkansas because they lived almost on the state line. Actually, if a person had married and died on the same day, each event might be accurately recorded in two different states because most couples went the few miles up the road to El Dorado, Arkansas, to get married, but people generally died at home in Louisiana.

"You said William lost his leg in the Civil War. I've never understood why they would fight for a way of life they'd left behind when they left Georgia. I'd always thought they were simply farmers in Louisiana."

"Maybe they wanted to bring that way of life with them," she said. "I don't know that young men thought much about issues. More than likely, it was just Them against Us."

Carine was looking through files in one of the boxes of research material. "Your Grandma's daddy was quite a bit younger than William, so he wasn't old enough to enlist in the war. He had to stay home and do what he could to help their father. You see, life held some mighty rough bumps for the settlers from Georgia."

Irena died in the spring of 1855 giving birth to twins, a boy and a girl. It wasn't at all unusual for childbirth complications to take the life of a young woman. She left behind eight children when she was only thirty-four.

Carine had located the item she sought, a newspaper clipping to give me a better picture of life back then. She cautioned me to remember that the war utterly destroyed most of the South. The same swift sword that cut a swath of destruction through the land slashed through people's lives as well. It sliced through time itself, severing the connection; nothing was ever again the same, and it was impossible for the next generation to clearly understand life as it had existed before.

She handed me a yellowed clipping, which read:

Mr. Editor:

The Gazette of last week contained a brief notice of the death of William Adam Dumas at his home a few miles east of Farmerville. The history of this old Confederate soldier, though never rising above the humble walks of life, has in it something that calls for more than a passing sigh.

Nearly fifty years have dropped into the silent past since the clash at arms between the States. But histories in the main deal with the deeds of the leaders and acts of armies as a whole, and only now and then is the valor of a private soldier or his suffering recorded. In relating here an incident or two in the life of William Dumas, I but record that which, in substance, has perhaps happened in the lives of hundreds of other old soldiers scattered through this South land.

In a battle between the Confederates and Federals in the neighborhood of Corinth, Mississippi, Dumas was seriously wounded in the leg. He was not able to drag himself from the place he fell, and while he was helpless on the ground, the Confederate and Federal soldiery in turn charged over his body.

When the battle was over, the Federals were in charge of the field, and Dumas, along with the Federal wounded, was moved to an improvised hospital for treatment. As he was of the enemy, he had to wait until the Federal wounded had been treated before he could be operated on. When they sought to take him to the operating table, they thought him dead and placed him in a room along with others who had died of their wounds, preparatory to burial.

19

While in this room of the dead, Dumas returned to consciousness and beat upon the walls with his hands. Someone passing by heard him, and he was removed, and his leg was amputated.

He was a prisoner until his leg began to heal, when he was paroled. By various means he attempted to reach his home in Louisiana. He was carried by one kindly disposed person or another from place to place. While thus making his way home, he had the misfortune to lose his parole, and he was taken by a company of Federal soldiers and again thrown into prison. Rough treatment while under arrest caused his healing wound to break afresh, and it was many weeks before the wound finally healed. At last, however, he was released, and after additional difficulties, he found himself back at his home.

And now, what did this Confederate soldier do, with one leg off close up to the body, with no learning, no money, no skill to do anything and no profession? Did he seek entrance to the alms house? Did he become a pauper and beg? No, verily. But with a resolution that carried him over obstacles which to other men would have proved insurmountable, he set to work to provide maintenance for himself and his family. Crippled as he was, he succeeded in doing most of the work about the farm. Many is the day, with crutch in one hand and plow handle in the other, William Dumas plowed his fields. And thus, each day facing adversity, this plain man reared his children, not in substance, it is true, not with finished education, but as law-abiding and respectable people.

The writer has known this old soldier, this plain citizen, for many years, has seen him hobbling along our streets attending to the affairs of life, but never complaining, has heard from his lips his record of service for the South, and now of respect for his manhood, lays this tribute upon his grave.

Let not ambition hear with disdainful smile
The short and simple annals of the poor. [sic]
R.B.D.

I handed the worn clipping back to Carine. "Grandma's father must have anticipated that his handicapped brother's family would need extra help, not the other way around. She never told me how difficult life had been while growing up. She made it seem that her childhood was a series of playful pranks, all set to music."

Carine quietly lifted another file from the box and sorted through photographs. In a confidential tone, she said, "Your great-grandmother was pregnant when her husband died; your great-aunt Frankie was born after his death."

She produced pictures of the family that included Jerry, Grandma, and Frankie when they were young. In the early photos, Frankie, the youngest sibling, is a petite dark-haired girl, laughing and vibrant. "She married young, but in the early 1930s, as the Depression was gathering steam and Frankie was expecting their sixth child after five daughters, her husband shot and killed himself."

I had heard whispers of something like that.

"I think that must have happened about the time my mother left for college," I said. "Isn't Frankie the sister who came to stay with Grandma? I'd heard she had a baby, but I thought there was only one."

"Yes, she stayed with your grandparents, Terry and Burch, after the new baby—her only son—was born. She was dead-set on getting her family back together, under the same roof and in their own home. All of her brothers and sisters wanted to help, but none of them could take in Frankie's entire family; their homes were already crowded with offspring. Simply providing enough to eat was now a serious problem." Carine cleared her throat and hesitated. "And Frankie didn't intend for her daughters to be separated. They were safe, as far as she knew."

"Where were they? Did they have to go to different homes?"

Carine had difficulty finding the right words. "Her brothers—my father included—finally convinced Frankie to let them leave her daughters at the church orphanage in Monroe, just through the winter. They assured her that the girls would not be adopted. It was the Depression; no one would adopt a family of older children, or so they thought, but people did continue donating to the orphanage any money they could spare."

"So what really happened?"

"In backwoods Louisiana in 1930, transportation and communication were still primitive, and when Frankie went back in early spring for her daughters, the girls weren't there. For some reason that was never satisfactorily explained, in spite of prior assurances, they had been adopted. And despite pleas and tears, no further information was allowed. There was no way to find out where they were or who had them."

"Did she ever find them?"

"The oldest daughter was eleven years old when it happened. Four or five years later, she ran away from her adoptive family and, remembering her mother's maiden name, eventually found Frankie. Together, they searched any and every avenue they could imagine, but Frankie never again saw her other daughters. There's a lot we'll never understand about this old earthly life. Frankie used to say she could only pray that God would take care of her little girls."

In July of 1990, when Carine's notice of the next annual family reunion came in the mail, Doug and I made plans to attend; Mother flew to Dallas and drove with us to Louisiana. There was added excitement because Carine promised there would be a surprise.

In the summer of 1989, the last adoptive parent of one of Frankie's daughters had died in Kansas. The daughter, Elizabeth, was adopted at age two and raised as an only child. Among her parents' records and papers, she located information regarding her adoption; now that her adoptive parents' feelings would not be hurt, Elizabeth wanted to know about her blood family. In a short time, she learned of her birth mother's death as well as that her oldest sister and her youngest sibling, her only brother, still lived in Louisiana.

In February 1990, on the West Coast, another woman, called Betty, answered a phone call that ripped open a part of her life she had buried in the past more than a half century earlier. She had closed a door in her mind and put it all behind her, never speaking a word of it to anyone, even to her own daughter.

But Betty did remember. She was nine years old, and some people came to get them at the orphanage right after they had arrived. She was aware that they were relatives of her father. His family blamed her mother for his death and wanted to see that the girls were given homes far away. They said her mother didn't love them and only wanted to be rid of the girls. Betty recalled protesting and weeping, being forcibly held and told that she would be taken where she would never, ever see that place again. She remembered the trip that seemed unending, along the narrow highway through far-spaced dusty towns, for days upon days until they finally reached California.

She eventually ceased to wonder and worry about what happened to her oldest sister, taken by the couple who said, "That one looks sturdy. She could be a big help around the house." Eventually, she ceased to brood about the look of helpless sorrow on her mother's face the last time she saw her.

Betty, of California—a petite, vivacious woman who strongly resembled the pictures of the youthful Frankie—was raised alone. Her beautiful daughter, who came with her mother to the family reunion, never knew aunts, uncles, or cousins. The women confided that before making the trip in the August heat to Louisiana, they wondered what these people were like, this unknown family, ready-made, out of the blue. "Do we want to be part of this family? Are they decent, law-abiding people? Are they a people of faith? For all we know, they could be atheists or even criminals."

The Dumas reunion of 1990 was an extraordinary, joyful occasion. Two more sisters were located, and four of great-aunt Frankie's five daughters and the brother they remembered as an infant were together after a lapse of sixty years.

Newfound relatives spoke of their mother and wished aloud, "If only she could know—"

Someone else spoke up. "God was answering even as she prayed. He was taking care of her little girls."

On the five-hour drive returning to Dallas, I wondered aloud if great-aunt Frankie's faith wavered when months turned into years and years to decades without an answer.

"Wavered? I'm sure her faith might have even completely failed at times," Mother said. "But we can pray for more faith, just as we pray for all of our weaknesses."

My own faith was at low ebb; Doug and I were facing a financial crisis with no obvious solution. In the eighties, America rode a wild roller coaster to dizzying financial heights; the downside plunge showed us it was a long way to fall. Only a short time ago, we'd planned on early retirement, but new a plan had to be made. Doug was nearing sixty years old, too late for a comeback, and he would never consider bankruptcy. My work alone could not support us.

"The Lord tells us to pray for our daily bread," Doug had said. "He means for today, not for tomorrow and the rest of our lives. He provides for our needs as they arise. We've been blessed with bread and also a lot of gravy. There will be a way. Let's wait and see. Maybe the bread and gravy will come out even."

We'd have to make dramatic changes; for a beginning, the two of us no longer needed the big house where we'd raised our children.

At the next Sacred Harp singing, I thought of great-aunt Frankie's heartbreaking predicament and my own wavering faith. The words to a song spoke with new meaning:

My spirit looks to God alone, my rock and refuge is His throne.
In all my fears, in all my straits, my soul on His salvation waits.
Trust Him, ye saints, in all your ways, pour out your hearts before His face.
When helpers fail and foes invade, God is our all-sufficient aid.

"Russia" #107 in *The Sacred Harp*
Words, Isaac Watts, 1719; music, David Read, 1786

CHAPTER 3

To Georgia—an Unclaimed Inheritance

THE Resolution Trust Corporation (RTC) was formed in 1989 as a temporary federal government agency to resolve the savings-and-loan crisis. Doug's financial background as a CPA and the Chief Financial Officer of a large company landed him a position in the investigations arm of the RTC, the department determining why specific savings-and-loan institutions had failed and attempting to recover some of the lost assets. This was the job Doug needed to take him to retirement age, and as a victim of the financial crisis, he was motivated to find the guilty parties.

Doug was assigned the southeast area, based out of Atlanta. We had to move from Dallas, from the comfortable home and neighborhood where we'd spent our entire married life, and from the church where Doug had been a charter member fifty years earlier. We'd been involved in nearly every facet of our community—even the store clerks were first-name friends—but life had taken a sudden, ninety-degree turn. I was heartsick thinking of how our old life had ended.

Mother advised me to trust God. "He hasn't forgotten you. The next phase of life might be even more interesting than anything you've ever done." She and I began to talk of new possibilities. Mother had thought her traveling days were over, but we imagined her flying to meet us in Atlanta or other cities for Doug's work. It was thrilling to speak of expanding horizons.

On a bright September morning, I could see from our Atlanta hotel room the contemporary high-rise condominium building that would be our new home. We had chosen the first place we looked because of its spectacular view. At the far end of the condo's living room, a wall of projecting windows framed the art museum, symphony hall, Alliance Theater, and the red-rock Presbyterian Church on Peachtree Street. The IBM tower a block south, the AT&T complex to the east and up the hill, and the old Victorian stone castle gave the view a three-dimensional collage effect. Doug had pointed out his office among a cluster of buildings, restaurants, and shops directly across from the AT&T complex. It was a steep climb a few blocks up the hill to work, but he insisted it would be good exercise. The crest of the hill was eye level with our living room window on the eleventh floor.

I walked onto the hotel balcony and looked down to the plaza of the IBM building across the street. Water no longer erupted from the prominent fountain; emptied, it became the impromptu stage for a group of instrumentalists blasting riotous sound in a musical frenzy. As a celebrating crowd gathered below, the early autumn air seemed buoyantly alive, and euphoria was contagious.

I stepped back inside when the phone ring. Doug, calling from his office, asked, "Have you heard? Atlanta has been named the site for the 1996 Olympics." My heart filled, knowing that our new life was already turning up good surprises.

I was startled by a knock on the door. The maid had come to clean the room.

"Excuse me, ma'am. I can come back later."

"No, no, come on in. I'm only watching the celebration about the Olympics. Isn't it fun? Atlanta must be an exciting place to live."

"I reckon so, for some folks," the maid responded. I looked back at the young black woman, seeing "Arlette" embroidered on her well-worn uniform, and asked how long she'd lived in Atlanta.

"About eight years, ma'am. I come up from near Tifton with my husband when he was looking for a better job. That was back when our children were real little." With each question I asked, Arlette's answer came as if she were setting down a great weight—a welcomed relief with a painful extraction.

"Then," she continued, "about four years ago, he left. He went looking for a better job in Florida, but he found another woman instead."

Arlette's husband now had children by the second woman and, with even more responsibility, didn't reliably send money to the family he'd left in Atlanta. Thinking of my own children, I admired the hard work Arlette withstood to maintain her children alone.

"I wake up in the morning and ask, 'Oh Lord, why me?' but I have to carry on," she confided, and I wondered if the upcoming Olympics might provide more opportunities for people such as Arlette and her husband.

It was comforting to begin unpacking our familiar belongings, and when I saw our favorite paintings and well-loved family photos in new surroundings, the move finally became reality. Unpacking boxes of books, I came upon the old Sacred Harp songbook; it had come back home to Georgia.

Realistically, Doug and I both viewed his position in Atlanta first as a way to provide our daily bread, but I was becoming aware that Georgia held opportunities for me too.

"Isn't it amazing that we find ourselves suddenly in Georgia?" I asked. "Why Georgia, of all places?"

"It could be anywhere," Doug said. "Why?"

"I mean regarding the close proximity to Grandma's family's former home. It couldn't be more that an hour's drive from here."

"Well, that is quite a coincidence."

"Perhaps. But I wonder. I've been thinking of trying to locate Dumas relatives."

I wanted to connect with my roots, to learn who my ancestors really were and how they'd lived. Here, Sacred Harp music had taken root and flourished, and I wanted to know what inspired this music. I wanted to walk where they walked, to smell the air they breathed, to experience life in the place my ancestors once lived.

"I came across Carine's book today," I said. "She wrote a couple of intriguing incidental notes, each involving an inheritance. I'd like to see if I can learn something more."

"What kind of inheritance?" Doug asked.

"Well, the first was for Grandma's grandfather, Jeremiah Dumas, who moved west to Louisiana. Carine says Jeremiah was named a beneficiary in his father's will. His father, Benjamin Franklin Dumas, died a few years after Jeremiah left Georgia for Louisiana with his wife and umpteen sons. Carine didn't try to find specifics of how the estate was settled. There are surely records filed somewhere, and they may hold a clue to why Jeremiah's family left Georgia in the first place. They held onto this old Sacred Harp songbook, so I know the music and its message were important to them. Surely, Jeremiah eventually came back home to claim what was rightfully his."

"He might have thought the inheritance wouldn't be enough to make the trip worthwhile. That was a long time ago, and traveling was a hardship. At this late date, I doubt there's a chance you could find out anything about Jeremiah Dumas. But you mentioned two bequests. What was the other?"

"Oh, it involves a much larger estate. It was from Jeremiah's brother, Davie, who also left Georgia a couple of years after Jeremiah. But we know his reason; he went to search for gold in California and apparently found it. Reportedly, he left behind an unclaimed forty-million-dollar fortune."

"Forty million dollars! Unclaimed? What happened to it?"

"No one seems to know. Carine's note referred to an old newspaper article that said the Dumas family would be the legitimate heirs, but, as none of the money was ever received by the family, it probably went to the State of California under the law of escheat."

"I'm sure someone was curious enough to resolve a mysterious forty-million-dollar fortune. Can you imagine how much that'd be worth today?"

Pulling her book off the shelf, I reread Carine's note. It said the newspaper article appeared in the *Monroe Advertiser* on January 24, 1929, under the front-page headline, "Dumas Heirs Get Legacy Reported to be $40 Million." The article mentioned that Davie's wife had not heard from him and, assuming he was dead, remarried. Their two children had died as infants. Davie Dumas reportedly died before returning to Georgia and left a very large estate. The article also said his heirs would have been his wife, but if she had divorced Davie, his brothers and sisters would be the legal heirs. None of the money was ever received as far as could be ascertained. Copies of the *Monroe Advertiser* for the given period were bound in volumes, kept in the office of the Probate Court at Forsyth, the county seat of Monroe County.

"I think I'll try to find out what happened. I'd like to find the old home place," I said. "I have a romantic vision of what it was like."

"Like the big plantation in *Gone with the Wind?*" Doug suggested in amusement.

I pictured something less pretentious, with a spacious back porch for the family to gather. Someone might churn butter or read stories to the children. They would sing, like Grandma, while shelling peas. They were real people who lived right here in Georgia. They sang, even wrote, the same music I'd come to love. Seeing their home might make this distant family as real to me as their music.

> *How charming is the place where my Redeemer God*
> *Unveils the beauties of His face and sheds His love abroad.*
> *Give me, O Lord, a place within Thy blest abode,*
> *Among the children of Thy grace, the servants of my God.*

"Nidrah" # 540 in *The Sacred Harp*
Words, Samuel Stennett, 1787; music, Raymond C. Hamrick, 1982

The frenetic pace of urban Atlanta dissolved into a tranquil rural setting as I drove south on Interstate 75. The rolling terrain of central Georgia slopes gradually from the north Georgia mountains to the sea. As I sped along the highway, undulating hills seemed to rise and fall playfully, kissing the billowing clouds, stark white against the bright blue sky. I pictured the surrounding deep green timberland as virgin forest and the road as a ribbon leading to the past. My mind slipped seamlessly into the previous century.

> *Grandma's songbook is my link to their home. I can hear their music*
> *echoing in the countryside. It's so beautiful here. Why, oh why, did Jeremiah*
> *leave?*

The exit to Forsyth led in a circuitous route to an aging red-brick courthouse on a central square. Before walking inside the courthouse, I paused to read a historical marker describing the first employment at the *Monroe Advertiser* of Georgia native, Joel Chandler Harris, author of the Uncle Remus stories. I located the appropriate office that housed old records and there met Judge Ben Spear. With a commanding appearance that suited his title, Judge Spear informally directed all office activity from a wheelchair.

I explained that I was interested in learning about the Dumas family, not yet knowing that Judge Spear was indirectly related to the family by marriage. I mentioned Edmund Dumas, the brother of my ancestor Jeremiah, who wrote music and preached as well.

Judge Spear nodded, "That same Edmund Dumas once held the office I hold now. However, back in that day, they called him the Monroe County Ordinary instead of the county judge. He also served in the Georgia legislature. He started teaching while he was still very young and was well liked by all the local families. A very interesting fellow. You'll be able to find something about him at the library."

"I'd especially like to find the family's old home place or, at least, see the specific piece of land where they lived."

"You might recall that Sherman's troops eliminated many homes around here. I know of only one old Dumas home that's still standing. I don't recall who built it, but it was inherited by S. T. Dumas."

"Maybe I can get in touch with him?"

"You won't be talking to S. T. Dumas," the judge said flatly. "He's done blown his brains out." After observing my shocked reaction, Judge Spear explained that the old gentleman had been terminally ill and preferred to make his exit from life while he was still capable of choosing the manner.

"If there are other Dumas descendants still living here, I'd like very much to talk with them. What would be the best way to contact someone?"

Judge Spear mentioned several names, but said Mrs. Charles Dumas was among the oldest and would best know the family relationships. I jotted down her name as the judge escorted me to the vault, the door as massive as a bank's. He reached from his wheelchair to lift weighty volumes off the shelves, insisting that they were much too heavy for me to handle. Placing one of the books on a wide counter, he began explaining how to trace the ownership of land and locate wills.

"That should keep you busy a few hours," he said. "We'll try not to lock you in tonight."

The land that had belonged to the family patriarch, Benjamin Franklin Dumas, from the 1821 land lottery until his death in 1852 is now part of

Lamar County, which was carved out of Monroe County. The sequence of county formation is very important to genealogy searches because most people searching their family line will have an ancestor who, in the country's westward migration, was in Georgia at one time or another. The Dumas land was near a small town, Barnesville, in an even smaller community, Goggins Station, which was once a regular stop along the railroad. The Goggins family donated land to entice the railroad owners to route the rail line through their property and assure a train station for their community. Goggins Station was among the earliest inland communities to be connected by rail to river transportation and, as such, held an economic advantage.

Eventually, in one of the cumbersome and elaborately hand-scripted books, I found Benjamin Franklin Dumas' will, recorded in March of 1852. His wife, Martha Ussery Dumas, was already deceased when the will was written in 1850. All of Benjamin Franklin's children were listed along with what they each were bequeathed, with a notable exception of only one son, Jeremiah's brother Davie. In fact, Davie was only mentioned specifically in item 7: "My son Aaron David Dumas has already received his full share of my Estate, and my will is that he receive no more."

At that moment, Judge Spear wheeled in to check on my progress.

"I am uncovering more questions. One Dumas son was effectively disowned. It says that he had already received his share, whatever that meant. I don't yet know how the will was ultimately finalized."

"That will be in a different book. The Executors are required to make a report to the court, which is recorded each year until the will is settled."

The judge showed me to books that chronologically listed all of the expenditures from estates through their final accounting and settlement. Great-great-great-grandpa Benjamin Franklin Dumas' estate had entries in multiple volumes, and the first entry showed that sums had been paid out to several of his children. But nothing was paid to Jeremiah. Although I searched carefully, I was unable to locate Book K, where subsequent entries would have been made.

Jeremiah must have returned to Georgia at some point, I thought. They wouldn't leave him out completely. *Or maybe they would.* I had mixed emotions regarding Jeremiah's possible omission in the settlement of the family estate. I identified with Jeremiah because I was his direct descendent, but the will revealed that Benjamin Franklin Dumas owned slaves who were considered "property" willed to the family, and I wanted Jeremiah to have had no part in that sensitive issue.

I made photocopies of everything I found, planning to later decipher the elaborate handwriting. A return trip would be necessary to examine deed books, riffle through old copies of the *Monroe Advertiser,* and continue hunting for Book K to gather some additional background on the deepening mystery of Davie Dumas and his gold.

I wished for Carine's guidance. If Carine met with Judge Spear and Mrs. Charles Dumas, they might be able to tie up all the historical loose ends. As soon as I reached home I phoned Carine, hoping she could clarify muddled areas regarding the wayward son, Davie.

"I don't remember anything about Davie Dumas that I didn't put in the book," Carine said. "I can pull my files and see if there's anything else about him. I did my research by correspondence; the documents I used were photocopied and mailed to me in answer to specific, narrowly defined requests. But, if you look closely, you might find additional information that I didn't ask for."

I asked about the other mystery. "I'm baffled about why Jeremiah pulled up roots and took his young family off west. His father was still giving hundred-acre plots away to the other children long after Jeremiah left. Do you suppose competition with his older brothers was the reason he left? Jeremiah obviously admired his brother Edmund, but Edmund cast a mighty broad shadow."

"And you think maybe Jeremiah longed for his own place in the sun? That's probably part of the reason," Carine said. "Sibling rivalry can be bitter; remember the story of Cain and Abel. But I think you already know the reason Jeremiah left Georgia. You touched on it when you wondered why Jeremiah's sons would fight in the Civil War for the life they left behind them in Georgia. I questioned whether their idealized dream of old southern plantation life really *was* left behind."

Maybe Jeremiah had wanted the same way of life to continue—but on a larger scale and under his own control.

"It is easy to assume Jeremiah joined the trend toward general westward expansion," Carine said. "After all, that's how his father acquired all that property in Georgia in the first place. Isn't it possible Jeremiah's father encouraged him to go? If Benjamin Franklin had been a younger man then, he'd likely have gone west himself."

I conceded that the five or six hundred acres Jeremiah ended up with in Louisiana would exceed a divided portion of his father's Georgia estate, but if Jeremiah wanted to continue the way of life he left behind, it meant he probably condoned slavery.

"Slavery was a fact of their day. If you erase the slavery element from Jeremiah's history, you erase him from his time," Carine said. "Don't you have a simple question for me that would require only a date or place answer?"

Carine was an excellent source for time and place answers, but I was now combating more difficult quandaries. "Since we know Jeremiah was in Louisiana and that Davie had to go through Louisiana on his way to California, do you suppose Davie stopped by for a visit?"

"That's another logical assumption, but we don't know that. If you're suggesting that Jeremiah might have encouraged Davie, I don't think so. The directions of their lives correspond in only one aspect—they both went west from Georgia. It sounds as if Davie left under a dark cloud of alienation. He must have done something outrageous to provoke Benjamin Franklin to write his son completely out of his will, but I don't know how you can ever learn that kind of information."

Benjamin Franklin Dumas had been exceedingly generous to the rest of his children. Most had received land while he was alive, but Benjamin Franklin also made provisions to equally divide his assets among all of his children— all but Davie, that is—after his death. Davie had somehow "already received his full share."

Several of the children had borrowed money against their inheritance. The will mentioned specific receipts that Benjamin Franklin maintained to be deducted from their share at the final distribution of the estate. Jeremiah's name was not listed there, which meant that he had not borrowed money from his father.

I told Carine that one of Benjamin Franklin's daughters—who was blind, the will stated—was singled out to receive his barouche and harness in addition to her allotted share. The barouche was apparently a fancy four-wheeled carriage with a collapsible hood, two double seats facing each other, and a box seat up front for the driver. A recent article in the *Atlanta Constitution* described the town of Barnesville, near the Dumas plantation, as the Detroit of the horse-and-buggy days. The stone building still standing in the center of Barnesville had been the largest buggy showroom in the country, and the Barnesville Buggy was known all over the South as the "doctor's" buggy. The writer also said close proximity to Barnesville gave well-to-do planters a wide choice of vehicles to display their wealth.

"Benjamin Franklin mentioned the barouche twice in his will," I continued, "It must have been his pride and joy."

Carine was amused. "So you think the old fellow was status conscious?"

"Well, it wasn't just a buggy. It was a *barouche*."

She laughed. "No, that doesn't exactly sound humble."

"Judge Spear told me that an estate's record of expenditures gives a good picture of a family. Each entry is like a snapshot of an important event within the family, and the Dumas heirs left a series of snapshots that showed their

31

respect for Benjamin Franklin Dumas—including the itemized amounts spent on lumber, nails, stones, and mortar to construct his grave. Then it listed amounts paid to workmen for five days' labor to build it."

"That sounds like an above-ground tomb, like those near the coast, down around New Orleans."

"When I find the church nearest their home, maybe I'll find the tomb in a cemetery nearby."

"Let me know how it turns out," she said. "Are you going to ask the new kinfolk if they know what became of Davie's money?"

Carine wasn't interested in probing the Georgia Dumas family about Davie's unclaimed estate, but if I was going to inquire about this matter, I first needed to know more of the facts. I returned to Forsyth the next day and, before resuming my search for Book K, I asked Judge Spear what he knew about Davie Dumas's reputed fortune.

"I was wondering when you would get around to that," he said, smiling.

He directed me to stacks of bound copies of the weekly *Monroe Advertiser*. The immensity of the mound was discouraging, but the volumes were well organized, and I located the issue January 24, 1929, that Carine referenced. Under a bold headline announcing the newly discovered, unclaimed fortune was a sub-headline, "Brother of Late Ordinary Edmund Dumas Said to Have Died in California Leaving No Immediate Family. Several Monroe County Groups Would Share Estate."

> ... The report originated in a letter from Sacramento, California, which was received this week by the postmaster at Barnesville, with instructions that it be delivered to some white member of the Dumas family. The letter [said] that a Mr. David Dumas had died in California leaving an estate valued at $40,000,000. The deceased was a bachelor and his estate would naturally revert to his heirs here.
>
> While a citizen of Monroe County, Mr. Dumas lived at Goggins. He was a man of considerable means at the time he left and did not keep in touch with relatives during his residence in California ...

I turned to the next issue's headline of January 31, 1929:

> Dumas Amassed Fortune in California Gold Rush: Interest in Reputed Wealth Left by Former Monroe County Man Grows. Legal Records Probed by Attorney.
>
> The heirs of Mr. David Dumas have been busy during the past week probing into every available source of information that might lead to a clearer knowledge of the facts relating to the vast inheritance.

According to . . . Dumas heirs, Mr. David Dumas left his home at Goggins in 1849 to go to California in search of gold, and thus joined in the famous gold rush of the "forty-niners." Mr. Dumas was married to Miss Winifred Collier, leaving his wife and two children here at the time he went to California.

Mr. Dumas was accompanied to California by Mr. William Horne, another gold-seeker of Goggins. After a lapse of ten years, Mr. Horne returned to Goggins for the purpose of carrying his wife and the wife and children of Mr. Dumas back with him to California. He found that in the meantime Mrs. Dumas had married again, thinking that her former husband was dead. . . .

. . . It is reported that the estate is being held by a California trust company pending distribution to the rightful heirs. Reports of this undistributed fortune have aroused deep and widespread interest, and people from different sections of the state have visited Forsyth during the past week seeking information in regard to it.

A second article about Davie also made the front page:

Legal Records Disclose David Dumas Excluded From Father's Last Will...

Through the efforts of Col. W. B. Freeman, an attorney who has been delving into legal records of Monroe County to determine the early history of the Dumas family, the *Monroe Advertiser* is enabled to give the following information. In the will of Benjamin Franklin Dumas, recorded in 1852, no property was willed to Aaron David Dumas, his father stating that he had already received his part.

The records show that on May 26, 1848, Benjamin F. Dumas, for and in consideration of love and affection, conveyed to his son, Aaron D. Dumas, a tract of land containing 'one hundred one-fourth acres' . . . in the 7th district of Monroe county. This deed probably explains why no property was left to Aaron David Dumas by his father's will, [if] it is to this property that his father is referring when he states in his will that his son, Aaron David Dumas, has already received his part of the estate. . .

. . . Mr. Freeman found in the deed books of Monroe County that on January 1, 1840, Aaron David Dumas sold a tract of land near Goggins to Owen J. Willis for the price of $600.00. Diligent search of the records does not reveal any other transfers of properties by Aaron D. Dumas.

Davie Dumas also made front page news in the February 7, 1929, issue though the story was more akin to gossip than news:

The fabulous fortune of the late David Dumas of California continues to be a source of interest among his heirs, a number of whom reside in Forsyth. The size of the legacy has been variously estimated at from forty to sixty millions of dollars as reports have continued to come in. While the matter has yet hardly advanced beyond the stage of speculation, there is enough of reality connected with it to cause ordinary citizens to believe they are occasionally having the privilege and pleasure of standing in the presence of and engaging in conversation with potential millionaires.

Reports have come in from prospective heirs so widely separated as the states of Texas and Massachusetts, and the descendants of the Dumas family are gradually becoming amazed at the wide expanse over which the family tree has extended its branches. It begins to look like a legacy of millions of dollars makes the whole world kin. About fifty would-be legatees have already visited Forsyth with the apparent purpose of removing obstacles to any further lack of division of the vast estate.

. . . A claim has also come in from a Mr. Phillip Dumas of Boston, who claims to be a descendant of David Dumas and who seeks to trace the family line back to the noted Alexandre Dumas of France, thus putting a crimp into the claims of the American branch of the family. . .

A family tree in the possession of a relative at Barnesville shows that David Dumas was born in 1819 and left Monroe County in 1849. It is contemplated that some member of the family, probably from Barnesville, will take a trip to California soon in order to get first-hand information regarding the estate.

The February 14, 1929, issue of the *Monroe Advertiser* recapped the ongoing investigation with little new development:

Dumas Heirs Begin Searching Fortune...

Progress in the investigation has been difficult [because] the place of residence of Mr. Dumas in California has not been revealed in any of the reports received. The heirs, however, are going at the matter now in a systematic way, and it is expected that definite information will be available in a short time. Inquiries on the part of the estate are being made by Col. B. S. Willingham, and results are expected at an early date.

I searched page-by-page through the following six months' editions and found only one short related column on page three of the February 21, 1929, issue.

Newsy Notes From Goggins…

The many friends in this section of the Abernathy-Dumas families are hoping that the much-talked of Dumas fortune materializes. There are a number of the family residing in and near this community, and we truly hope that reports of the fortune are factual and that ere long now they may be reaping the benefits. Should the fortune materialize, Lamar County can easily lay claim to being one of the richest in all of Georgia.

After turning the last page, I closed the book and returned the large volume of the *Monroe Advertiser* to its place. Judge Spear passed by and asked, "How are you coming with your research?"

"The only thing I've learned for sure is that human nature hasn't changed. I haven't solved the mystery of Davie's fortune yet, but if it's waited this long, it won't go away."

The day was gone and again I would leave Forsyth with unanswered questions and a research to-do list that would have to wait. I decided to contact Mrs. Charles Dumas before returning to Atlanta. Dialing the number listed in the local directory, Mrs. Dumas' warm, cheerful voice answered, and she was happy to help piece together family connections. Unfortunately, it quickly became clear that the time span was too great to supply unknown links without extensive first-hand knowledge or notes, but Mrs. Dumas had a suggestion.

"One of the cousins, Mary, knows much more about the family's history than I do. We're having a family reunion next Sunday in Barnesville and she will probably be there. I think you ought to come. And bring your husband, too. After all, we're a big family, and you're part of it. It will be in the old depot building, right downtown. You can't miss it."

Blest be the tie that binds our hearts in Christian love;
The fellowship of kindred minds is like to that above.

"Fellowship" #330b in *The Sacred Harp*
Words, John Fawcett, 1782; music, Paine Denson, 1935

CHAPTER 4

The Home Place, 1822

IN Georgia in the autumn of 1990, only a few months after the Dumas reunion in Louisiana, Doug and I found ourselves attending the reunion of another family branch, descending from Benjamin Franklin Dumas' son Edmund. We were welcomed warmly and introduced throughout the chatty crowd as "long-lost kin, from the brother who went west." My pictures from the Louisiana occasion were examined with interest, and several newfound "cousins" delightedly commented on seeing resemblances to other known relatives.

As I attempted to catch up, not on the past year's events, but on the past century and a half, I was disappointed when no one could locate the original Dumas home. Despite having deep roots in the state, I found this branch had little knowledge of their ancestry—these descendants of Edmund Dumas were not aware that he had composed Sacred Harp music or music of any kind. One woman who was familiar with the music told me that her mother, Edmund's great-granddaughter as well as an accomplished musician and vocalist, had been classically trained and therefore looked down on the shape-note music and its "country" roots.

Most of the family had not heard the story of Davie Dumas' California gold either. The oldest great-aunt recalled that the Davie Dumas uproar occurred about the time she married, but she could not remember how the story ended.

"No one ever got any money, as far as I know," she said, laughing. "It's obvious we didn't."

Finally, I struck an easy friendship with a recently retired teacher from an Atlanta suburb. Barbara was interested in documenting her personal family tree, a project initiated by her long-deceased mother. She mentioned an elderly cousin, Mary, who had in her possession the Edmund Dumas family's Bible with a page listing all the children's birth, marriage, and death dates.

"Mary couldn't come today because she's having hip problems," Barbara said. "She lives in Roswell, north of Atlanta. I'll get in touch with her, and we'll see what Mary and the old family Bible can tell us." Barbara, who was

Edmund Dumas (1810-1881), county ordinary (or judge) of Monroe County, Georgia, was a circuit-riding preacher, singing school master, and composer of shape-note sacred harp music. Edmund Dumas also served in the Georgia legislature.

eager to join in my search for the original home site, then promptly contacted her cousin Mary.

Early the next week, Barbara and I met to begin our exploration at the depot in Barnesville and together examined the Edmund Dumas family's Bible, borrowed from Mary. Thoughtfully Mary had made copies of the handwritten documentation for Barbara and me to keep, but we were eager to look at the real thing. Barbara carefully opened the box, lifted the large Bible onto the table, and turned to the Family Tree. Tied with a dainty thread, an unidentified lock of golden hair fell from between the pages. I pictured Edmund's wife, Isabel, clipping the delicate strand of baby's curls and tucking it into the Bible for safekeeping. That lock, placed there with the list of her babies, spoke of a tender moment in time. Perhaps Isabel had clipped the curls from the head of her first born, before she was constantly busy with one new baby after another.

"Edmund left tracks all over history," I pondered, "But did you ever hear about Isabel? Other than having all these children, I mean?"

Thinking of my daughter Elise's long-ago disagreement with Edmund Dumas' view on a woman's role in marriage, I wondered if Isabel would agree that a woman's role should include obedience. At a recent Sacred Harp singing, I'd heard other singers object to the words of Edmund's controversial song, "Edmonds" #115 in *The Sacred Harp*: "The woman is commanded her husband to obey, In everything that's lawful, Until her dying day." The song was seldom sung, and some suggested that it should be omitted from the songbook's next edition.

Someone had taken great care to insure that the Edmund Dumas family of thirteen children was well documented in the family Bible. The delicate handwriting appeared unhurried and flowed smoothly across the page with an assured flourish, indicating a well-educated writer with sufficient time to practice penmanship. I assumed it was Isabel. If so, she undoubtedly had help caring for the house and children, perhaps in the form of slave help.

Barbara responded, "Mother did a lot of research tracing our roots and was particularly interested in the women. The Dumas women—and men— were strong proponents of education for women, which was not generally accepted at the time. Many of the Dumas girls could boast of attending Pleasant Grove Academy, a noted school of the day."

Barbara's mother believed Isabel had maintained an exceptionally strong yearning to learn, which she passed on to her daughters as well as her sons; Edmund, too, solidly supported that position. He wrote that as a small child, he witnessed his mother's baptism in Little River.

"Of course, it was a full immersion baptism," Barbara said, "which must have frightened little Edmund half to death, because he later asked his mother if the preacher was trying to drown her. She sat Edmund down for a serious talk about his spiritual life that affected him so strongly, he took it with him the rest of his life."

Edmund's mother was illiterate as were most women of her time, but she begged him to study diligently so he could read the Bible to her. "So, it was his mother who first stressed to him the importance of a good education. Edmund later wanted his wife and daughters to have the freedom to pursue what his mother had been denied."

Barbara opened an envelope with other photocopied memorabilia. One item was a letter from Edmund to a cousin, William Andrew Jackson Dumas, whom Edmund counted as a former student. I saw a reference to his brother, Jeremiah, my Grandma's grandfather, with news that he had moved his family to Louisiana "and was doing well."

Mary had also provided Barbara with vague directions to the Dumas' original home; she believed they would have lived within walking distance of their church since the family patriarch had donated a portion of his own land for the church to be built. Mary remembered the church being a building with very tall windows and an adjacent cemetery, located a short distance from Barnesville on the road to Forsyth. We could be sure we'd found the right church by reading the tombstones, many of which should be Dumas monuments. She couldn't remember the name of the church, other than that it was Primitive Baptist.

We figured there couldn't be too many Primitive Baptist churches along a thirteen-mile stretch of country road, but after Barbara and I had hunted through six different Baptist churchyards without success, we suspected that we lacked at least one vital clue. Barbara pulled over at a convenience store to phone Mary.

Returning to the car, Barbara shifted into reverse and said, "I grew up in Barnesville and thought I knew everything about my home town. It seems there's more than one road that leads to Forsyth and we should have taken the old road instead. It runs right next to the railroad tracks through what was once the community of Goggins Station. Mary says we should be able to find the church right across the road from where the station used to be."

After we retraced our route and took a few specified turns, we spotted a steep-roofed church on the left, set far back from the road in a grove of pecan trees. We turned into a curving drive and passed a marble marker that read, "Union Primitive Baptist Church, established 1837."

Landscaping of the grounds was informal, though well tended. Small, neatly trimmed shrubs were centered between sturdy red brick foundation piers. Tall windows along the length of the church emphasized the building's height and the long, dark wood shutters contrasted sharply against the bright white exterior. Beneath the peak of the shingled roof was an arched opening with fixed louvers. A half-dozen steps, bordered on each side with sturdy metal handrails, led to double doors of the entrance.

"So much attentive care—" Barbara began, but her words fell away into silence like evaporating raindrops of a summer shower. The silence seemed alive, holding its breath. There was no need to state what we each knew to be true; we were on hallowed ground.

We walked wordlessly to the rear of the building toward a graceful metal fence around an assortment of monuments. As we passed through the open gate, a mass of stones with deteriorating mortar caught my eye. It measured about seven feet in length, four feet wide, and four feet high. I walked around the strange mound, but found no identifying marker.

Barbara, who had turned to face an adjacent marble obelisk, exclaimed, "Oh, it's engraved all around: Benjamin F. Dumas, Died 1853, Age 70 Years." She moved closer to read carving of a smaller size, "Donater of Five Acres of Land for Church." Continuing to the left adjoining side of the stone, Barbara read, "Martha Urcery, Wife of Benjamin F. Dumas, Died 1838."

I was appalled. "Her last name was *Ussery*. You'd think they would check spellings before carving into stone."

Barbara smiled and shrugged, turning to the next monument—a taller, thinner spire. "This one is for Thomas Dumas, and his wife was Sharlot."

"Thomas was the second oldest brother after Edmund," I said. "Thomas was Edmund's right-hand man, and the two of them were the executors of the Dumas family estate. They were the older brothers my ancestor Jeremiah wanted to emulate."

"You sound just like my mother, talking as if you knew them personally."

"I feel like I do know them. And I think I know something about this strange unidentified heap of stones. It's the only above-ground tomb here; it must be the tomb of our great-great-great-grandfather, the family patriarch, Benjamin Franklin Dumas."

"But his name is on the large monument. It says—"

"I know, but the monument was erected at a later date in honor of both parents. See, it was placed as close as possible to his grave. Benjamin Franklin's wife's grave must be unmarked also, but of course, she would be right here, too."

"So we've found the home place," Barbara said softly. "And this is where they gathered to worship, to marry, to be baptized, and to commit these souls to eternity. Sorrow is a common denominator; joy, too. They gathered here together in God's presence, in life and death. It's peaceful, isn't it? Like home."

We walked among the monuments, trying to place family members in our own frame of reference. Barbara found the family grouping for Edmund Dumas, with Edmund and Isabel's similar markers standing side by side, Isabel humbly in her husband's shadow.

I was suddenly amused, remembering when I told my grandchildren that Edmund Dumas was a circuit preacher who traveled by horse over 100,000 miles, five-year-old Colin's eyes opened wide and he blurted out, "Wow. What was his horse's name?"

Over his forty-year ministry, Edmund must have been away from his home and family a lot of the time. It was easier for the preacher to ride alone on his horse to his parishioners than for entire families to travel the distance. It was hard to imagine that Edmund was the county judge and a traveling, singing preacher at the same time. He served as pastor for two churches simultaneously, and the congregations alternated their Sundays. If they had a Sacred Harp singing, Saturday might have been taken, too. Perhaps Isabel and the children went along some of the time but surely not every time Edmund left. Grandma once told me that families gathered pillows and quilts and piled into a horse-drawn wagon, sometimes staying for days with seldom-seen relatives. Singings were their social life.

"With their thirteen children, Edmund and Isabel would have had a mighty crowded wagon," Barbara said. "There's no way he could have managed to do so much without an equal commitment on Isabel's part. Her half of the partnership required a lot of unsung responsibility."

Edmund acknowledged that commitment of providing for his family in his controversial song:

This woman, she was taken from under Adam's arm,
And she must be protected from injury and harm.
This woman was not taken from Adam's feet, we see;
And she must not be abused, the meaning seems to be.

"Edmonds" #115 in *The Sacred Harp*
Words and music, Edmund Dumas, 1869

We stood quietly for a moment near the monuments placed side by side for the couple who had together completed their work on earth.

"They must sometimes have thought of coming generations, of us," Barbara said. "Their lasting contributions make me feel humble and unworthy. Mother often spoke of the 'balcony' people, the ones who've gone before. She said they never really leave us." She turned again to read Edmund's chosen inscription. "He felt unworthy, too. See how he sums up his life: a sinner saved by grace. He wasn't boasting of righteousness but admitting his human need for forgiveness."

This was what I'd wanted to see and experience—to be in the place of my ancestors' earthly home, to be where the words and music of Sacred Harp songs were composed, and to *feel* it. I felt I was part of something with no beginning or end, stretching from the primordial to the everlasting. Though the voices of those whose names are engraved on these headstones are now silenced, their songs continue to be sung and their souls have found another home, "a brighter world on high."

On the drive back to Atlanta, I thought of what finding the Dumas home place meant to me. Nothing there had my exact name on it, but still I knew I had received an incomparable heritage through Grandma's cherished Sacred Harp songbook. The man, Jeremiah Dumas, who bequeathed it to her had formed his love of the music where his family's roots were—where the music's roots were—right here in Georgia. They continue to communicate with me through the music, our shared faith, and a far-reaching, familial love.

When I arrived home, I sifted through the details in my copies of new information now strewn across the dining room table. I was eager to report to Doug what I'd learned from the day's expedition. As I chattered on, Doug glanced over the tabletop where the copied pages of Edmund's letter to his cousin William were lying beside the copied Bible entries. He asked if the two documents were written by the same person, and I matter-of-factly told him Edmund wrote the letter, but it was likely Isabel who listed the children's names.

Doug frowned and sat down for a closer examination. He showed me that the letters *B* and *E* were made with the same characteristic curvature. Carefully comparing other scripted letters, Doug reached the same conclusion; it was Edmund, not Isabel, who had meticulously documented the details of each child in the family Bible. These family milestones were not exclusive to Isabel's world. Perhaps they had together hidden away the lock of baby hair because the tiny keepsake was cherished by both partners in the marriage, because this was evidence of their love and the home they'd made together. I realized that Edmund and Isabel saw heart-to-heart.

I pictured Edmund Dumas as he sat at his desk writing to the cousin who'd moved away.

Barnesville, Ga., March 1st, 1870
My dear beloved cousin,

Your last letter is before me, and its contents duly considered and, I will assure you, very highly appreciated. It is true that I have received two letters from you since I've written to you: yet you ought to do that well every time I write to you, and if you but just knew my condition and you could travel with me just one month and see the labors that I have to perform in a religious sense; and then see what I have to do in what little time I am at home, I am sure that you would say to me, Cousin Ed, I ought to write four letters to your one. I want you to write to me often; and I will write to you as often as I can. I am rejoiced every time I can hear from you, for I do know that I love my kinsfolk, wherever they may be, and do wish them well in time and in eternity. Cousin William, I am proud of you bearing my name Dumas, for I know that your opportunities have been bad in procuring of an education, yet you have by industry and the dint of study grown up to considerable scholarship. You recollect you went to school to me when a little boy, and I often present to my children your letters in its hand writing and beautiful construction of sentences, in order to show them what the dint of study can do, and I tell them to imitate you.

Cousin William, your poor old cousin is now growing old. A few more beating rains and chilling winds, and the storm of life will have blown over with me. I feel that in the end of life's journey, Heaven is my home. How is it with you, Cousin William? Have you a hope in Christ, that when you die and go hence, that you will meet your poor old cousin in Heaven? If you have no hope, may God through our Lord Jesus Christ give you one, I pray.

Cousin William, on a preaching tour some six weeks ago, while returning home during a cold snap in January last, I got very cold—and the next day I had a paralytic stroke in my head and face that twisted my head and mouth about considerably. I have been confined at home nearly ever since. I am much better now, but am very nervous as you see by my writing. My family is moderately well. My girls, all but my baby girl, are all married off. Jane, you know married Wiley J. Sikes, Nannie married Mr. W. S. O'Neal, Lucinda married Mr. W.G. Smith, Mattie married Mr. James M. Horne, all of whom are of the first families in this county, and are doing well. My son Thomas is living about four miles from me, his wife has seven children and is doing well. I have my sons Frank, Eddy, Moses, Alex, and Newton, with me. Frank and Eddy are grown and working for themselves. Brothers Thomas, Moses, Covington, and Jeremiah are all yet living and doing well. Brother Covington is living in Terrell County about 150 miles south of where I live. Brother Jeremiah is yet living in Louisiana. My two sisters, [Nancy] and [Frances], are yet living in this section of the country, and doing well.

The farmers are fixing up to plant corn next week. The farmers made a good crop of cotton last year, which has greatly relieved the country. But oh, the sad rule of radical reconstruction in Georgia under the Morton Bill—if you were here, I am sure you would say that you wouldn't give a fig for the government, but enough of that.

You will please give your dear Mother and all of my kindred my best wishes for their present and future prosperity through life. May God bless you all I pray. All of my children and kindred send their love to you all.

Yours in the bonds of kindred ties,
Edmund Dumas

His writing revealed a person who was much as I'd imagined—warm and good humored but serious. The handwriting of the letter no longer flowed as effortlessly across the page as it had in the family Bible, but Edmund had himself explained the reason.

Several major lines of thought stayed with me, and I, too, agreed that I wouldn't give a fig for the government. The remark that son Thomas' wife had seven children showed that women were viewed as possessions and responsibilities, with lives quite apart from a man's world. From my vantage point, looking backward in time, I managed to put my bruised feelings aside and see Edmund Dumas clearly as a product of his time.

Slavery was another issue that cast a dark shadow despite its not being addressed. Attached to the letter had been a recent note from a descendent of Edmund's cousin, William, who was seeking information about her family before leaving Georgia for Missouri in the 1850s. She wondered if her descendants were considered renegades by their southern relatives for fighting on the Union side in the Civil War. Her comment was followed by a quickly drawn smiling face, but I noted the date of Edmund's letter, 1870, and I knew undoubtedly that both men chose to leave relevant and heartbreaking war stories untold. The letter's date told me the "storm of life" had raged fiercely around them, and its penalties continued through the Reconstruction era as Edmund Dumas persisted in his postman-like rounds as a traveling preacher.

In addition, the "beating rains and chilling winds" he'd braved over a forty-year ministry had sapped his strength and his health. With my new experience of living through the seemingly incessant rain of Georgia, I easily understood the words Edmund Dumas dedicated to his traveling, singing-master colleague, B.F. White:

> *I'm a long time trav'ling here below,*
> *I'm a long time trav'ling away from home,*
> *I'm a long time trav'ling here below, to lay this body down.*

"White" #288 in *The Sacred Harp*
Words, *Dobell's New Selection*, 1810; music, Edmund Dumas, 1856

As I hummed the words, I imagined Edmund singing aloud to his faithful horse. I felt its steady, trotting pace and the powerful rhythm of hooves, beating in sync as the words and music merged in the preacher's mind. Edmund reportedly wrote the song "White" #288 in 1856, but I found no first-hand account of how or when he met B.F. White, publisher of *The Sacred Harp* in 1844, or how he met composer and preacher J.P. Reese, for whom he wrote the song "Reese" #418 in *The Sacred Harp*. At a singing,

"White" #288 in The Sacred Harp, shown here in the 1991 revision, was written by Edmund Dumas in honor of his friend and mentor, B.F. White.

the Sacred Harp historian, John Plunkett, handed me a copy of a song by Edmund Dumas he had found in his research that had been published in *The Organ*, a newspaper B.F. White founded in 1852 to promote interest in Sacred Harp music. The men—White, Reese, and Dumas—shared a love of the music and were among the stalwarts in both the Southern Musical Convention (1845) and the Chattahoochee Musical Convention (1852). The growing popularity of the music had made it necessary to form the second convention. The Chattahoochee is the oldest continuing shape-note music convention, having met every year, even through the years of the Civil War, since its organization in 1852.

A page preceding the appendix of additional tunes in Grandma's worn songbook placed Edmund Dumas on the committee headed by White that was appointed in 1869 by the Southern Musical Convention of the State of Georgia to revise the previous 1859 edition of *The Sacred Harp* and select new songs to be added. It seems natural that Edmund would seek White's and Reese's advice about his latest compositions. Perhaps they "swapped tunes" with each other for respected critiques.

These two conventions, the Southern and the Chattahoochee, established the form and procedure for Sacred Harp singings that has continued into the present day. Because the strong traditions of rural southern—primarily Primitive Baptist—churches have kept the singings virtually unchanged, we

45

(top) "Rees" #418 in *The Sacred Harp*, 1869 revision, was written to honor Dumas' friend and musical colleague, J. P. Rees. Names given to compositions were often simply names of places or people. ("Rees" in later editions was spelled "Reese".)

(bottom) "Dumas" #426t in *The Sacred Harp*, 1869 revision, is Rees' reciprocating composition.

may assume that the singers' emotional connection with the music is the same. Our voices sing the same notes and words, fully convinced that if we were to suddenly change places with a singer from the nineteenth century, we would not miss a beat.

This inner knowledge assures present-day singers that, as early singers faced each other across the hollow square, they can also experience the same profound sense of all-inclusive spiritual union. Though a perfect tone might not be achieved, our voices are accepted as they are, as from our souls, bare, unashamed, and in fervent communion with our Creator.

NEW APPENDIX TO THE SACRED HARP.

THE Committee appointed by " The Southern Musical Convention of the State of Georgia," at its last session, to whom were referred the revision and enlargement of the SACRED HARP, beg leave to make the following report. In discharging the duties of said appointment to the best of their ability, they carefully examined the work, and corrected a few verbal and typographical errors which had escaped detection in the previous edition. In this Appendix they have introduced a large number of new compositions from the pens of the most eminent teachers and composers of vocal music. They have also displaced several pieces in the body of the work for others which they think will prove favorite compositions. In the judgment of the Committee THE SACRED HARP is now fully suited to the wants of the singing public, and will meet the taste and feelings of the Southern people.

All of which is respectfully submitted.

B. F. WHITE,
EDMUND DUMAS,
ABSALOM OGLETREE,
R. F. M. MANN,
MARION PATRICK.
Committee.

NOVEMBER, 1869.

Page introducing the Appendix of 1869 revision of The Sacred Harp showing Edmund Dumas on the committee appointed by "The Southern Musical Convention of the State of Georgia" to revise and enlarge The Sacred Harp. B. F. White chaired the committee and was personally involved in selecting like-minded committee members to advance his collection of shape-note music.

As Joe Dan Boyd quotes the black Sacred Harp singer, Dewey Williams, "You go to an all-day singing and, by the middle of the next week, those songs will still be ringing in you. The music is one of the greatest things I know of. It's sung with a joyful noise—so much so that it raises the hair on your head once in a while and makes it feel like you got a hat on. It sort of stirs you up. . . . People wrote the old hymn songs under the authorization of the Holy Spirit, and after this generation come on, they put them in *The Sacred Harp* and put notes on them, like signs on a road. *The Sacred Harp* wasn't written for no price. It was written to have it sung."

The music has never stopped. We still see three or four front-row tenors pouring into the music everything in their being. In unison, their emphatic arm gestures drive the pounding, pulsing beat that is the lifeblood of the soul to the Sacred Harp singer.

On the Rock of Ages founded, who can shake thy sure repose?
With salvation's wall surrounded, thou mayst smile at all thy foes.

"Jefferson" # 148 in *The Sacred Harp*
Words, John Newton, 1779; music, *Tennessee Harmony*, 1818

CHAPTER 5

Revelations—Settlement of the Will

MARRIAGE records at the courthouse revealed that Aaron David Dumas and Winnie Collier were married in January of 1847 in a ceremony performed by his brother, Edmund Dumas, pastor of Union Primitive Baptist Church. I wondered about the young wife Davie left behind on his adventure to California, and I turned again to Carine for answers.

"I've been imagining," I began, "what I would have done if my husband had abandoned me back in the 1800s? That's really what we're talking about, you know. Winnie couldn't simply go out and get a job back then. I think she might have gone home to her parents. One news story said they had two children who died before reaching their first birthday. Where should I begin looking for them?"

"Why, that's easy. You're right there in Atlanta, the state capital; the Georgia State Archives are right at your fingertips. You'll need to find the 1850 census. If you find Winnie Collier, you'll find any children they had. The census is about the only place I know to find anything at all about a child—unless there's a gravestone somewhere. If an infant died, the matter was never discussed publicly in those days as the subject was too intimate; it was a personal, private matter."

"And losing a child wasn't uncommon back then, was it? It must have been even more painful than today when we can grieve openly." I suddenly remembered the tragic death of Carine's son and caught my breath. "Oh, Carine, I'm sorry. It was thoughtless of me to speak of losing a child."

"I don't avoid the subject. I've found it to be a comfort when others acknowledge my loss, and I agree that perhaps Winnie's sorrow was especially hard to bear, suppressed as if it never happened."

"Why would Davie leave her at such a difficult time? Did he try to comfort her somehow? Maybe she didn't want to get pregnant again."

"Well, pregnancy was virtually synonymous with marriage," Carine said.

"Maybe Davie Dumas didn't want to be married in the first place. He might have been 'encouraged' with a shotgun wedding."

Carine, softening my cynicism, said, "We'll never know. We can only assume that on that winter day in 1847, they both had hopes for happiness like any other couple who makes a commitment based on their love and desire for each other."

"Do you suppose Davie left because of alienation within the family? We already suspect that his father, Benjamin Franklin Dumas, was unhappy with him about something of critical importance."

"We could speculate anything," Carine said. "However, you first need to establish some facts. Find her parents. Your assumption that Winnie went home to her folks is a fairly safe guess."

"They might have lived a long way off."

"Then you're out of luck, though it's more likely that they were neighbors. Young people didn't have many opportunities to meet prospective mates from too great a distance. You might also check for records of Winnie's family in the counties adjacent to Monroe County. And you could try to find out something about the old Union Primitive Baptist Church. There might be some helpful information in the church minutes."

"Minutes? Would they keep records back that far?"

"I have copies of the minutes from Shady Grove Baptist Church all the way back to when it was first organized," Carine said. "That's roughly the same time frame. Make a list and start looking with an open mind."

Because Georgia was a major stage in the westward migration of America, there is always a full house of genealogy seekers at the State Archives, a large utilitarian building in the shadow of the gold-domed Georgia capitol. And as soon as I learned how to access microfiche records, I began combing the 1850 census for *Dumas* and *Collier*.

There was no evidence of Winnie's whereabouts in Monroe County, but in the adjacent 1850 Pike County census, in household No. 791, I found: Randolph H. Collier, age seventy-one, male; Nancy Collier, age fifty-five, female; and Winnie Dumas, age twenty-four, female. So Winnie did go home to her folks, but there were no other family members listed—no children. The compilation continued with the unrelated household No. 792.

I felt a pang of sadness for the absent babies, but I also felt a thrill of accomplishment as a rookie detective. If Winnie had returned home, then perhaps the wife of Davie's prospecting buddy, William Horne, had done the same. I repeated the process with a search for *Horne*. I found a surprise in the Monroe County household of Thomas Dumas, who along with his brother Edmund, was administrator of their father Benjamin Franklin Dumas' estate. Thomas' age was given as thirty-nine and his wife, Charlotte, was thirty-five. The remaining members of the household were

Martha Dumas Horne, age nineteen; Mary Horne, age three; and Simeon Horne, age one.

In finding that Martha Dumas Horne, the wife of Davie's partner, had also returned to her parents' home, I also discovered that William Horne had been married to Davie's own niece. Martha Dumas Horne, who was possibly named for her grandmother Martha Ussery Dumas, also had two documented children. Could the newspaper's source have been mistaken that Davie and Winnie were parents?

Winnie went home to her family, and Davie left for California never to come back. The bare facts I discovered suggested a troubled relationship but were too few to reveal more than a sketchy trail. There were, however, additional public records in Monroe County that I'd not yet checked.

On arriving at the courthouse, I stopped by Judge Spear's office to say hello. "So you're back at work. What's the first item on today's agenda?"

"Some unfinished tasks. I haven't exactly pinpointed the location of the Dumas home, but I think I'm close enough since we found the church. I'm afraid there's no longer a house. This time, I'm planning a more systematic search of chronological transactions. I need to get the right sequence to understand what was going on."

"One thing you might keep in mind is that the normal land grant from the Georgia land lottery—called a 'lot'—was exactly 202.5 acres. I understand that Benjamin Franklin Dumas bought several additional lots from owners who'd acquired lottery land with the sole intent of selling for a tidy profit to planters who wanted to acquire larger land holdings. So his lands were not strictly contiguous."

I thanked the judge and proceeded up the echoing stairway to locate the legal recordings of property transactions. When I examined the books, I found that the penmanship was not the same fastidious hand I'd seen before. Instead, the handwriting of the transcribing clerk appeared hurried and somewhat careless, so I would have to be especially attentive.

Focusing only on the deeds involving the father and a son or daughter, I uncovered one such documentation stating that Benjamin Franklin Dumas deeded "on May 26, 1848, for and in consideration of the natural love and affection that I bear to my son, Aaron David Dumas, *one hundred and one-fourth acres* of land, it being the *west* half of lot number 189 . . ."

If a lot of land were 202.5 acres, then each half would be 101.25 acres; the transcribing clerk had omitted part of Davie's lot description, a minor discrepancy but irritating, nonetheless.

About six months later, on November 18, 1848, Benjamin Franklin Dumas deeded "in consideration of the natural love and affection that I bear to my daughter Frances Adams (wife of William Lucas Adams) one hundred one and one-fourth acres in said county and state it being the *east* half of lot of land whereon Aaron D. Dumas now lives."

This proved that Davie was still in Georgia in the fall of 1848. His sister had apparently married and was given the adjacent farmland.

I found other deeds from Benjamin Franklin Dumas, both as grantee and grantor, for he had numerous land holdings; however, in all the recorded transactions, I located only one other deed involving Aaron David Dumas. I closely examined the original pages on which the entries were posted. The last recorded transaction that Aaron David Dumas left behind in Monroe County was made "the first day of May in the Year of our Lord One thousand Eight hundred and forty—"

Forty-*what?* The clerk had made another careless error, but each prior and succeeding entry on the same page claimed the year to be 1849. I had to find out if this was the same transaction mentioned in the *Monroe Advertiser.*

"Aaron D. Dumas of the county and state aforesaid witnesseth that for and in Consideration of the sum of Six hundred dollars . . . do convey unto Owen J. Willis of the same county and state . . . all that parcel of Land . . . known as the *west half of lot number 189* containing One hundred One and One fourth acres."

There was the answer. The land that Davie sold—the only land he ever owned in Monroe County—was the same parcel his father had given him only months before. His father, Benjamin Franklin Dumas, gave Davie and his bride Winnie a hundred acres for their home. And something happened that caused Davie to disregard his father's wishes, sell out, take the money, and run. It's no wonder Benjamin Franklin got mad.

Perhaps Davie's public reason for leaving was to join the gold rush, but he did leave abruptly, sell the home he shared with Winnie right out from under her, and he never came back. It seems too tame to simply say he left to join the gold rush.

Deep in thought, I gathered my notes and prepared to leave. It was the end of another day spent reading tedious records at the courthouse, and there was still no Book K. Perhaps it had slipped behind a bookcase. I was only faintly aware of the noisy clicking of my heels on the granite steps of the stairway. I hesitated a brief moment before pushing open the right side of the double doors to exit.

The sun, still high in the sky, had begun its setting toward the west and beamed its blinding rays into my eyes. At that moment, I recalled my last visit to the courthouse and a chance encounter at the building's lone copy machine.

A woman named Jane Newton had asked if I was researching genealogy and, after my positive response, said she had genealogy files for nearly everyone in town at her office, the tax assessor's office, right across the street. Doug was out of town, and with no pressing need to rush back to Atlanta, I crossed the street to see if she had any Dumas information.

Jane Newton had a Dumas file, all right; she had a trove. In the file were many copied pages from the missing Book K, and Jane generously allowed me to make copies of my own.

Facts were accumulating, and puzzle pieces were beginning to fit together. I felt I should follow Carine's suggestion to locate the earliest church records—if such records still existed. Doug and I planned to attend a service at Union Primitive Baptist Church soon. Until then, there was more ornate script of legalese to translate.

I couldn't examine the pages in detail until late that night. There were thirty pages that covered the final settlement of Benjamin Franklin Dumas' will. I settled comfortably in bed to read through my collection of copies, and with Doug away, without concern I kept my lamp burning into the morning hours.

I discovered that Jeremiah Dumas did indeed return to Georgia for the final distribution of assets under the terms of the will. Jane Newton's file included copies of an itemized auction inventory of Benjamin Franklin Dumas' estate, listing the amount and buyer of each item sold, complete with detailed reports to the court stating exactly what each heir received—*including Jeremiah's own sealed signature in acknowledgement.*

These new revelations, however, unearthed deeper misgivings. Here I read indisputable evidence that Jeremiah was not only a beneficiary of the labor of slaves but used nearly half of his inheritance—eight hundred dollars of eighteen hundred—to purchase a "prime" slave from his father's estate, a young man of about twenty-five years named Phil.

When I finally turned out the light, I found only fitful sleep. In the hazy, floating obscurity where the mind, more agile, races ahead of the body to escape uneasy slumber, I sensed that a spirit from the past had escaped those scripted words on the long-silent pages. From habit, I reached for Doug. Instead of his comforting form, my arm fell upon the stack of papers that had been sleepily laid aside, and I inadvertently brushed them to the floor. Startled by the intrusive sound, I roused, aware of an eerie presence in the room.

"Who's there?" I called aloud.

As my body tensed in alarm, the mantel clock in the next room chimed a half-hour and familiar objects began to take shape around me. I realized

I had awakened in the middle of a disturbing dream, one in which I'd been transported back in time.

The year would have been 1837, for the patriarch of the plantation, Benjamin Franklin Dumas, was pacing off the placement of the new church on the five acres of land he'd donated for the purpose. His sons, Edmund, the church's future pastor, and Thomas, the next oldest, were actively engaged in the discussion. Jeremiah, my direct ancestor, followed and listened attentively.

The men pictured the church building set in a grove of trees at the crest of a rise at a bend in the road. Directly across the road was the railroad station for the Goggins community, a convenient location for transporting crops to market. The plantation had its own gin-house, and the cotton fields stretched out behind the church and beyond the area earmarked for a cemetery. A large wagon was almost overflowing with cotton being picked by slaves in the field. I walked, unseen but all-hearing, with the men toward the wagon.

As we approached, I looked more closely at the slaves and saw they were all faceless but one. A slender black boy about ten years old struggled with every sinew in his body to lift a long, trailing sack of cotton into the wagon.

Benjamin Franklin walked admiringly to the wagon. He patted the child on the head and said, "Good work, boy. You can out-pick anybody out there." The boy's perspiring face beamed with pride. The plantation owner continued, "No doubt about it, you're going to make me a prime field hand. You'll be the prime man, Phil."

The boy was Phil, the slave Jeremiah would buy from his father's estate fifteen years later. As morning light filled the room, I lay in bed and contemplated the reality of the scene I'd dreamed.

In the years since Benjamin Franklin Dumas had acquired his plantation in the 1822 land lottery, the land had been cleared and become productive, as expected. Benjamin Franklin, in his early fifties, was at the zenith of his life. His son Edmund would have been twenty-seven years old, already a teacher, songwriter, and orator, if not yet a preacher. Thomas was following Edmund's example and had become his brother's able assistant. Jeremiah, at age twenty, would be formulating his own dreams, perhaps to become a plantation owner, like their father.

Over the following fifteen years, the plantation would continue to prosper. Union Primitive Baptist Church would become firmly established and grow in membership. Jeremiah would follow his dream and take his family to Louisiana. The slave boy Phil would reach adulthood and perhaps have a family of his own.

Then in March of 1853, that world changed forever. Jeremiah bought Phil to further his dream in Louisiana.

The eyes of the slave child, Phil, seemed fixed on me, imploring me to finally set him free. If anyone would ever know his identity, it would be up to me.

I am a poor, wayfaring stranger, while journ'ying thru this world of woe,

Yet there's no sickness, toil, nor danger, in that bright land to which I go.

I know dark clouds will gather o'er me, I know my way is rough and steep;

Yet beauteous fields lie just before me, where God's redeemed their vigils keep.

"Wayfaring Stranger" #457 in *The Sacred Harp*
Words, Bever's *Christian Songster*, 1858; music, John M. Dye, 1935

CHAPTER 6

The Minutes

I was unable to escape the specter of a direct link with slavery. It seemed that I was swimming a river with a treacherous undertow. My questions demanded answers, and this time, Carine had none to offer.

"Of course, I'm aware there were slave owners in our family's early history in America. In fact, you'll find I've made note of it all the way back through North Carolina to the beginning in Virginia. But for the most part since we've been here in Louisiana, our history has been post-Civil War. I'm sure you can find records that document answers to what you're asking, but remember that slavery harmed everyone—black and white—and the South has been trying to put that sorrowful chapter behind us."

When Mother came from Texas for a visit in the spring, I questioned her regarding possible Dumas slave ownership.

"Good gracious, I don't see how Mama's family could have ever owned any slaves. The Dumases were too poor to own much of anything, just the land they farmed to barely scratch a living. My father's people were said to have been wealthy, but I don't remember hearing about anyone who ever owned slaves."

"Where did all the slaves go after the war? Did they stay there, maybe to work?"

"How would I know that? That was a long time before my parents were born, a whole generation before they were born; your Grandma was born in 1881—" Mother's hands, rarely idle, had found a kitchen towel with a raveling hem. She reached for a spool of thread on the lamp table, unrolled an arm's length, clipped the thread with a quick motion, and handed the thread and a needle from her purse sewing kit to me.

"Here, honey, will you please thread this for me? I might as well have you thread half a dozen needles for me so I won't be asking you for help over and over again."

"Don't scoot away from the subject so quickly," I said. "It's important for me to learn what our family was doing at the time of the Civil War. Grandma always said she looked on great-uncle William as a father, and the Civil War was certainly real enough to him; that's where he lost his leg."

"That's right, but again the Civil War was over long before your Grandma was born. I suppose William had stopped talking about it and just focused on trying to support the family."

"You say Grandma's family was poor, but they owned land. How did the black people there support their families?"

"They had a hard time, like everybody else. I used to feel sorry for the little Negro kids; their school was in such bad shape. They couldn't go to school when the weather was freezing cold because the school didn't have enough heat. One of the rich old farmers finally built them a new school on his land. They still had to walk a long way. But then, we did, too."

"How did so many black people begin living in Louisiana in the first place if their ancestors hadn't been slaves to the landowners?"

"Maybe some of them were slaves once. I don't know. There was a very good relationship between whites and blacks in north Louisiana where we lived. Do you remember Aunt Sally? While she was still alive, I never failed to take you to see her when we were down home. I don't know what Mama would have done without Aunt Sally those years when she had little ones who were still babies when the next one came along."

"Oh, yes, I do remember Aunt Sally," I said. "I must have been about four or five years old when she died. She used to help Grandma with the laundry, didn't she?"

"Yes, with all the chores. Mama helped her, too. Of course, Aunt Sally didn't have any children of her own at home in those days. She was old from my first memory of her, always the same sweet old lady. Mama shared whatever she had with her; when Mama canned food, there was always some for Aunt Sally, and if the boys caught fish or if Papa killed a hog, she had a share. Then, when Aunt Sally's health was so bad before she died, Mama took care of her."

"Did you ever wonder why she was called *Aunt* Sally? That has a pretty strong connotation."

"Why, it was out of respect for her age. That was the custom. We loved Aunt Sally as much as if she had really been family."

"Do you think Aunt Sally's parents were slaves?"

"Maybe they were, but I don't know. I'm sorry I can't tell you something I don't know." Mother paused and furrowed her brow. "You know, I do remember—maybe before I started to school—there was an old colored man who lived up on the Meeks' place. I remember hearing that he had been a slave. Poor old man—he had to use a cane when he hobbled around. He didn't have any family at all, as far as I know, and the Meeks family took care of him. The grownups used to whisper that he was a eunuch. I didn't know then what that meant. I thought that was his nationality."

"Oh, Mother!"

"I don't think you'll find a pretty story tucked inside such an ugly chapter of history. It has passed and should be put to rest, so why are you pursuing these memories of slavery?"

"It's the other way around. It's pursuing me. I can't explain why, but this is something I know I have to do. It began when I *happened* to see a magazine article about Grandma's old Sacred Harp music, and then we *happened* to find ourselves here in Georgia where her family and the music originated. There has been one coincidence after another, and—"

When I'd gone with Doug to Washington, DC, a few weeks earlier, I'd spent my time at the Daughters of the American Revolution library, only a few blocks from the White House. Carine's book was there, and she had wanted me to go see their main library where she'd done much of her research.

"I now understand that I've seen only one slim dimension of our history, and it's all lily-white," I continued. "I want to go back to take a closer look at some of the records."

"Legal records won't tell you about personal relationships like that of Mama and Aunt Sally."

"That's true most of the time. But Benjamin Franklin Dumas' will provided for the care of his slaves. He listed each one specifically, like Barney and Nelly, who were of particular concern to him. Barney and Nelly were to be inherited by his daughter Nancy. Apparently, they were house servants because Nancy is the daughter who received the home, the gin house, and the orchard and garden. She also got his fancy carriage, the barouche."

"How do you know his wishes were carried out?"

"That's where Judge Spear's snapshot of the family comes into play," I said. "In the interval between Benjamin Franklin's death and the final disposition of his estate, there's roughly a year in which all expenditures of the estate were recorded. It's like reading someone's checkbook."

Periodically, sums were spent for provisions and clothing for all of the slaves until they became the responsibility of their new owners. There was an intriguing payment for $26.75 to a Dr. James Wynn to cover his bill for nine visits for the care of a "decrepit Negro woman" named Nelly. The amount included charges for medicine—three boxes of *vegetable* pills—and for the doctor's transportation. The frequency of the doctor visits indicated a desperate hope for a cure, but the medications didn't work and Nelly's coffin was listed as a subsequent expenditure.

"But what I find most fascinating is that one of the very first payments out of the estate was also to Dr. James Wynn for the care of Benjamin Franklin Dumas himself. The Dumas heirs evidently cared enough to give the house servant the same level of medical care provided to the master of the plantation."

"They both died," Mother said dryly.

"The point is they were both cared for and in exactly the same way. Nelly was like Aunt Sally. Maybe they even called her Aunt Nelly and buried her at the same cemetery."

"Oh, the Union Primitive Baptist Church probably had a slave cemetery. They had separate churches and schools and everything else," Mother said. "I would like to go see that country church; you've lamented so long about my ancestors leaving such a beautiful place, I'd like to take a look for myself."

When Doug arrived home from the office, I was trying to find how to contact the Union Primitive Baptist Church to find the time for Sunday's service, but the church did not have an office or even a phone listing. After a series of calls to Barbara and her cousins, I learned that services were held only on alternate Sundays, and the upcoming Sunday was a scheduled "church" day.

On arriving at Sunday's service, we were welcomed warmly by the small congregation, who greeted each other even more heartily, like long-lost kin. A number of people had traveled a considerable distance, and apparently, the membership was made predominantly of descendants of a single Willis family. I'd hoped to find a link to the Dumas family, especially to Edmund Dumas or his music, but their hymn book was not *The Sacred Harp* or any other shape-note version.

At the close of the service, everyone was instructed to gather in the room at the rear of the sanctuary. The destination was a dining room and kitchen, already set up for serving food that had been brought in abundance and stored in the kitchen prior to the service. The pastor's wife leaned the backs of folding chairs against one of the tables for Mother, Doug, and me. She said, "Please sit here by us so we can get acquainted."

In response to polite questioning, Mother and I explained our familial connection to the church. The pastor, Elder W.E. Evans, was aware that land for the church and cemetery had been a gift from Benjamin Franklin Dumas.

"I do know some Dumas descendants in Barnesville," he said. "And some descendents live in Forsyth, but I think most of them belong to Ramah Church. We have a lot of small churches in this part of the country, and families have always tended to go to the church nearest their home.

That is to say, that's how it was at one time." He raised his eyebrows and looked around at his flock, many of whom had come from afar.

Someone at our lunch table mentioned his family's long history with Union Primitive Baptist Church, and I took the opportunity to ask the question foremost in my mind.

"I'm interested in church history—specifically, this church's history from when it first began. I've heard that many churches recorded minutes of the sessions of the church from its beginning. Are there such early records for this church?"

"As a matter of fact," Elder Evans said, "Another descendent of one of the charter members has already asked about the minutes. She came back home recently for a visit and asked to see them. You'll find some interesting anecdotes there. Some of the early members got called on the carpet quite often for things we generally let pass today."

"Ooh, that's right," a woman's voice said. "We'd be told today that it's none of our business. But whose business is it, if it isn't the business of the church?"

Elder Evans smiled amiably and cleared his throat. "Well, the minutes are in a big bound volume, and frankly, it's old and not in the best condition. Because the volume was so hard to read, the lady researching volunteered to take it home with her and have it all transcribed. I haven't heard from her in a while, so I don't know how the project is coming along. We'll probably hear from her in the next month or so. Give me a call in a few weeks, and I might know something."

I could not get this close to possible answers and let them slip from my grasp. "Is there a way I could contact her? I'm interested in mainly the first few years. If I could have her address, I could write her a letter."

"That would be fine, but now that I think about it, there might be a better way," he said. "There was a historical project some years ago to put early church records on microfilm. It seems, right offhand, that the records would be at the Forsyth courthouse, but it was a statewide project, so you might find the film in Atlanta."

There had also been a historical project to track down all of the cemeteries in the county and to record the names and dates of those buried there. "They listed everybody buried in our own little cemetery," he said. "You'll find a lot of your Dumas family there. You might want to take a walk out back. It's a mighty pretty place."

"Yes, we'd like to do that," Mother said.

The pastor's wife walked to the cemetery with us. Mother noted a large grassy area past the stone monuments and commented that there was still much room for expansion. Mrs. Evans explained that although there was still room available, the area that Mother indicated had been the burial site for slaves. "Originally, slaves were accepted as members of the church. It was only after the war that they came to have their own church."

While the others examined epitaphs, I walked to the slave burial grounds. There were no visible signs of markers; they must have been made of wood— plain wooden crosses. Where was the family to remember those lives? Were Nelly and Barney here? Would the minutes divulge anything about church members who were slaves?

The segregated burial plot of unmarked graves revealed more than I wanted to know. I was suddenly eager to leave.

I tried to coax Mother to extend her visit in Georgia, but she insisted she had her own busy schedule she didn't want to neglect. I thought of her discomfort in our non-smoking household and recognized that it was more difficult to take the elevator to the pool level than to step onto the patio at our old home to have a cigarette.

"I have to get someone to fill in for me when I can't be there to teach my class. I do have a life of my own, you know. I needed to see for myself that you do, too. I'm satisfied now."

"But we haven't even been to a Sacred Harp singing. We're right in the thick of Grandma's shape-note music. The singings are in surprising, off-the-beaten-path places. I wish you could've gone with me to Holly Springs— not only so you could hear the music, but because I needed a navigator. The little church was hardly fifty yards from the interstate, but it was tucked so thoroughly away in the woods that anyone on the highway would never suspect a church was hidden in there."

"Why did they try to hide it?"

"They weren't trying to hide it. That's where the church has always been. The interstate happened to choose a route that came near its location. There are a jillion little churches nestled deep in the woods all through Alabama, Georgia, and Mississippi, and many still sing Sacred Harp. The music followed the path of the churches, which followed the path of newly available land."

Early one Sunday morning before daybreak, Doug and I had tried to follow directions to a church near Ozark, Alabama, where we hoped to find Brother Dewey Williams, who'd been in the PBS film *Amazing Grace* and whose grandfather had been a slave. We found the church as the service was concluding, and we located Brother Dewey and his family just in time for lunch. He showed us his shape-note songbook, *The Colored Sacred Harp*. He and a few family members treated us—right there in the restaurant—to

Ozark, Alabama, 1991. I met Brother Dewey Williams of the Alabama Wiregrass Sacred Harp singers. Brother Dewey told me his church sang from *The Colored Sacred Harp*, first published by Judge Jackson in 1934. (Photo by Doug Webb.)

an unforgettable demonstration of the distinctive, syncopated rhythm of African-American Wiregrass singers.

Wiregrass refers to native vegetation in southeast Alabama. At a later Atlanta-area singing, I told Hugh McGraw, whom I'd first met in Texas, about meeting Brother Dewey Williams and complained about the confusing "mis-directions" I had been provided. He grinned and said, "Well, you found him, didn't you?"

As Mother packed her bags for the plane home, she said, "I'll admit I'm not musical, but from what I remember, Mama's old music sounded too mournful for me. The young people I knew liked smoother, more melodic music. I'll be back soon. I'll give you a few weeks to do some more sleuthing. I want to hear what you discover when you find the minutes."

After a trip to the Georgia Archives early in the following week, I had news for Mother and Carine, but I wanted to consider the facts in my own mind before asking their interpretations.

Elder Evans had been right that the Union Primitive Baptist Church minutes were available at the archives in Atlanta. He was also right that they were difficult to read, even more difficult than he'd imagined. The minutes existed as photographic negatives and were far more difficult to read for that reason than an unwieldy book might have been.

The records were divided into two sections: the first portion related to documenting the membership, and the second recorded the business sessions of the church. New members' names and joining dates were entered on left-side pages. Corresponding lines on right-side pages gave the date and reason for dismissal—whether deceased, released by letter to membership in another church, or excommunicated. The practice of entering a death date was not consistently followed, and it illogically appeared that many of the earliest members were still alive and active.

I jotted notes as I read, although many pages were so dark that they were illegible. Among the thirty or more charter members on August 18, 1837, were Edmund and Isabel Dumas, Thomas and Charlotte Dumas, Nancy Collier, and Winifred Collier.

On March 18, 1838, a Martha Dumas was accepted into membership. I wondered which Martha Dumas had asked for membership that Sunday. Edmund's mother Martha, who he feared was drowning in the baptismal river? The year 1838 was when that Martha Dumas died, so perhaps she joined the nearby church to put things in order. Or was this a very young Martha Dumas, the granddaughter who would within the next decade marry her uncle Davie Dumas' prospecting partner?

Numerous slaves were listed as members. Barney, "a colored man, property of Benjamin Franklin Dumas, received by letter in 1837," was one of the earliest. Nelly, presumably his wife, became a member on the same date. On the page to the right, across from the beloved Nelly's name, was a notation in careful florid script, "Nelly deceased January 30th, 1852."

I scrolled down the roster without recognizing additional names until I came to July 29, 1842, when David Dumas was received into the membership, telling that both Davie and Winnie were members of Union Primitive Baptist Church before they married.

Another name caught my eyes. *Phil, property of Benjamin Franklin Dumas*, was received by experience on September 1, 1851. The corresponding line across the page stated that Phil was excommunicated March 26, 1853. The same handwriting—the only entries made by a different hand— continued on the following line. Caroline, property of Benjamin Franklin Dumas, was also received into membership on September 1, 1851, and excommunicated on March 26, 1853. What had they done to incur the wrath of the church?

The excommunication date was immediately after the final settlement of the estate—when Jeremiah had purchased Phil, and not Caroline. For them, this could not have been a casual separation. What did they do? What happened to them? They joined the church together, and they were excommunicated together; that could only mean that Phil and Caroline saw heart to heart. Surely there was more to the story of their looming separation—something so dramatic as to cause their banishment from Union Primitive Baptist Church.

I scribbled hurriedly and scrolled to the business section of the minutes to look for more details. Proceedings of church business in the early years primarily concerned reception of new members, but I began to notice that they also enumerated reasons for expulsion. A member who was charged with a sin was cited to appear first before the committee and after proper renunciation of his offending conduct was usually immediately forgiven, but some accusations of sinning did lead to excommunication. Such a charge was lodged against "a colored sister, Mary, the property of Brother John Poe, for fornication." After investigation, Mary was unanimously excluded from the church.

Later, the business session considered charges relative to reports against Brother John Poe. The church filed a charge against him for "repeated inebriation and profane swearing, and upon due investigation of said charge, he was unanimously excluded."

I read through years of receiving new members, their falling from favor if not from grace, and being expelled if they would not repent of their sins to thus be restored to full fellowship in the church. As I read matter-of-fact reports through month after month and year after year, the proceedings of one particular business meeting caught my attention.

Wednesday, January 25th, 1868
After divine worship the Baptist Church at Union met in conference, Brother E. Dumas moderator. After the usual invitations . . . took up the reference from last conference relative to the ordination of Brother Barney Tate, a freedman. The presbytery being formed, consisting of brethren E. Dumas and John E. Duke, the church then set the said brother before the presbytery. They proceeded to examine the brother, and finding him orthodox and orderly, brought him under the imposition of hands and set him apart to the ministry.

Inquired for miscellaneous business, the church then granted letters of dismission to the freedmen of this church, and then adjourned.

That final abrupt statement marked the beginning of segregation in Union Primitive Baptist Church. The tidal change was so simply reported, yet the declaration fell like a guillotine. Brother Barney Tate, the new freedman pastor, was one of the earliest members of the church; he was also willed by his former owner, Benjamin Franklin Dumas, to his blind daughter, Nancy, who had married Jeremiah Tate.

We have no record of what went through the church members' minds, and we cannot fairly judge them by our own standards. We do know that they sang Sacred Harp music—all of them, the freedmen and their former owners. The freedmen took the Fa-So-La's they'd sung all their lives and, setting the music to their own distinctive variations and rhythms, developed their own unique gospel music. While pondering how Sacred Harp music had been severed as the once united church body split, I scrolled to the end of the microfilm reel and read, "Elder Edmund Dumas departed this life on October 23, 1882."

While carefully rewinding the film, I stopped repeatedly for a closer look. A significant clue I'd missed on the first review suddenly popped out. On January 27, 1849, a charge was brought against Brother David Dumas for the sin of "drinking intoxicating liquors to an excess," but because Davie was not present, the charge was deferred until the next session.

On February 22, the church again took up the case of Brother David Dumas, who duly acknowledged the charge, apologized and vowed "to be on his guard more particular for the time to come." The church restored him to fellowship.

No additional infractions by Davie or any other Dumas in the related time frame were found, so I returned to the beginning section that listed the roll of church members and examined again the entry for David Dumas. On the opposite page was a corresponding entry, "August 23rd, 1853, deceased."

I phoned Carine as soon as I arrived home.

"What could it mean? You'd think I would have found another reference somewhere to his death. I found nothing at all to offer an explanation or shed light on how or where he died. There is no marker for him at the cemetery."

"That must have been about the time Winnie had given Davie up for dead," Carine said. "He'd been gone since 1849. Since they gave a specific date, maybe they'd had news to indicate he had died, perhaps in a letter, or a letter that came back."

"But the newspaper said his partner, William Horne, returned ten years later, about 1859, to take Winnie to Davie in California," I said.

"It seems the church was under the assumption Davie was already dead. All you really know is that he'd been an unhappy young man who had turned to alcohol months before he decided to run from the predicament."

When he was called on the carpet, Davie resolved to try to do better. He couldn't seem to stay on the right side of the righteous. I wondered if his drinking caused the problem with his father, or if the problem caused his drinking.

Carine continued, "The couple definitely had a problem, and when Davie didn't return in a timely fashion, Winnie was ready to move on with her life."

Desertion would've been sufficient grounds for divorce, but divorce was an unthinkable disgrace in those days. However, a widow could gracefully remarry. And Davie and Winnie's marriage was already over when he walked out the door.

I pictured Davie and Winnie, back to back, resisting the bond between them like the repelling poles of two magnets. In contrast, the slaves Phil and Caroline, who were pulled apart by outside forces, seemed to be the powerful attracting poles, reaching desperately to touch the other's outstretched fingertips.

The marriage wasn't over for Phil and Caroline on the day they were excommunicated though the Dumas estate had been settled and Jeremiah had purchased Phil. Others' decisions created circumstances in which Phil and Caroline would never again see each other. The couple faced a dilemma with no feasible options. Running away must have seemed the only solution. But there was nowhere to run and there was no mercy for runaway slaves.

Whatever Phil and Caroline did, wherever they ran, they took with them what mattered most. They were willing to pay the price for love, regardless of the cost, and decided that their love would never be over.

> *Come, humble sinner, in whose breast a thousand thoughts revolve;*
> *Come, with your guilt and fear oppressed, and make this last resolve;*
> *We're marching through Immanuel's ground,*
> *And soon shall hear the trumpet sound,*
> *And all shall then with Jesus reign, and never, never part again.*
> *What? Never part again? No, never part again,*
> *What? Never part again? No, never part again,*
> *And soon shall hear the trumpet sound,*
> *And never, never part again.*

"Never Part" # 94 in *The Sacred Harp*
Words, Edmund Jones, 1787; music arranged by John Carwell, 1850

CHAPTER 7

The Prodigals

ON a Sunday afternoon near the end of summer, Doug and I drove from Atlanta to Birmingham and checked in at a hotel near his branch office downtown. He planned to be in Birmingham all week, thus allowing me to continue the next morning on a long drive to visit Carine in Louisiana. I headed west on the interstate at daybreak. Summer was now full-blown and stretched out across the Alabama landscape in a shimmering haze, but the foliage of the forests already held a subtle bronze hint of autumn. The barely perceptible change made me take a deep breath to fully absorb this pregnant Monday morning. This was Sacred Harp country, and the rustic roads that headed invitingly into the woods beckoned me to their hidden chapels.

I was grateful for the pleasant distraction because I had heavy issues on my mind. I'd wanted to go to Louisiana for many weeks, since my research in Forsyth revealed that Jeremiah Dumas had bought a slave from his father's estate. Before I had read what those records contained, they were merely innocuous pieces of paper with marks of ink upon them. Once the real significance of those marks was transferred from the page to my mind, I had been tormented by curiosity about a black man who'd been dead for more than a century.

Mother tried to remain supportive but avoided the subject. Doug seemed impatient when he asked, "What difference can it possibly make today?" So alone, I searched for information in Georgia, where both Jeremiah and his slave were born and raised. Jeremiah was thirty-three years old when Benjamin Franklin Dumas died and had undoubtedly known Phil, born eight years after Jeremiah of slaves brought with the Dumas family in their move from North Carolina, for all the young man's life.

Now that I knew Phil's name, he became a real person who might be traced. If Phil was with Jeremiah, he should be listed on the slave schedule of the 1860 census in Louisiana. Many Louisiana records were available only in Louisiana on original documents, and I wanted to see everything that was available. I expected the 1860 census to tell me that Jeremiah owned a male slave, about thirty-two or thirty-three years old. Then I would find him on the 1870 census after the war, and thus a free man, perhaps listed as Phil Dumas, a black male approximately forty-three years old. From there, the next step would be to identify and locate his descendants.

Traffic was marvelously light and soon I'd left Alabama behind. I stopped in the Mississippi Welcome Center because it seemed the responsively polite thing to do, and it provided a safe rest stop for a woman traveling alone. The hours and miles clicked away, and as I neared Vicksburg, I spotted a billboard advising I'd reach Pemberton Mall in three more exits. The mall would be a good place for a brisk walk to stretch my legs and have some lunch—southern vegetables and corn bread from the cafeteria, a staple restaurant not often found outside the South.

I reflected on the comparative ease of our age and how dramatically circumstances of everyday life have changed from the previous century. As Jeremiah and his slave traveled to Louisiana, neither could have imagined that a century and a half later, a lone white woman would be making the same journey in a fraction of the time. Nor would Phil have guessed that the purpose of my trip was to follow *him*, wondering what had gone through his mind.

When I returned to the car and approached the bridge across the Mississippi River, I imagined Jeremiah and Irena's first crossing in 1846 with their brood of little boys. Great-uncle William, the oldest, was only six years old, and their seventh son was born soon after they reached their destination. I wondered how a pregnant woman could manage so many children in a cramped covered wagon. On second thought, maybe it was easier traveling with them—like a continuous campout—than it would have been to contain them in a house.

I assumed Irena was a willing partner to Jeremiah's dream. The evidence of her life proved her commitment to marriage and family. Because her parents were moving west in the same wagon train, it was unlikely that she felt isolated. The move had necessarily been planned for a lengthy time, and most likely, with a great deal of excitement. They had high hopes. I tried to imagine their dreams.

The highway I traveled traverses the same fertile soil that's now tamed and producing the crops Jeremiah envisioned as he made his way westward. Jeremiah undoubtedly talked with his father and sought his advice. The older sons had settled nearby and were established and well respected in their own right. There could have been a place for Jeremiah in Georgia, but he must have wanted more.

Benjamin Franklin Dumas had been successful in settling a new land, and Jeremiah would expect no less. With a loving wife and an encouraging father, Jeremiah would have been enthusiastic in his vision of what the venture could offer. He and Irena left behind a life of abundance, not for reasons of necessity, but with prospects of an even better life ahead. Life was good in Georgia. He would recreate it.

He wanted to be like his father and his older brothers. When his father died, Jeremiah was already without his presence in the affairs of daily living, so his was a different grief than that of his brothers. Perhaps after Benjamin Franklin's death, Jeremiah felt even closer to his father because of the inheritance that served to further the plans they'd discussed together. On his return to Louisiana after the estate was settled in 1853, Jeremiah brought with him a thousand dollars cash, as well as the slave he'd purchased with his remaining share of his father's worldly goods.

In Jeremiah's eyes, the slave was a key element in his plan for achieving his American dream. With seven growing sons, he could count on homegrown help in a few years, but Jeremiah needed the help of a grown man now. He knew Phil, knew the kind of work the man produced, knew him well enough to invest nearly half of his inheritance to get that help.

Did only the two of them, Jeremiah and Phil, make the return trip? Great-uncle William would have been twelve years old. William could likely have been more help to his mother back home, but perhaps he and the next oldest son accompanied their father. The boys would have seen the Mississippi with eyes like Tom Sawyer's. Great-uncle William still remembered his first crossing in 1846, as a six-year-old; the abrupt change of terrain from Mississippi's hilly cliffs to the low delta land of Louisiana made a dramatic, unforgettable impression.

Great-uncle William crossed the great river at least twice more—before and after losing his leg. Ominous echoes along the route can still be heard. Cannons now fixed in place and looking down from Vicksburg give stark testimony to the bitter conflict on the same southern soil.

Now on flat delta farmland, I noticed the plants growing in the fields were not of the "tall cotton" variety. Instead, I saw a bumper crop of shorter, stunted-looking plants with bursting bolls. Agricultural technology had made a significant breakthrough. Glancing at the clock, I saw that I would arrive earlier than expected at Carine's house. There was time to drive leisurely into Monroe on the old highway, so I turned off the interstate at the exit to the small community of Start, Louisiana, where Grandma lived after Grandpa died.

Although much had changed, reminders of the community's former life remained. I passed the old Methodist church, and across the road sat an empty lot, home to Start Baptist Church back when the two churches held services on alternate Sundays. Mother said this custom was born of necessity because neither congregation had a full-time pastor. People were thus able to attend church each Sunday if they wished.

I reconstructed in my mind the white frame Baptist church I'd attended with Grandma, recalling a favorite tree near the back entrance and the tart sweetness of its plums. I pictured Brother Deal, Grandma's silver-haired pastor and next-door neighbor, in his blue-and-white striped seersucker suit as he pleaded with sinners to "come home."

Start Baptist Church was now housed in a newer, larger brick building on the other side of the highway, and the few buildings that remained nearby seemed to have shrunk and aged the way people do. Venerable pecan orchards could still be seen, but even those large trees seemed ancient and tired.

Memories of Grandma lingered intensely, and I could hear her voice ring out, "I am bound for the Promised Land, Hallelujah. O who will come and go with me, I am bound for the Promised Land."

Grandma's music is my link to Jeremiah's world. His music is still alive and has been passed to me. Sometimes I feel I know him well, and I long to see the joy in his eyes as he sings. Other times, I hear an uneasy discord.

When I arrived at Carine's home, I saw that the graceful landscaping wore a new robe. Blooms of an earlier season had retreated to give center stage to bright red spider lilies.

On the phone, I had told Carine of Jeremiah's purchase of the slave and of my determination to learn what happened to him. She had long ago obtained a copy of Benjamin Franklin's will, but she'd not seen the accounting of the final settlement of the estate, which revealed the purchase.

On answering my ring at the door, Carine hugged me and kissed me on the cheek. "I haven't been home more than half an hour. I didn't tell you what was going on when you called because I knew you'd decide not to come, and I've been counting on this visit."

"What do you mean? Are you all right?"

"Oh, I'm fine. I was visiting Miss Dettie McGough, who'd been a close friend to my mother as well as a good friend to your grandmother all her life. She was taken to the hospital, and for awhile it looked like she wouldn't make it. Let's sit down and have a glass of sweet tea while you fill me in on your family. I have some lady-food in the icebox—I know how it is to be involved in a project—and we can grab a bite when we feel the urge without having to observe mealtime."

Carine's lady-food—chicken salad, sliced cantaloupe, raw vegetables, and a pound cake—was prepared ahead of time to allow for whatever an erratic schedule might dictate. She placed coasters on the coffee table, took a chair near me, and leaned forward attentively.

"Now, tell me about the slave and what it is you're hoping to learn."

"I want to find Phil in the census. He should be listed here in Union Parish. I need to find the slave schedules of the 1860 census."

Carine frowned and straightened in her chair. After a long sigh, she said, "That's going to be a problem. You see, I was never able to locate Jeremiah's family on the 1860 census."

"But your book says they were already here in Louisiana in 1850."

"Oh, I found them in 1850, all right. But if you take a closer look at what I said about the 1850 records, you'll see that Jeremiah's family lived up the road a little piece across the state line in Union County, Arkansas. That's *county*, not *parish* like we say in Louisiana. It's in a different state. The names and dates and birth places corresponded with what I found here in Union Parish in the 1870 census, and for a genealogy search, that was all I needed. I was never able to find them in 1860 in either state, but because the names and birth dates were consistent from '50 to '70, I truly thought a question would never arise."

"So there's no way to know exactly where Jeremiah's family was in 1860?"

"Well, I know that the land I own here— the subject came up when I recently sold the timber—has been in the family since before the Civil War. But I'm every bit as sure that Jeremiah and Irena lived in Arkansas for a short while because that's where I found them on the 1850 census. My personal opinion is that Jeremiah bought this land with his inheritance—probably around 1855 or so, soon after his father died. I've never checked deed records for the exact date. I obviously missed his name on the census tabulations at one place or the other. Some of the handwriting was very difficult to read, and another eye might see it differently. I suggest you take a closer look at the lists for 1860. Their names have to be recorded somewhere. That was the last year of listing slaves, so it's the last chance you'll have to find what you're looking for."

I referred to the steno pad with my notes. Carine smiled indulgently. "Go ahead," she encouraged, and I decided to begin with my least touchy issue before considering Jeremiah's situation on the eve of the war.

"Okay, let's talk about Davie. On the drive over here, I tried to compare his journey west with Jeremiah's. Davie was still living at home when Jeremiah was making his plans, and he could hardly have avoided overhearing. That might have given Davie his first thought of leaving home. Gold had been discovered in Georgia at Dahlonega, and when news of fabulous finds in California reached them, Davie came down with gold fever. But their father, Benjamin Franklin Dumas, was more likely to approve of acquiring land than of prospecting for gold, which was akin to gambling and not in keeping with the beliefs of the Baptists."

"Mmm-hmm," Carine agreed. "Benjamin Franklin would've approved of Jeremiah's plan to stake a claim for more land farther west. After all, that's why he'd uprooted his family from North Carolina when land was first available in Georgia. Jeremiah would be continuing their shared dream."

I knew I must confront my more troubling thoughts. Louisiana held Jeremiah's dream, but what about the slave, Phil? Back then no one considered the feelings of slaves, but didn't they also experience the same deep sentiments? According to the expenses paid from the Dumas estate, three slaves died at the home place between the time of the old man's death in March of 1852 and the final settlement in January of the following year. What was Phil's relationship to those who died? Nelly could have been his mother.

Phil might have been coping with something more painful than grief for a departed parent. I suspected that he was being forced to leave behind those he loved most dearly. Jeremiah purchased only Phil, not Caroline. If Phil had left his wife behind, was he also forced to part with their children?

My pent-up misgivings spilled out. I paused to take a breath, not yet expecting a response. "If we're unable to feel emotion in the cold hard facts we piece together, is the grief of forced separation any less real?"

Carine absorbed the question thoughtfully before speaking.

"Even with the advantage of hindsight, I don't know that we can divine the motives or conscience of someone who lived a hundred and fifty years ago any more than we can see inside anyone today. But the way you describe it—"

"I found conflicting messages in the Georgia records," I said. "Benjamin Franklin Dumas provided land for the church, but he also owned slaves, though it seems he did provide for their physical needs. Can we at least assume Jeremiah had a comparable attitude about his own responsibility of caring for a slave?"

I was sure that Carine could hear in my voice a plea for reassurance, yet she said nothing. She tapped two fingers lightly on her lips.

"I thought I had begun to know Jeremiah through our shared love of music. I thought he was like Grandma, who would never knowingly hurt anyone. Maybe he was. But I'm disturbed about Phil—especially if he might have had a family that was torn apart by Jeremiah's hand."

"I'm going to have to think about this. Let's sleep on it," Carine said carefully. "Go see what the courthouse records can show you tomorrow and I'll go back to the hospital to check on Miss Dettie McGough."

Tuesday morning I went to the Union Parish courthouse alone though Carine offered last-minute suggestions all the way out to the car. "Now remember, Jeremiah's second wife's name was Jane. I think she, too, must have died because I never learned what happened to her. By 1870, he had married his third wife, great-grandmother Julia Ann. She was still in her twenties when they got married. They had one child, a daughter."

"Oh, I know about Great-grandmother Julia Ann," I said. "Grandma told me a lot about her. She came for long visits to their house. They called her the Supervisor."

Great-grandmother Julia Ann took it upon herself to give detailed instructions for every mundane chore to be done. She once arrived in a wagon as Grandpa and the boys were stacking a few last logs of firewood. Great-grandmother Julia Ann climbed down from the high seat and strode over to judge the day's work. After scrutinizing the stack up and down, she finally said, "I don't know, but you boys do just about as good a job when I'm gone as when I'm here to tell you how!"

Carine's expression turned serious as she asked, "Do you know why she came for those long visits? Without a will, Jeremiah's land went to his sons. That's an example of Louisiana's Napoleonic laws of succession. Great-grandmother Julia Ann was left with absolutely nothing. She had no choice but to stay with one son or daughter after another."

Carine said she had not looked at deeds, so I would check those records at the courthouse before crossing the street to the library to examine census tabulations. She had cautioned that relevant items would be prior to 1876, the filing date for the succession papers of Jeremiah Dumas after his death. When I found the final accounting of Jeremiah's estate, I began to understand the effect of Louisiana's default inheritance laws. His widow, Julia Ann was left with nothing at all to raise her young daughter. Jeremiah's land holdings, which included the home, were left to his sons. There was mention of "money owed to J. Dumas for land sold to M. Taylor and S. Tucker" of which only a small fraction had been paid, but none of that sum, if ever collected, belonged to Julia Ann. It was understood that widows were to be supported by surviving children.

I made copies and moved on to check the earliest recorded conveyances in the parish. Jeremiah was the grantor of land deeds on February of 1863 and December of 1865. But when did he acquire the land so that he could sell it?

In the index ledger for grantee conveyances, the first entry for Jeremiah Dumas was from the James Taylor Estate. On January 2, 1860, Jeremiah Dumas bought 580 acres at $1.50 per acre with a purchase price of $870.00.

So Jeremiah was officially living in Louisiana in January of 1860, proving that his family should be listed on the 1860 census in Louisiana, not Arkansas. I read on to see if Jeremiah acquired any other property at the auction of the estate of James Taylor. The accounting of all that was sold included three parcels of land, followed by a listing of eight different purchasers of slaves or groups of slaves. Next were purchasers of hogs, cattle, a mare and colt, and finally, the remaining personal property.

The balancing breakdown listed:

Sum total of Sale of personal property	$ 837.50
Sales of Slaves	18,210.00
Sales of Land	1,624.00
Total Amt. Sales	$20,671.50

The largest proportion of an estate was by far the value of the slaves, many slaves.

During a meditative lunch break—a sack lunch packed by an insistent Carine--I reread a photocopy of the original James Taylor estate document. I noticed that the purchaser of a "Negro man Jerry @ $340.00" was David Nolan, grandfather of David Burch Nolan, whom I call Grandpa. So, Phil was joined by another black man.

I turned to another page and made an effort to merge the new facts with the old to obtain a clearer picture of life in Louisiana on the eve of the Civil War.

In 1853, life must have looked rosy. Jeremiah and Irena could have returned to Georgia at the death of his father if they had wished. Some of Benjamin Franklin Dumas' land was sold for settlement of the estate, evidence that land was available. There was no indication of family alienation keeping Jeremiah away as there was with his brother Davie. Jeremiah's interests in music and church undoubtedly bonded him with his brothers, Edmund and Thomas, but Louisiana must have offered a more enticing opportunity. Jeremiah's dreams of a flourishing plantation life were drawing near, supported by his seven growing sons and the "prime" slave from his father's estate, twenty-five-year-old Phil, to help Jeremiah make his dream come true.

But in 1855, Irena gave birth to twins on April 27. That same day, thirty-five-year-old Irena and one of the twins died. Jeremiah's bubble burst. Who would now care for the motherless family? Jeremiah married again, but apparently lost his second wife, too, although almost nothing is known of their brief marriage. Carine had noted that Jeremiah married a third time on January 1, 1863 to Julia Ann Smith, who raised the brood and outlived Jeremiah himself.

However, my major question remained unanswered: where was the slave, Phil? If he had been with Jeremiah in 1860, that would mean he had been right here in Union Parish. The census should hold the answers.

I spent the afternoon at the library combing census records, but the search was fruitless. I, too, was unable to find a listing for Jeremiah's family. How could both Carine and I overlook his name? This was not the news I'd hoped to deliver.

Carine placed two tall glasses of sweet tea on the coffee table and added sprigs of fresh mint while I leafed through my growing sheaf of papers. I complained that I had read page after tedious page through the entire parish, scanning microfilm all afternoon in vain.

She responded, "How can you say you didn't find anything? What you found simply isn't what you wanted to find, but based on the land purchases, Jeremiah *must* be listed in Louisiana. We've simply missed him. Give it one more try. Be especially diligent in the area near Cherry Ridge up the Marion road where our family owned land. You can't give up so easily."

"Maybe I did scan hurriedly because I continually expected Jeremiah's name to be on the next line. The handwriting was not always legible. I might as well look again; it is why I made this trip."

"While you're at the library, I'll check on Miss Dettie McGough. Then I'll come back home and meet you here about noon."

I began with a fresh start Wednesday morning. I read each line slowly and carefully, refusing to become impatient. When I reached household No. 578, dated July 18, in the Cherry Ridge community, I found, *J. Dumas!*

The *J* and *D* on first glance read together as one letter, but with close examination, there could be no doubt that it was definitely *J. D-u-m-a-s.*

J. Dumas, 40, (meaning forty-ish. He was 43, but maybe he wanted to appear younger.), *Male, Farmer. Value of Real Estate $1500.00; Value of Personal Estate $4180.00; Born in Georgia.*

The next lines continued with his mysterious second wife, Jane, age twenty-two, and a long list of children, the oldest six sons being born in Georgia. From the top, I read that great-uncle William was nineteen; Covington, seventeen; Sidney, fifteen; and James Franklin, thirteen and the future father of my Grandma, Terry Louisa. The household contained a total of nine children. I allowed for inconsistencies such as Jeremiah's age and was convinced that I'd discovered a distinct snapshot of Jeremiah's family on July 18, 1860.

On the next line, household No. 579 was the home of Robert McGough, a fifty-nine-year-old farmer who also came from Georgia. I wondered how he was related to Miss Dettie McGough and if the families had traveled west together. The value of McGough's real estate was $4,000.00 and his personal estate was $18,125.00. How many slaves did that figure represent?

The slave schedules were on a different reel, but because I'd found the area where the family lived, locating Jeremiah's name in the owner column should be easier. I obtained the proper reel and nervously prepared to read.

What did I expect to find? The information had lain here undisturbed for more than a hundred years. It could scarcely seem of any importance today. But the first part of my hunch had been right, so Phil—who would be about thirty-three years old—should be on that schedule.

Schedule Two, labeled "Slave Inhabitants in the Parish of Union" was not nearly as lengthy as the regular census. There was a column for the names of slave owners, but to my dismay, the form held no given names that would identify individual slaves. Additional columns asked for the number of slaves of a stated age, sex, and color—black or mulatto. The remaining columns were labeled "fugitive from state," "number manumitted," "deaf and dumb, blind, insane or idiotic," and finally a column for the "number of slave houses."

The top of page twenty-one began with the slave owner name J. Dumas. His listing contained only two lines, one slave on each line. First listed was one sixteen-year-old *female*, black, and one slave house. The second line listed one one-year-old male, black.

Where was Phil? If he had run away, he would have been listed as a fugitive.

And who was the female? Could she have been Phil's wife? Had she also come from Georgia? They didn't ask the birth origin of slaves. I supposed it had not mattered.

There had been no conveyances of slaves on record for J. Dumas at the courthouse. Had Jeremiah traded Phil verbally? Perhaps after Irena died, he needed help in the house more than he needed Phil.

But who was the one-year-old child's father?

The latest revelation was too much to digest at one time. I made copies of the pages, knowing I would reread them many times. I dreaded having to report the day's results to Carine. She had spent much time and money tracing our family. They were all her children. What would she think about this new baby—a slave baby?

I had still not found Phil. Maybe he was on an adjacent farm.

The slave owner listed on the next line was R. McGough. He owned fifteen slaves, the bulk of his personal estate. I scanned the column for ages. R. McGough did indeed own a black male who was thirty-three years old.

My heart took a leap. It could be Phil, I thought. But without given names or birth origins, there was no way to prove it.

I looked for a pattern to indicate relationships.

There were three slave houses. In the first house, I imagined lived the forty-eight-year-old and the forty-three-year-old, whose children were males, ages twenty-one, nineteen, and fifteen. The sixteen-year-old girl owned by Jeremiah Dumas could have been a sibling in the family.

In the second house, lived the thirty-three-year-old male (possibly Phil) and a thirty-two-year-old female (possibly Caroline), whose children were males, ages eleven, eight, six, five, three, and the seven-year-old female.

For the third house, there remained two thirty-year-old males who might have lived alone, or perhaps they had wives on another farm. Weekend passes were often given for conjugal purposes, but the marriages of the slaves, though valid and holy as anyone's, were not recorded.

I wanted to cry. I came here for answers, not more screaming questions.

Carine met me at the door and asked, "Did you find him?"

"I found Jeremiah. I might have found Phil, but I know of no way in the world to know for sure. But there's more."

I related what the census had revealed, as well as my irritated bewilderment at finding a single black female owned by Jeremiah. "And she had a baby. A mother at sixteen—hardly more than a child herself."

"Could Phil have been the baby's father?" Carine asked and quickly answered her own question. "No, I don't think so. She'd have been too young for him."

"They don't tell us enough," I said. "The only concrete documentation about slaves is whether they were bought or sold. We can't even find out if a slave died, or whether he was married, or anything else. You'd think, at the very least, they could have listed their names. I want to assume it was Phil and Caroline who belonged to the McGoughs at the next farm. The age fits, but so far, that's all I have to go on."

"We need a breather," Carine said. "If you still want to take a drive up to El Dorado, I'd like to go, too. I know the way, so I'll drive. An ambulance will bring Miss Dettie McGough to the nursing home sometime in the afternoon. Then the medical people will be with her for awhile, and I would only be waiting."

I wanted very much to see the area where the family lived. I'd have no clue how to find it on my own. The original land had been divided between the brothers, so all of them lived in the same general area. Carine said we could check the big parish wall-map at the courthouse to know exactly where to look.

We quickly finished lunch and hurried to the courthouse to pinpoint the location of the land Jeremiah bought from the Taylor estate. The Cherry Ridge community was on the way to El Dorado. Carine turned onto a graveled road and shaded her eyes from the glaring sun as she pointed out the Dumas land.

I was surprised by the similarities to Monroe County in Georgia—the same red clay soil, the same sweet gums and pines, and the same rocky, rolling terrain in the hills above the delta. It was easy to guess why Jeremiah chose this place. It seemed like home.

On our return, we pulled into the parking lot at the nursing home as the sun was disappearing over the treetops. We learned that the ambulance had arrived within the last twenty minutes.

Dettie McGough was a tiny, fragile woman with translucent skin. She was tired and weak from the ordeals of the past week, yet she was cheerful. When Carine introduced me as Terry's granddaughter, she tried to sit up to greet me, though she hardly had strength to speak.

"Terry's granddaughter," she said, weakly. "Yes. You have her smile. Carine says you sing Sacred Harp."

"Don't try to talk, Miss Dettie," Carine said, as she busily arranged necessities within easy reach of the bed. I could do little more than hold her hand and say that her friendship had been important to Grandma. Suddenly, her doctor breezed in, and we had to leave with only a quick hug as our goodbye. Brief as our meeting was, Miss Dettie furnished a reassuring connection with Grandma and the music we now shared.

Upon entering the house, Carine headed straight for the study. "Shu-gah, why don't you fix us something cold to drink while I gather up some things I want to show you? Meet me in the living room." She returned with several boxes and albums in her arms. To make room on the coffee table, I moved the tray I'd brought from the kitchen.

Carine had old pictures, letters, clippings, and church records.

"I understand the reasons you're troubled about slavery. Slavery was a tragedy for everyone connected with it in any way. But it isn't as though slavery was something new; it was in effect long before the United States came into existence. They had slaves way back in Bible times, though I certainly won't argue that made it acceptable for our country. We've lived with the repercussions here in the South all our lives. You were right when you said Thomas Jefferson should never have allowed slavery in the Louisiana Purchase, but we can't rewrite history. A young white man born to a southern planter was born into the existing institution of slavery as surely as were the slaves."

"The war was a terrible price to pay to change it."

"God works in mysterious ways." Carine's voice took a tone of assurance and authority, an indication the remarks to follow were to be significant.

"After I went to bed last night, I was concerned that because of your disturbing discoveries, you were forming an unflattering opinion of our forefathers. It finally came to me that I should show you what's in my files."

She clasped a group of notebooks in both hands and handed them to me.

"Here are all the records of Shady Grove Baptist Church, where Jeremiah's sons were charter members. In these pages, you'll find their names recorded as deacons, teachers, committee members, and other positions of responsibility in the church. Here is solid testimony of where they stood to be counted, continuously and consistently, through the march of time. Jeremiah raised them right, or maybe I should say *someone* raised them to honor God, the Creator of us all, meaning every last one of us. This is the heritage they passed to following generations—to your grandmother, your mother and me, and to you."

I sat quietly for a moment, searching for the right words.

"Carine, I'm so sorry. I'm ashamed of the questions that are reverberating in my mind. I can't explain why I'm bothered by what happened, or what might have happened, so many years ago."

"What do you think might have happened?" Carine prodded.

"I can't help wondering about the slave baby's father. If the sixteen-year-old slave girl belonged to Jeremiah, then he was responsible for her, like a daughter."

"Maybe she had a husband on another farm."

"If so, it's wrong that such knowledge was denied to their descendants—and to the rest of us." I bit my lip, but I couldn't hold my tongue. "The real issue with me is of a wrong that has no color. We have to recognize that slave women sometimes had children by owners who forced sex upon them."

"Not Jeremiah!" Carine gasped.

"I don't want to tie those two threads together any more than you do. But someone fathered her child, and Jeremiah was responsible for her. Her baby wasn't much older than Jeremiah's son by his second wife."

"What are you saying?"

"After Irena died, did he find his slave girl attractive and available? Obviously, the teenage slave was sexually attractive to someone." Though I wanted to put the subject behind me and forget I'd ever found names for any of the slaves, I knew the questions would not simply fade away. "Slavery in itself was shameful enough, but to think that slaves could be used as a sexual outlet is even more degrading than prostitution. At least, prostitution is consensual."

"I realize that sort of thing happened," Carine said firmly, "but surely not in our family. We were raised to know better. There aren't any secrets in a small town, especially about shameful deeds. Jeremiah taught his sons that a man's reputation—good or bad—doesn't die with him. Oh, they don't need me to vouch for them. Look at the evidence of their lives." Carine's stricken expression implored me to listen with an open mind.

"They left a trail of faith—not of perfection, but of faith and humanity and hope," she said. "That faith didn't begin here at Shady Grove Baptist Church. Jeremiah and his family brought it with them. That's the trail you should follow. You've told me how you found it in Georgia. Benjamin Franklin's family brought it to Georgia with them. Follow it back to the first Jeremiah Dumas who came to Virginia. He was a Huguenot refugee who came here to escape religious persecution in France. And the trail doesn't stop there. Follow it through the family line of the colonial girl who married Jerome Dumas, the first Dumas to arrive in America. It will take you directly to the first English-speaking church on this continent, the old church at Jamestown. What richer heritage could they leave us? They brought us the Bible—direct from King James."

The room was alive with the sound and substance of Carine's words. I yearned to share the older woman's confidence and commitment. But my heart was heavy with doubt.

The night brought only intermittent sleep. I sought comfort in the knowledge of Jeremiah's second marriage. Surely, such a young bride would be enough. Suddenly, I was wide-awake again. Jeremiah's house was filled with motherless teenage boys. The young slave girl and all those healthy sons Irena left behind had come to the age of sexual awakening.

Yes, love could have happened, but such love was forbidden. *But, are not lust and forbidden love at home in the human heart?*

The soulful eyes in an unidentified photograph of one of Jeremiah's sons haunted me. Carine had thought he was James Franklin Dumas, Grandma's father. He was a handsome young man whose countenance spoke of gentle refinement. I closed my eyes, but could not block out his tender expression of open honesty, baring his own vulnerability. His eyes seemed to say to me, "Do not be afraid. I will not hurt you."

Where will I find the answers? Will I ever know the truth? God, help me.

I finally fell into a deep sleep. When the alarm clock rang, I awakened refreshed, with a renewed confidence. I was aware that although the road ahead might lead through controversy, I must go there. The sky became brighter through the east windows of Carine's guestroom. A sunrise brings assurance that the earth itself is God's and hallows His name.

When Carine refilled our coffee cups at breakfast, she sat down and spoke purposefully.

"I think I see what's at the core of your search. You feel the weight of grievous sin. You're trying to find justification for Jeremiah."

She leaned back in her chair and spoke with gentle yet assured conviction. "We've also wondered about Davie. Davie was a rebel when he left, and we picture him as lonely and tormented, but God looks upon our hearts. He alone knows what was in Davie's heart and what was in Jeremiah's heart. We each have our own confrontation with God and are responsible for what He sees; we cannot absolve the sins of another, nor can our judgment cast another into hell. If you're debating which son was the prodigal, look no farther. We are all prodigal."

God of my life, look gently down, behold the pains I feel;
But I am dumb before Thy throne, nor dare dispute Thy will.
I'm but a sojourner below, as all my fathers were;
May I be well prepared to go when I the summons hear.

"Poland" #86 in *The Sacred Harp*
Words, Isaac Watts, 1719; music, Timothy Swan, 1785.

CHAPTER 8

Crash Course in Slavery

ALTHOUGH the colors of the forests hinted more strongly of approaching autumn, my return trip to Birmingham did not offer the same carefree spirit. I had to acknowledge disappointment and ask myself what I'd expected to find. With an embarrassing naïveté, I'd imagined the best of all worlds, gathering rosebuds of Huck Finn, Tom Sawyer, Scarlett O'Hara, and Rhett Butler for a preconceived, dried flower arrangement that would provide a happy ending for the discomfiting search I'd begun.

I'd wanted to find dusty records of Phil Dumas, a black man, with a wife named Caroline and a half dozen children, living on land that would someday be theirs. Then I could have traced their family and perhaps find that their great-great-grandson fought as a Marine in Vietnam and saved the life of a white Dumas, or that their daughters were sorority sisters at some southern university.

I was keenly aware that my shallow swipes at the subject were woefully ignorant. I recalled a conversation with a young black woman who worked at the courthouse in Forsyth. She spoke of insurmountable difficulties blacks often find in tracing their families, because slaves were counted namelessly on the 1860 census. I could now more fully appreciate that her frustration was more than a mere annoyance.

I feared I might hurt someone who could no longer defend a good name. The trail one leaves behind is important, and the time we live is the only time we can influence what it reveals about us.

A face from the past suddenly popped into my mind—a drunk at a 1960s social gathering in Dallas. He began a story of a hunting trip, or perhaps they were fishing. It didn't matter which, because the sporting party's efforts were primarily focused on liquor consumption. But this was a tale of loyalty, loyalty of his "nigger." He used the term like a weapon, garnering maximum attention and indignation.

"My nigger always got me through a bad spot and got me home. I could count on him. He was my best friend. He was a damn good nigger—the best you could find anywhere. He was a Geechee blue-gum nigger."

He had relegated his best friend to a position most assign to a beloved pet. And we've advanced no farther than the estate auction of the 1800s, when only a minor distinction was made in listing the number of slaves to be sold and the cattle of the field. But this loyal pet was not a mixed breed. He held an impressive pedigree. He was a Geechee blue-gum.

I arrived in Birmingham tired and fending off a mood of melancholy. Catrena Carter, the attractive college student who was the hotel concierge, called me over as I entered the lobby. Doug had left a message explaining that he was involved with a deposition that could last awhile, and that Mother wanted me to phone.

Mother was excitedly preparing for an unexpected visit from Elise and wanted to postpone a planned trip to Atlanta. She asked what I'd found in Louisiana. It wasn't as hard to tell her about the latest discoveries as I'd expected. But like Carine, she held fast to evidence of strong Christian principles that had been passed down.

"Times have changed, but principles are the same. Your grandmother always said everything changes but the Word of God. I've heard her say that a jillion times. I'm aware that when my grandparents were born, the economy depended on slave labor, but I have to believe my grandparents were taught the same basic belief they taught me: to treat everyone decently."

When I countered that buying and selling other humans could never fit those guidelines, she agreed and said that's why times had to change.

Doug had been told that the Tutwiler Southern History Library, directly across the street from the hotel, was one of the best in the South. He figured I'd want to spend some time there and asked if I had a need to hurry home to Atlanta. A person he wanted to interview would be in town over the weekend, and as it developed from one day to the next, Doug needed to stay more than another week. The Tutwiler's resources were at my fingertips.

There could be no better place than the Birmingham libraries to seek a beginning knowledge of slavery. African-American studies were appearing in campuses across the country to answer the demand of young black students. *What were they learning that I, too, should know?*

I figured "Geechee" was a tribe name, if it was actually a name at all. Through the library computer's subject classification, I was unable to locate the word, "Geechee," "Gheetchy," "Guichi," or any other spelling I could devise.

There were many more relevant topics, however, and I began skimming books on slavery, its origins, and origins of the slaves themselves from the time they were first captured by other Africans and forced to march in *coffles*—lines of captives linked at the neck—to reach the waiting slave ships on the coast. One of the most surprising discoveries was that John Newton, who wrote the words to the beloved hymn "Amazing Grace," was a slave trader who kept a journal detailing punishments aboard his ship. Over the next days, my crash course revealed more human depravity and suffering than I wanted to know.

I continued to read and make notes one day while I waited for Doug in the hotel lobby. Catrena Carter, who was again working at the front desk, was entertained by my frazzled expression.

"What are you studying, Mrs. Webb? You look mighty serious when you start writing, like something fierce is in your notebook."

I hesitated, embarrassed to discuss the subject. Catrena was an African American, but I decided to be frank.

"I'm in over my head in a self-study project on the history of American slavery. I want to know what life was like for slaves, what they faced on a day-to-day basis."

Catrena appeared only slightly surprised. "I've taken some black history courses. I'd be happy to try to help with any questions you have. What part are you on right now?"

I glanced at the steno pad and again felt self-conscious. "I've encountered a word that's new to me—*miscegenation*. At first glance, I thought *misogyny*, but it didn't take long to figure out that the hatred of women didn't fit the context. Then, Webster acquainted me with the term for—" I looked at my notes and read, "Marriage or interbreeding between members of different races, especially in the United States, between whites and Negroes."

She said nothing. I was shocked at my thoughtless blunder, but when I looked into the girl's clear hazel eyes surrounded by her light and creamy complexion, I understood that Catrena had her own interpretation for the word.

I nervously attempted to steer the conversation in a lighter direction. "While I was delving into the issue of miscegenation, I came across a biographical sketch of Alexandre Dumas, author of *The Three Musketeers*. His father was a mulatto and one of Napoleon's generals. The writer took the surname Dumas not from his father, but from his grandmother, who was a black slave. His grandfather—also a French military official—lived with her as his wife while stationed in the island territory now known as Haiti."

I told of my own Dumas family connections and the 1929 uproar regarding Davie Dumas' unclaimed fortune in California gold. "I was amused to read of one man who hoped to trace his ancestry to both the white gold hunter and the famous mulatto writer. In reality, the two Dumas men lived in exactly the same time period on different continents."

Still, Catrena made no comment.

With a faltering smile, I continued, "I guess I'm concerned about something that can't be changed, but I see the continuing racial tensions as the legacy slavery left our society."

"But you want to know how the mixing happened," Catrena assessed.

"Yes, I suppose that's the way to put it."

"I'll bring my black history class notes tomorrow. I do know that there were more mulattos in the free population in towns and cities than on plantations. Racial mixing was much more likely with the free blacks than with the slaves. That's because in cities, there were more white men than white women, and there were more black women than black men, especially free black men. And freed mulattos gravitated to the cities, because where else could they go?"

"Did slave owners ordinarily free the children they had by slaves?"

"Only some of the time. Maybe it was because of guilt, or maybe the slave owners or their wives wanted to get rid of the reminders."

"I suppose a wife would get plenty angry looking at a daily flaunting of her husband's infidelity, but in that day a woman couldn't go out and file for divorce."

"No, she just had to live with it. But a betrayed wife wouldn't always take it out on the mixed child. They say sometimes the wife was like a kind stepmother. We'd only be guessing at an owner's reasons for getting rid of his mixed-race children. Sometimes they were set free, but sometimes they were sold."

"They *sold* their own children?"

"Sure did. There was a court case up in South Carolina where it came out that one plantation owner had a dozen or more children by the slave-mistress who lived with him in the big house. He sold off one of the children nearly every year when they got to be about nine or ten years old. Actually, few mixed-race children were either freed or sold. Most of them just lived out their lives as slaves."

Catrena said mixed-race children didn't get any special privileges and usually had difficult lives. It wasn't unusual for a slave girl to serve her own half-sister, "and you can be sure there was none of the great loyalty they talked about with a 'pure' slave. Obvious blood ties made for some bitter situations all the way around."

Her voice revealed no emotion, but her eyes suddenly took a glint of laser brilliancy. "One of the interesting sidelines of the slave trade was called the 'fancy-girl' market. A beautiful fancy-girl could bring five times the price of a good blacksmith. And blacksmiths were always in demand. Fancy-girls were mulatto girls sold as house servants with special services required for the pleasure of the richest planters or their sons. People thought it was outrageous because the girls were nearly white, but it was generally looked on as an indulgence of the upper class."

Catrena sighed as if reaching a foregone conclusion. "An owner who was so callous about sex with girls who couldn't even object showcased his own depravity. The owner disgraced himself first, then the pain he inflicted was felt in ever-widening circles—the fancy-girl herself, the betrayed and humiliated wife, and the families, especially the children, of both."

As I began to gather my papers, I saw that a yellow stick-on note clung to the top page. "Oh, yes. Maybe you might know something about this." I pulled the note off the page and handed it to Catrena.

"*Guichy* or *Geechee*. What does it mean?"

"I don't know," I admitted. "I think it's an African tribe. It isn't especially important that I find the meaning. I'm just curious."

"It sounds familiar. Now, I'm curious, too. I'll see what I can find."

Catrena asked how I became interested in African-American history. I gave a quick summary of my discovery of Phil and Caroline and my worries about a forced separation.

"That sort of thing happened all the time. Separating families was one of the cruelest things done to slaves. It's now generally accepted that forced separation was the beginning of the black matriarchal society; single mothers just had to carry on."

I thought of Jeremiah's slave girl, alone with her baby in the slave house. Then I thought of Arlette, the hotel maid in Atlanta. That was the term she used, she "just had to carry on."

The following day, Catrena came well prepared for an in-depth discussion. "I rearranged my lunch hour so we can really talk. This is going to help me with a class I'll be taking next semester, so I boned up on the subject last night with a personal interest."

Catrena outlined a general history of the black family which was as personal and specific an ancestry as most blacks ever find. Sometimes, advertisements referred to a family for sale, meaning the owner wanted a stated amount for the "lot," and if his price wasn't met, the family would be sold as individual slaves. Basically, he was interested in getting the most money possible. Young mothers were usually advertised as "female with first child" or "breed woman" to indicate many productive years ahead. Although slaves might have originally been captured as a family, they were rarely sold as family units. If they had been taken together, the traumatic voyage was likely the last time the slaves would see their family members.

"Historically, the American black male has not held an authoritative position in the family," Catrena said. "That's what I meant by the beginning of the matriarchal society. It wasn't caused only by forced separations; often blacks didn't have a two-parent home to start with."

Phil and Caroline's dilemma loomed in my mind. "Didn't plantation slaves generally stay in the same vicinity? Sometimes, a slave was married to another slave on a neighboring farm, and the family remained intact."

"Yes, but if one slave owner decided to move, he took his slaves with him, and those owned by someone else stayed behind. There was the westward migration going on in the country, so it was not at all unusual that families were split. Maybe a child had been sold to a neighbor, or sometimes a son or daughter who had already moved west inherited a slave. There was no realistic way to escape from being a slave. It was passed to their children and to their children's children."

So Phil and Caroline's predicament was not at all unusual.

"Separation was devastating to a slave," Catrena said. "Having the love of a family tie was the single, solitary thing a slave could live for—the only thing in the world worth living for. Letters written back to the old plantation were like newsletters with messages from various family members. Sometimes, a letter might include a request to buy a slave who'd been taken from his wife, or for an old mother, or for children left behind. Then, the slave would cooperate and work hard because that's all he had to go on. Most of the time, slaves were looked upon as nothing more than livestock."

Catrena said slaves were sometimes sold off to speculators who came rounding them up in late December for the big January market. Four or five slaves might be chained together at the ankles. The drivers rode horses, but the slaves, "looking for all the world like a drove of turkeys," had to run along with bare feet on the frozen ground, right on through icy mud puddles. "The women wore nothing but thin dresses and maybe a petticoat. Icicles hung from their hems like fringe balls. When they got cold, the driver made them run to warm up."

The loud ring of a telephone interrupted Catrena, and she rose from her chair to take the call. After a few words, she turned to me. "It's for you. I left a request with the school research librarian asking the meaning of the word you wanted to know."

The librarian was able to tell me that "Geechy" is a derivation of Gullah. Gullah refers to dialect, as well as ancestry. The slaves who were brought to rice growers on the islands off the coast of South Carolina and Georgia remained isolated, and they kept their native language and customs. The situation was the opposite for slaves taken to the mainland. They were often thrown among other slaves speaking different dialects, and they, of necessity, learned to understand and communicate in English, the language of their masters.

"Gullah" rang a bell. Hadn't I read an article in last Sunday's newspaper about Gullahs?

I thanked Catrena and went through the conscious physical motions of walking back to the hotel room, all the while tingling with the anticipation that something was clicking. I was amazed to find that the newspaper section from the *Atlanta Journal-Constitution* had not been discarded. The date was Sunday, October 6, 1991.

The Associated Press headline read, "Lullaby ties Georgia Gullahs to Sierra Leone." The story told of a woman in Georgia who sang lullabies to her children. An anthropologist, Joe Opala, who had traced a group of Gullah descendants in Georgia, heard her songs. He'd previously heard a scratchy recording of the same song sung by another Gullah woman, documented by a researcher in the 1930s. No one had known the meaning of the words, and the songs had been simply passed down from generation to generation as melodic keepsakes. Now, the songs were passing to another generation of grandchildren.

The anthropologist could determine enough of the words to associate the language to the Mende region of the southern part of Sierra Leone. When he went to the remote Mende villages to play the recording, the villagers were astonished. They understood the words. The song was not a lullaby, but a funeral dirge, written centuries before. The villagers couldn't believe the song came from the United States. The article closed by saying that the melody had returned to the village where it originated and is no longer simply a sad funeral lament. "It can now truly be called a lullaby."

I thought of great-aunt Frankie's reunited children and of Barbara's mother describing the balcony people who've gone before. We all have balcony people. Perhaps we're missing clues to the spiritual world. Who can explain great-aunt Frankie's answered prayer? Or the Gullah lullaby? Or Grandma's worn Sacred Harp songbook that reached to me from a page in a magazine?

Before going to bed, I organized the latest accumulation of notes and photocopies in preparation for returning to Atlanta the next day. I made a rough spreadsheet to catalog what I'd discovered. A jumble of isolated facts whirled through my mind. While I removed my makeup, I looked in the mirror and saw with a flash of recognition the haunting eyes in Carine's photograph of the young man thought to be Jeremiah's son, James Franklin Dumas, Grandma's father. Strange, I thought. I must have seen a fleeting family resemblance.

I'd barely begun to drift off to sleep when I suddenly thought of a descriptive column in the slave schedules. I bolted from bed to find the copy of the 1860 Slave Schedule for Union Parish. I hurriedly looked for the page beginning with *J. Dumas*. This time, I saw the page as a whole, and the "Color" column jumped out at me. Most of the entries in the column were marked "B" for black, but farther down the page were entries for slaves labeled "M," for mulatto.

The female, age sixteen, belonging to J. Dumas was black, and yes, also the baby boy.

Black, not mulatto, and not the child of Jeremiah or his sons.

Perhaps that was truly the case. But what about those who were labeled mulatto? Racial assignments were subject to the judgment of the census taker. It was not a scientific determination but a personal opinion based on skin color, physical characteristics, some other racial profiling, or perhaps based on other secret motives or prejudices. Maybe the census taker never even saw the slave and simply asked the owner. The question was effectively unanswerable—another dead-end for African Americans who might wish to trace their ancestry.

It wasn't Jeremiah's sins or the sins of his sons that I saw in the eyes in the mirror. It was my own sin; I was the accuser. With scarcely more than cynical suspicion, I'd placed full blame on Jeremiah and his sons for the centuries of sins committed by abusive slave owners. The sins—whether adultery, rape, or loving a slave while keeping her and her child in bondage—had happened countless times, and there was no way to know when, where, and by whom.

There still remained solitary evidence of a teenage mother with no father figure in her home. And Phil, the slave I'd sought so long, was still missing—a man who could, and should, have been a father figure in some child's home. I could only hope that Phil had been given his freedom and for that reason was not on the 1860 slave schedule.

I glanced at the clock. My night-owl mother would still be awake. She listened to the story, commenting an "mmm-hmm" at appropriate intervals before making her own observations.

"So you suspected that someone in the household fathered a child by the slave girl. I suspect something even worse. I'm afraid I know the answer you've been looking for."

Mother paused before continuing. "I've been wondering if the old former slave I'd remembered seeing as a child might have been the same slave you've been trying to find, Phil."

"You don't mean the eunuch!"

"He'd have been about the same age. He didn't have a family. The poor old man wasn't born that way. Somebody did it to him. Somebody punished him for some perceived misdeed—something else we don't know. Maybe it happened before he ever came to Louisiana."

The possibility made me feel ill. Mother's suspicion could be right. Phil had been judged guilty of something that caused him to be excommunicated from the church, although we don't know what the unforgiven act might have been. From our place in time, it's hard to judge which could have been the greater evil, the unknown crime or its punishment.

When I again put my head on the pillow, I thought of the Sacred Harp music Grandma had inherited and passed on to me. Jeremiah sang of God's amazing, redeeming Grace. He passed to us melodic guideposts from his time and before. The song-prayers were for such a time as this, when we need something to hold on to as we stumble blindly in the dark, when words alone cannot describe the centuries of inflicted pain nor God's redemptive mercy. A song came to me, its remembered chords sweeping over and around me like soothing strokes from heaven:

> *Beneath the sacred throne of God I saw a river rise;*
> *The streams where peace and pard'ning blood descended from the skies.*
> *I stood amazed and wondered when or why this ocean rose;*
> *That wafts salvation down to man, His traitors and His foes.*
> *That sacred flood from Jesus' veins was free to make a-way;*
> *And Mary's or Manasseh's stains, or sins more vile than they.*

"Sacred Throne" #569 in *The Sacred Harp*
Words, John Kent, 1835; music, Hugh Wilson, 1764-1824

PART TWO

■

THE AMERICAN REVOLUTIONARIES

Rocky River Baptist Church, organized 1776, in Anson County, North Carolina. Edmund Lilly, son-in-law of Benjamin Dumas I (1705-1763), was the founding pastor. Lilly was still pastor of the church in 1791 when he was "carried" to preach after a serious injury in the American Revolution.

THE AMERICAN REVOLUTIONARIES

1756
BENJAMIN DUMAS (III) born in Anson County, North Carolina;
ca.1780 married Susannah Hutchins(on) in North Carolina;
died in an American Revolution battle,
leaving behind a young widow with three small sons
Children: David, Benjamin Franklin, Moses

1730
DAVID DUMAS born in Hanover County, Virginia;
ca.1750 married Sarah Moorman in Virginia;
the newly-married couple moved with his parents from
Virginia to North Carolina the same year;
ca.1803 died in Anson County, North Carolina
Children: Andrew, Benjamin (III), Unity, Frances, Jeremiah,
Sarah, Obediah, Zachariah, Nehemiah, Azariah

1705
BENJAMIN DUMAS (I) born in New Kent County, Virginia;
ca.1730 married Frances Clark in Virginia;
ca.1746-48 they sold their flourishing Virginia
plantations and moved their entire family,
including married children and their spouses, to Anson County,
North Carolina; 1763 died in North Carolina
Children: David, Frances, Sarah, Jeremiah, Benjamin (II)

CHAPTER 9

Aunt Izzie

ALMOST as soon as Doug and I returned home to Atlanta, I received news that Mother had lost the vision in her left eye. Despite her objections, I left home again and made a quick trip to Amarillo to see for myself that she was all right.

Apparently the deterioration of Mother's vision had occurred gradually, and she had already made adjustments. Still watching her closely, my worry shifted to her continual wheezing and coughing. My suggestion that she should see a pulmonary specialist received an unexpected reaction; she'd already done so.

"He merely told me to quit smoking," she said wryly. "Then he prescribed an anti-depressant that was supposed to help me quit. I tried taking it, but those pills were like poison to my system. The day I took two, I vomited until sundown. And if I were to seek second or third opinions, I already know what they'd say: quit smoking."

"Well, why don't you seriously think of quitting?" I asked.

Tears welled in Mother's eyes. "*Think* of it? I think of it all the time, and I pray about it constantly. Quitting smoking is the hardest thing I've ever tried to do in my life. Nothing seems to help. I've tried chewing gum instead. I even went to a hypnotist."

Looking into Mother's helpless face I realized for the first time that quitting smoking was no longer a matter of choice for her. I wondered when the line of freedom to choose had been crossed. The binding tentacles of addiction had tightened slowly and subtly. Smoking had long been seen as sophisticated and glamorous; dire warnings have been a recent development.

When I returned to Atlanta once again, I realized that Barbara had phoned three times while I was away. In her last recorded message, received the prior evening, her anxious voice said, "For heaven's sake, Chloe, have you left town for good? When you get home, please call me as soon as possible. A box of my mother's old research material led me to someone I want you to meet."

My curiosity piqued, I phoned Barbara before unpacking. "How long has that crucial box of your mother's been lying around?"

"That isn't what's most important. There are some letters from a newspaper editor up in North Carolina who was doing a genealogy search for her. We have only his letters, not hers, but it's fairly easy to conclude what her questions were."

Thinking of the mountain of dirty laundry trapped in my suitcase I said, "I don't know that I'll have time to get over to read them right away. Doug's going up to Raleigh for a couple of weeks for an investigation, and I'm going along."

"To North Carolina? Why, the timing couldn't be better. North Carolina is exactly what Izzie was talking about. That's even more reason you must come with me. It's very important that you meet Izzie, and by all means, bring your tape recorder."

Barbara said Izzie was "shirt-tail kin." Though she'd never fully figured out how she was related to us, Barbara knew Izzie was named for Isabel Dumas, wife of Edmund Dumas.

Barbara explained, "I found a reference to *Aunt Izzie* Ingram on one of Mother's notes. I had not seen her in twenty years or more, and she was old and white-haired way back then."

Barbara had phoned an elderly cousin in Marietta who told her that Izzie is still living. "She's one hundred years old, and she's in a nursing home in North Cobb County. She was a schoolteacher, a history teacher. After I failed to reach you last week, I went to see her, and I was sorry you missed it."

"Why? What did she tell you?"

"Oh, I won't be able to tell it like she does. She was born a few months after Isabel died, and her mother had promised Isabel that if the baby were to be a girl, she'd have a namesake. Izzie said her folks loved to go to Sacred Harp singings with their *Aunt* Isabel and *Uncle* Edmund. They were like godparents, I suppose."

"Does she have some of Edmund's original music or something?"

"No, but Izzie remembers the past as if it just happened. She can tell some amazing stories about what was really going on—such as why Edmund's mother, Martha, wanted to learn to read so badly, and—when can you go with me to see her? I promise you won't be disappointed; stories that are passed down orally are every bit as important as those you'll find in a history book."

It was useless to protest further, and I agreed to go the next day. Barbara's enthusiasm didn't waver overnight, and she continued her praise as we drove. "You're going to love Izzie. Her mind is sharp as a tack. I won't pretend she keeps up with the news on CNN, but she remembers the past as if it were only yesterday. Seeing her will reassure you about your mom living by herself;

Mabel Dumas Crenshaw (1906-1989), great-granddaughter of Edmund Dumas, "pretty as a boll of new cotton." (Photo courtesy of her descendants.)

Izzie lived alone in the house where she raised her family until only a couple of years ago. Her vision isn't what it once was, and she tripped and broke her leg while she was mowing the lawn."

"A hundred years old and she's mowing the lawn?"

Barbara's eyes sparkled with glee. "She said she'd hardly had a sick day in her life, but once she hit ninety-five, she started falling apart."

With Barbara at the wheel, I sifted through the box of her mother's papers that Barbara had brought for me to borrow and photocopy. She explained that most of the material documented the Dumas family's journey from Virginia through North Carolina. "Mother was particularly interested in what the women were doing. She said the effects of what women did were not as obvious, but were often more lasting than a man's work. 'The hand that rocks the cradle,' you know."

A letter written to Barbara's mother, Mabel Dumas Crenshaw, was on top of the pile in the history box.

Rockingham, N.C. February 27, 1956
Dear Mrs. Crenshaw:

Now let's digress and trace the Martha Ussery branch, inasmuch as you know the Dumas line of her husband.

The USSERYS (or Usserey as sometimes spelled, French). William, John, and Thomas Ussery migrated from France, through England or Scotland, and eventually settled in North Carolina in

Richmond County, but later moved inland and northward into the area that is now Montgomery County. (All of Richmond and Montgomery counties had been part of Anson County at that time. Anson was later divided. Use of the eventual county names will identify their place of residence.)

The USSERYS were wealthy and owned much land. The DUMAS family lived in and along the border of Richmond and Montgomery counties. It was but natural that the two families should intermarry.

I have in my possession the original will written June 10, 1811 by Thomas Ussery, son of the Thomas who came from overseas. In the will, he names his nine children. Martha (who married Benjamin Franklin Dumas) is listed as one of the four daughters.

Thomas Ussery was a Regulator of the 1760s and fought in the [American] Revolution. He was a big man in Montgomery County (formed in 1779 from Anson County, Richmond formed same year from Anson). Thomas represented Montgomery County in the North Carolina Legislature 1788 to 1795.

I hope the above is of some value to you.

Isaac S. London

"That's from the newspaper man who did research for Mother," Barbara said. "It isn't often that we learn much about mysterious daughters mentioned in wills, but in a few minutes, you'll see why I insisted you hear about our great-great-great-grandmother Martha and the role that women played."

We approached a red brick building with wings extending from a central core. The driveway circled a stately magnolia tree and passed beneath a broad portico at the main entrance. We entered the nursing home and walked down a long corridor, passing several aged wheelchair-bound residents who greeted us eagerly.

Isabel Ingram, thin and frail, was seated in a chair near the window in her room. The warm sunlight streamed down her halo of snow-white hair, and a metal walker stood within arm's reach of her chair. When Izzie turned in response to Barbara's greeting, I was struck by her glowing expression of contentment and peace, as though the woman's delicate shell was a prism reflecting rays of the sun.

"Barbara...oh, yes, Mabel's girl. You were here last week, weren't you? I have a hard time keeping you young folks straight. Mabel's always been such a pretty girl. Pretty as a boll of new cotton, they used to say. It's hard to believe she has a grown daughter." Barbara winked at me and smiled. I asked for permission to turn on my tape recorder as we took seats near Izzie.

"This is the relative from Texas I mentioned to you. She wants to hear about your quilting days and what you heard about the American Revolution."

"The quilting days." Izzie paused to shift thinking gears, fine-tuning her focus to specific dates and occasions. "Now you girls know that Mabel wasn't a quilter. It was Mabel's mother, Minnie, who was my quilting partner. And it was Minnie's aunt, Aunt Sarah Dumas, who taught us how to quilt. All of Minnie's friends called her Aunt Sarah, even if she wasn't our real aunt."

Barbara addressed Izzie in a louder volume than her usual speaking voice, "Please tell us about learning to quilt. Chloe wants to hear about the little scissors."

"Oh, yes, indeed. The little scissors. They were passed down to Aunt Sarah, our quilting teacher. They were pretty little scissors that she fastened to her waist so they'd be handy when she needed to cut a thread. They hung down at her side, and I remember how they'd shine like a Christmas ornament when the sun hit them. That's when I was still a bitty girl, and I'd be sitting next to Mama's legs under the quilting frame while the ladies were quilting."

Izzie's eyes darted playfully to Barbara and me, and in a lighter tone she continued, "Well, a few of those ladies didn't sit very lady-like, and sometimes their underdrawers were cut pretty loose. When Minnie and I got to giggling about what was exposed, our mothers ran us outside to play so we wouldn't be jostling the quilt. But when the ladies hushed their voices, we made sure we stayed real quiet and still because that's when we learned about the birds and the bees. We learned all sorts of things when we napped under the quilting frames. And not all of it was naughty."

"You didn't learn to quilt from that vantage, did you?" I asked with a smile.

"I suppose we absorbed more than we realized at the time. I remember watching closely to see how soon I could make out the shape Aunt Sarah's stitches were forming. Her stitches became drawings of objects from a story or an initial of a main character in her story. I liked the way she stitched, a continuous chain of connecting *S*s. Some ladies liked to make hearts or flowers, and some just sewed straight lines. To this day, I still like to turn my quilts with the underside up because you can see the pattern of stitches better against a solid field. To me, that's the prettiest part."

Izzie reached for the edge of a quilt folded at the foot of her bed, flipping the corner up to reveal the hidden top side.

"It was Aunt Sarah Dumas who pulled Minnie and me up close enough to see how the top side was taking shape. Every time we saw her reach for her scissors, we knew it was all right to interrupt because she was soon going to have to rethread her needle. If we were quick enough, we might be allowed to use those dear little scissors ourselves to clip the thread."

"Describe them for us," Barbara said.

"They were small silver sewing scissors attached to a chain and a belt clip. She let us look at them up close sometimes. They had an inscription that said, 'Sarah Dumas, 1776.' She made sure we understood that it referred to a much older Sarah Dumas—more than a hundred years before her time. She didn't want us to think she was that old, even though it was all the same to us."

"Did she tell you about the first Sarah Dumas, the original owner?" I asked.

"Oh, yes. We called her *Old* Sarah. Minnie and I always wanted to hear about her. Sometimes Aunt Sarah's quilt stories were about Old Sarah or something that happened way back then. Besides making quilts, Old Sarah used the scissors when she made garments for the Continental soldiers—you know our men weren't as well-supplied as the redcoats—or sewed on buttons or whatever else was needed to help the patriots in the American Revolution.

"They lived up in North Carolina then, where the Rocky River runs into the Great Peedee River. The patriots had to work in secret so the British troops or loyalist sympathizers wouldn't find them out. Old Sarah came from a Quaker family, but she married into the Dumas family. It was well known that the Quakers wouldn't bear arms, but the Dumas men weren't held to that belief. There was a lot of religious discussion mixed in with their heated politics, it seems."

Barbara prompted Izzie to continue, admitting, "We want to hear everything Aunt Sarah told you."

"I guess I ought to make the connections clear to start with, because there are two women named Sarah Dumas at the beginning and end of this chain of remarkable mothers-in-law. Aunt Sarah is the one who told the stories to Minnie and me, and Old Sarah lived them.

"Aunt Sarah Dumas came by the little scissors from Isabel Dumas. Isabel died right before I was born, but she passed down the scissors' history to Aunt Sarah. Isabel had heard that same history first-hand from her mother-in-law, Martha Dumas, who personally knew a lot of the people involved."

Izzie relished having an audience. She took a sip of water, blinked her eyes rapidly before returning the glass to her bedside table, and continued, "Isabel was smart, but she often admitted that she got most of her education after she married. Her mother-in-law, Martha, taught her sons when they were growing up that girls ought to have book learning, the same as boys. So Isabel's husband, Edmund Dumas, the preacher-songwriter, made sure that his daughters were properly educated, and that Isabel's education wasn't left behind either.

"Edmund was always preaching and teaching singing schools. He taught shape-note music—wrote a lot of it himself. Even people who couldn't read could recognize the shapes and sing their matching syllables. But that brings me back to his mother, Martha Dumas, who never got to go to school when she was a girl. Her father was a judge up in North Carolina when the struggle for freedom from England was going on. Her brothers learned how to read, but Martha's family, like most people, didn't think it was wise to waste an education on a girl.

"Martha learned soon enough that wasn't always the case. She married a man named Benjamin Franklin Dumas. With a child named Benjamin Franklin, it isn't hard to figure out which side of the fight the Dumas family was on. The original Benjamin Franklin—the real, historical leader—had a hotbed of followers in that neck of the North Carolina woods. They started out loyal followers of the King of England like everybody else, but they were soon fed up with being cheated and mistreated by the King's representatives. It's true that some of them on both sides were no more than scoundrels or ruffians, but that's often the way it is. Even so, I'm glad the American Revolution turned out the way it did.

"Anyway, when Martha married into the Dumas family, she got herself a legend for a mother-in-law. Her name was Susannah; she seemed bigger than life and could do no wrong. I say that because she died while Benjamin Franklin Dumas and Martha were still courting. So all the great things Susannah did while she was living were only polished brighter every time they were told."

Barbara interrupted, "But didn't you say last week that Martha admired her?"

"Yes, that's what they said. Still, I don't know how anyone could keep from resenting having to measure up to a real do-er like Susannah."

"What sort of things did she do?" I asked.

"Why, Susannah could read and write! She could do anything she set out to do. She did about anything with her brain a man could do, and she knew how to use her sweet-talk charms, too. Her father-in-law, David Dumas—the first David Dumas—owned the only public ferry along the Great Peedee River for about twenty-five or thirty miles, and he had a prosperous tavern with a general store right next to it. There weren't any bridges back then and you had to take the ferry to cross the river. The tavern was more than a place to eat and drink. We'd call it a hotel or motel; it was the best place for travelers to stop for the night. The tavern and store were the main headquarters to catch up on the latest news. During the war, it was a regular beehive for both sides. All the fords and ferries swarmed with activity, like the tavern. The British tried to keep a close eye on the place, but they were outsmarted.

"Susannah knew almost everything there was to know about her father-in-law's business of running the tavern and general store. She signed as a witness to all his legal dealings, and you might say she was his right-hand woman. David Dumas knew he could rely on her to winnow information to help the patriots' cause. I guess she was clever enough to know when to play dumb. David's wife, Old Sarah, sweetly went about her own activities, which were many, considering she was still having new babies of her own at that time. Old Sarah wasn't really old back then.

"Susannah became as close as any daughter to her in-laws. Her real mother had died in childbirth, so Susannah's care was left to her father. He came to work in some close capacity for David Dumas, and he brought Susannah with him. She grew up right alongside the Dumas children. Old Sarah offered a mother's love long before Susannah married their son, Ben III, and the bond between those two women was never severed. Susannah must have watched those little sewing scissors being used, just like Minnie and I did. Years later, when I watched Aunt Sarah stitch a border of interconnecting *S*s, she explained that they were for Susannah and Sarah."

A pained expression crossed Izzie's face. She stopped talking, and with the twisted fingers of her age and work-gnarled hands, she rubbed her

"Vain World, Adieu" by Edmund Dumas, #329 in *The Sacred Harp*, 1869 revision. Edmund Dumas was born in 1810 near Rocky River Baptist Church. The first music he heard was likely the church's camp meeting songs and slave melodies echoing in the river valley.

forearms. Barbara asked if she should call the nurse, but Izzie just said, "Oh, no, dear. It's only a touch of arthritis, and they bring my pills around more often than I like. I'm doing fine, plus I have more to tell you. History was the subject I taught. Please bear with me."

As she secured a snap fastener of her loose-fitting dress and raised a determined chin, Izzie continued, "Let's see, now...David Dumas and his brother, who farmed the plantation, were both deeply involved with the militia, but they had to keep their activities above suspicion from the redcoats and any loyalist sympathizers. David and Old Sarah's son, Ben III, who became Susannah's husband, signed up to fight on our own Continental side. His assignments were fairly close to home because his knowledge of the rivers and wooded terrain was invaluable.

"His name was Benjamin—the same name as his grandfather and his uncle, and later his own son—but they called him Ben III. I don't have any idea why there was such a shortage of names back then. Anyway, Ben III took some cattle and horses to a big island they owned out in the middle of the river. Horses for the soldiers were scarce, and meat the cattle provided was critical to being able to feed the troops. Salt for curing the meat was in short supply, so occasionally, Ben III slipped through the British lines to go get what they needed."

Barbara interrupted to elaborate on the difficulty of such a task. "Even today, the woods in that remote part of North Carolina are rugged wilderness. They say it's still possible for a survivalist who knows it well to hide out there and never be found."

"Well, Ben III certainly knew the country well," Izzie said. "He came from a family of explorers, so finding his way over the rivers and through the wildwoods was natural to him."

A nurse's aide came to the door with a reminder that lunchtime was approaching. Izzie asked to be called again at the last moment. "I'd rather talk to you girls than eat, anyway," she said with a bright smile.

Her voice took a tone of confidentiality as she continued to speak, "The British had already documented all of the public ferries on official maps, and there was no way to keep them from using the ferry crossing at the Dumas Tavern. However, a private ferry was a different matter."

Izzie described a smaller ferry that was kept submerged in an obscure location a few miles upriver until the resistance soldiers needed it. Then, it was pulled up to the surface with hidden ropes. After safe passage, the ferry was sunk again in the secret cove. She told of Ben III's adventures taking munitions and supplies from the general store to hide in caves unknown to the British. There were enough Dumas brothers or cousins to assist when needed or hinder suspicion that someone was missing.

Izzie frowned before continuing. "Shortly before Ben III and Susannah's third son was born, his company was in a terrible blood bath to the south of Anson County, in South Carolina. He didn't come home from that one, but David and Old Sarah continued to take a special interest in the welfare of the young widow Susannah and her fatherless boys."

The second of those three sons was my ancestor Benjamin Franklin Dumas, who grew up, married, and eventually moved to Georgia. He and his wife, Martha, were the parents of the preacher-songwriter Edmund.

"I don't really believe Martha resented Susannah because she could read and write," Izzie said, "She admired her. Susannah set the goals."

Izzie blinked her eyes again, and then closed them for a long moment. We saw that she was tired. Barbara and I thanked her and moved the chairs back into place. Izzie reached for the metal walker and pulled herself erect.

"I don't often get a chance to talk to anyone like this, and I do like to talk." She laughed softly at herself, her energy spent. "I expect I'll have a nice long nap this afternoon. You girls come see me again real soon."

After saying goodbye and walking into the hall, I turned for a last look at Izzie, who took careful, labored steps in the walker toward the doorway to her bathroom. The aged woman's fragile frame appeared to be in a stage of metamorphosis, her spirit poised to shed its mortal husk, spread its wings, and take flight.

> *Ye golden lamps of heav'n, farewell, with all your feeble light;*
> *Farewell, thou ever-changing moon, pale empress of the night.*
> *And thou refulgent orb of day, in brighter flames arrayed;*
> *My soul which springs beyond thy sphere, no more demands thy aid.*

"Last Words of Copernicus" #112 in *The Sacred Harp*
Words, Philip Doddridge, 1775; music Sarah Lancaster, 1869

CHAPTER 10

Dumas Tavern and Mount Gilead

DOUG had planned to drive to Raleigh and stay in North Carolina for the time his business required. We'd heard that autumn color was spectacular throughout the northern Georgia mountains and into the Carolinas. There might never be a better time for such a trip.

Soon after sunrise on Saturday morning, Doug and I were leaving the outskirts of Atlanta behind. I gazed contentedly at the passing scenery, thinking Mother had been right: this might be the most interesting stage of life. Doug's business trip could provide an opportunity to flesh out more of Carine's documentation of our family tree. There was no time to thoroughly sift through the box of research material Barbara had brought me, but a cursory once-over was enough to show that Mabel Dumas Crenshaw had heard the same stories Izzie told Barbara and me. But Mabel, who had constructed a loose outline of significant events for the Dumas family in the time they were in North Carolina, left behind numerous questions of her own.

She highlighted the way they arrived in the area, beginning with a man named John Clark, an explorer of the Virginia-North Carolina region in the 1730s and 1740s, who was described as a "loose-footed" Scotsman. Around 1730, John Clark's sister, Frances, married Benjamin Dumas I, the eldest son of the Dumas line and the first son born in America.

Reading her notes, I understood that Mabel was attempting to establish a family link between the explorer John Clark and the later William Clark of the Lewis and Clark expedition, who was from the same vicinity of New Kent County in Virginia. Mabel noted that the Clarks who lived there had long been known to have had an insatiable curiosity about the land of Indian legend, the land west of the mountains "beyond the Blue Ridge." John and Frances Clark's father had even drawn an early map of Virginia along the James River, and the family was on friendly terms with the Native Americans nearby.

Mabel's documentation of the Clark family focused on one specific expedition. In the late 1730s, John Clark left Virginia with a Native American guide to visit the sacred mound and abandoned village of the Siouan and Creek Indians in present-day North Carolina. Clark had come upriver to the Siouan village, following long-established trails. They carried lightweight, but strong, birch bark canoes with them. The Native Americans had taught John Clark that a canoe was highly maneuverable in turbulent rivers and streams, as well as in shallow waters. And on this trip, the explorers could use it to ford rivers at low water crossings, or they could even swim across and pull the canoe loaded with supplies.

When they reached the abandoned village, John Clark was undoubtedly impressed by the area because he made a land claim there in 1740. When he returned to Virginia, Clark had a rapt audience who wanted to hear details of his adventures. One of the most interested was his brother-in-law, Benjamin Dumas I.

By 1750, Benjamin Dumas I and his wife, Frances, had decided to pull up their Virginia roots and move to the long-deserted Siouan village. And Mabel wanted to know why, as Benjamin Dumas I neared the age of fifty, a ripe old age in his time, he chose to sell his comfortable home and two large Virginia plantations to move his entire family, including his grown children, into the wilderness frontier. Her theory was that it was directly related to his Huguenot ties.

Benjamin's father, Jerome Dumas—pronounced Jer-o-may—had come to Jamestown in 1700 as a Huguenot refugee, a French Protestant seeking religious freedom. The Dumas family would naturally be in sympathy with the plight of fellow Huguenots who had scattered all over Europe after the revocation of the Edict of Nantes by Louis XIV in 1685. The Edict of Nantes had offered a measure of protection to Protestants since 1598, but upon its revocation, Protestants were forced to flee France or face execution if they did not renounce their faith immediately.

Mabel had concluded from her extensive research that Benjamin Dumas I and his family had moved from Virginia to the deserted village not for a more prosperous life but to provide a refuge for their fellow Frenchmen who would never again see their homeland. The North Carolina site, once chosen by the natives as their home, must have sounded to Benjamin Dumas like an answer to his prayers for the refugees. He and Frances, with their married children and their spouses, sold their flourishing plantations along the James River, left the security of established society in Virginia, and came to settle on Clark's Creek near the site of the village left behind years before by native tribes.

They must have felt like Adam and Eve in the Garden of Eden. The virgin land had everything they would need—notably, easy availability of navigable water for transportation. Carine's book had stated that their new lands were on both sides of the river where the Rocky River flows into the waters of the Great Peedee River. The rivers could supply power for a mill for the settlement to become self-sufficient. The surrounding area would provide fertile land to raise crops and livestock. And the expansive holdings included a sizeable island—just like Izzie had said.

After arriving at the hotel in downtown Raleigh, I bought a city map and asked directions to the North Carolina State Library and Archives. The large complex was only eight blocks away, and as I walked to the library the next morning, my mind was filled with questions of how I might locate the Dumas lands. I failed to notice the name of an imposing building until I reached the end of the block, but as I paused at the crosswalk, I glanced at the cornerstone: State of North Carolina Department of Transportation. In a flash of inspiration, I spun around and walked in the main entrance.

A receptionist directed me to an office down the hall. With the help of Carine's and Mabel's accounts of the ferry and tavern, the department supervisor and I were able to locate on a state map the general area where the Dumas family had settled. Then he pulled out an old ferry map and was able to pinpoint precisely the original location of the ferry and tavern downriver from a clearly-defined island above the juncture of two large rivers, the Great Peedee and Rocky River.

He said, "Highways typically followed established trails, usually trails that had been used by Indians for centuries. And I believe this Highway 109 bridge is where the Dumas Ferry once crossed." And with new found confidence, I purchased detailed road maps for the three contiguous counties which had been formed of the original Anson County, where the Dumas family had owned land.

At the North Carolina State Library and Archives, I asked a resourceful librarian for book recommendations about pre-Revolutionary history of the North Carolina frontier to better understand the context of my Regulator ancestor, Benjamin Dumas I. The librarian explained that the Regulator movement was a taxpayer rebellion during North Carolina's colonial days. "Regulator" was a buzz word that meant one of the earliest rebels, and later, those who were most committed to the American Revolution. She listed books on a notepad, and when she handed me the torn paper, I read the listing highlighted at the bottom: *Battle of Alamance—1771.*

"It would ordinarily be considered more of a skirmish than a battle, from a later perspective," the librarian whispered. "Some scholars now consider it to be the first battle of the American Revolution."

Flipping through *The Regulators in North Carolina, A Documentary History 1759-1776,* I found that the Regulators were not a formally organized group. They were landowners and farmers protesting the arbitrary abuses of power by appointed officials who represented the interests of King George. In the beginning, it was not the English government that the protestors found objectionable. They were simply calling for reform or *regulation* of misused authority of appointed, not elected, officials who levied taxes and fees at their whim.

The call for reform was especially volatile on the western frontier region of North Carolina, where the Dumas family had settled, compared to the established cities along the coast. The king's agent had the sole power to make rules and establish the amount that was payable. If the property owner was unable to fork over the required tax in hard cash immediately, his property—including household goods or anything else of value—could be confiscated, and it often was. In flourishing cities to the east, warehouse certificates or receipts for goods on an account were accepted in lieu of cash, but there were no warehouses on the western edges of the colony, so the settlers were at a distinct disadvantage. They had to have cash on hand. Land was often purchased by a friend of the agent, who *happened* to be nearby with the precise amount of cash that was needed.

The Regulators themselves were controversial too. Most of them owned only small plots of land and were dismissed in the orderly populated areas as a mob of ignorant backwoodsmen. However, in retrospect their protests seem valid, and most likely the other colonists agreed with the complaints, even if they never considered taking a public stand against the king.

I imagined that the Dumas Tavern, in western Anson County where the issue was inflamed, was a scene for heated discussions. But I could find no link of disorderly Regulator incidents that involved any family members, although David Dumas and his brother, Benjamin II—the one who operated the plantation—signed a pledge in 1769 with other Regulators refusing to pay taxes until satisfied that the levies were lawful and would be used for stated purposes. The Anson Petition, as it was called, asked that Doctor Benjamin Franklin, or some other known patriot, be appointed as their agent to present the grievances to His Majesty. The lines of communication on the western frontier were more closely linked to Philadelphia and Boston than to Virginia, and Benjamin Franklin gave voice to concerns of the North Carolinians.

There was no acknowledged spokesman for the Regulators' reform movement. The most widely known of the Regulators was a supporter of Benjamin Franklin named Herman Husband, who circulated political pamphlets with writings by Franklin and others objecting to "taxation without representation." Husband was actually a Quaker pacifist, but because he distributed Franklin's pamphlets, he was known as a troublemaker. Any time there was a disturbance, authorities automatically assumed that Husband was the instigator.

Most of the Regulators intended for reform to take a peaceful course, but victimized farmers needed crops to feed their hungry families immediately and had no time to wait. In several counties, their frustration and outrage erupted in violence. Husband often found himself negotiating for peace among the Regulators arguing to resolve the situation by force.

In the county north of Anson, on the morning of May 16, 1771, the day of the Battle of Alamance—the battle in which the governor's troops defeated the unorganized mob in only two hours—Husband met with a crowd of protestors, trying to calm them down. Many had already lost everything they owned and saw no reason to wait any longer for justice. When it became obvious that Husband's arguments were falling on deaf ears, he mounted his horse and rode away with the few others who wanted to avoid the ensuing confrontation.

There had never before been armed resistance to royal authority anywhere in the colonies. The Regulators had crossed the line, and the struggle for independence had begun in earnest in North Carolina.

By this time in 1771, Benjamin Dumas I had already died; David Dumas was forty years old, Old Sarah was in her late thirties, and their sons, Ben III and Andrew, were fifteen and sixteen. I wondered what they anticipated would lie ahead; they could not have foreseen the role the Dumas Tavern would play in the coming struggle.

I went to the archives division the next day and asked for assistance regarding taverns in colonial times. I was told that even in pre-Revolutionary days a tavern owner was required to post bond for a license and that I should first search the old records. One of the earliest recorded was a bond and license issued to David Dumas dated "this 9th day of April *anno domini* 1792" and was signed by the bond holder, Walter Leake. The bond had originally been posted prior to 1753 by David's father, Benjamin Dumas I.

Whereas the above named <u>David</u> <u>Dumas</u> hath obtained a licence to keep an ordinary in <u>his</u> <u>own</u> <u>house</u> and provide in the said ordinary, good, wholesome, and cleanly lodging and diet for travelers, and stabling, fodder, hay, corn, oats, or pasturage, as the season shall require, for their horses, and shall not suffer or permit any unlawful gaming in his house, nor on the Sabbath day suffer any person to tipple or drink any more than is necessary, then this licence shall remain in full force and virtue.

Apparently the responsibility of those serving alcohol to those being served was not a new development at all. Travelers were also protected from price gouging. Tavern rates were listed in pounds and shillings for the year 1771. A guest might indulge (to a certain extent) in a wide choice of Madeira, port, or claret wine; West India rum punch or grog; beer or *crab-cyder*, brandy, whiskey, Indian corn liquor, or rough seed barley rye.

After the British blockade during the American Revolution, the tavern was especially hard-hit by the shortage of sugar and rum from the West Indies, a staple on the menu. Scuppernongs, a popular variety of grapes, were plentiful in the region, and the Dumases began to make wine. Because they always had an overabundance of peaches and corn, they distilled their own brandy and whiskey. There was a shortage of everything they needed that came from somewhere else, and they had to improvise. The Dumases kept bees, so they used the honey for a sugar substitute. The blockade cut off their supply of textiles, but they could produce more cotton. There was no way to make salt, so that's why Ben III had to slip through to get it.

I found in a file of loose articles a description that gave a vivid picture of the tavern, which was constructed in the same manner as most log and clapboard buildings of colonial times. Beams were made of round logs—some as much as twenty feet in length. The framing was of hand-hewn pine logs, and the rafters were fastened with wooden pegs. The interior walls were hand-finished boards of heart pine about a foot in width, and the floor was also made of wide pine planks. Immense fireplaces, both upstairs and down, boasted handcrafted English style mantels. The chimneys were of hand-formed brick and a well, dug near the kitchen, was lined with similar brick, sculpted into a curved shape. The kitchen was a separate structure—in case of fire—connected to the main building by a covered passage. A smaller dairy house next to the kitchen held a shallow well for storing milk and butter. The tavern complex also included separate barns, grain storage bins, tool houses, and even a blacksmith shop.

The tavern served as a general store and became the local gathering place where the latest news could be debated, as in Williamsburg's well-known Raleigh Tavern. The Dumas Tavern could not lay claim to such refinement, however, for North Carolina's frontier reputation was as rough as the Wild West after the Civil War; there was only a semblance of law and order.

I read of an inquest to investigate an unusual death that occurred at the ferry. "A transient person accidentally drowned in the Peedee River on June 12, 1753, after drinking overmuch rum at the tavern of Benjamin Dumas. The man attempted to cross the river. While beating and cursing his horse, the man and his horse fell into a deep hole in the river and both drowned."

The case of law reminded me of Izzie's recollection that Martha Ussery Dumas' father had been a judge in North Carolina. It occurred to me that perhaps his court cases could reveal closer views into personal interactions.

The computer referred me to archive files that yielded numerous documents signed by Usserys in various official capacities. The first Ussery case I pulled, however, proved that few in the region, neither men nor women, were educated enough to sign their own names. The case noted a transaction in the sum of fifty dollars for the sale of a slave to be transferred to the new owner after the death of the seller. It was signed with the seller's *X*, his mark, as a signature.

A corroborating document from the original owner's son stated that he had heard his father say that he had made a bill of sale for the slave Sandy; "that he was acquainted with his father's mark and believed the mark to the bill of sale to be his; it was such a mark as he made when drinking, though heavier than he was accustomed to make it when sober."

I reviewed my notes and wondered if the meager additions I'd found would help in obtaining a clearer picture of the Dumas family in their years in North Carolina. There appeared to be many layers of stories being played out beneath a one-dimensional surface. The country was in an unpredictable state of transition. It was dangerous to reveal a differing political allegiance. Slavery was not even an issue. I would do as Mabel had done: catalog facts with the hope that the next discovery would allow me to see truth behind their carefully constructed façade.

Carine had cited old records of a family cemetery located about a mile north of the Peedee River on Highway 109. As I'd discovered in earlier research, their homes would have been nearby; people didn't transport a body a great distance for burial. The highway department maps showed that Mount Gilead was the closest town to where Highway 109 crosses the river.

On the drive to Mount Gilead, I followed winding roads over rolling hills through towering long-leafed pines. And as the road continued, I saw large forests of sweet gums and oaks separating cultivated fields of tobacco or grain. Numerous abandoned stands advertised peaches for sale; apparently, it had been an abundant year. I'd read that one of the first things a new settler in the Carolinas planted was an orchard. Fruit trees thrived in the virgin soil, and peaches were so plentiful they fed them to the hogs.

Colonial farmers didn't plant crops in the neat rows and irrigated circles that we now admire from airplane windows. They planted corn in hills or mounds like the Indians did, without bothering to clear their fields or even to remove stumps or fallen trees. They didn't plant marketable crops; they simply planted what they needed for their own consumption because the only preservation methods were drying or making brandy. Nearly every seed they put into the ground sprouted quickly and grew well, and the colonists became careless. Since fruit was so abundant, the orchard was left untended and unfenced, and animals were allowed to roam freely. Livestock thrived, but they were neglected. Pigs adapted best to the conditions. If the frontiersmen lacked refined tastes, they developed a healthy taste for the bounty of the land. A coon was said to be hunted for its hide and a possum for its meat, roasted and served in its own rich gravy. Sweet potatoes completed a fine feast. And as I drove, I observed that nearly every house I passed had a garden.

When I finally entered Mount Gilead, I stopped at the central grocery store for their public telephone and local listings directory. With my change purse handy, I dialed the first of five Dumas listings and explained that my grandmother was also a Dumas, her family had been early settlers in the area, and I was interested in talking with someone knowledgeable about the history of Dumas families currently living nearby. The man who answered the phone referred me to Asia Dumas, and the woman who answered my next call said, "Why, yes, Asia's here. He's walking in the door right now, but I'm afraid he won't be here long. He's heading back up to church for a gospel singing at a revival service after lunch."

I was anxious to talk with him, and I couldn't resist the prospect of gospel singing, maybe even Sacred Harp singing. The woman agreeably gave instructions to Asia's house where we could chat a bit to get acquainted. Mount Gilead is a small town, and in hardly any time at all, I was inquiring of two black men laughing good-naturedly near a driveway if this was where I could find Asia Dumas.

Could it be that Asia was black?

Yes, Asia was a black man with a smile so warm and welcoming that I felt at ease in spite of my unmistakable whiteness. Asia had just begun his meal and invited me to join him. Embarrassed at my mealtime intrusion, I accepted only iced tea, explaining that I planned to meet my husband later for a burger.

"A burger!" Asia laughed incredulously. Then I noticed the mouth-watering southern vegetables on his plate, and a burger did seem ridiculous.

"Asia, are those *speckled* butter beans? Speckled butter beans are my all-time favorite; I like them even more than black-eyed peas, but I haven't been able to find them at the produce markets in Atlanta though I'd thought they'd be plentiful all over the South."

Asia said he raises his own, so the family could have what they wanted. "But I only plant one row 'cause they're so hard to pick. Come on, fix you a plate."

"Well, maybe I could have just a bite or two." I knew that Doug would not pass up delectable home-grown squash prepared the same way his mother did. He'd understand.

I felt at home. Anyone would feel at home. Anyone, that is, who would like a dining table in the kitchen, a picture on the wall of a grandfather saying grace, and the last few dishes or pots not in use washed and left to dry on a rack by the sink—a tidy, functioning kitchen.

Asia's wife, Shirley, came into the room, and he made introductions. Shirley had been searching for the family tree they had made for a reunion held over the Fourth of July.

"It goes a long way back," Asia said. "It has my Granddaddy and all his brothers and sisters and all the next generations."

Asia spoke of the presiding elder of his church association, Reverend Dumas, "originally from Alabama, who came to see me to talk about the Dumas roots. Reverend Dumas and I claim kin, but we don't *know* it for sure."

"We're probably kin to a lot of people we don't know we should claim," I commented, "and I read somewhere that in going back ten generations, we have more than 1,000 ancestors—1,024 to be exact. Going backwards, it's only addition. If you start with them and come forward, you have to multiply, so we'd come up with a mind-boggling number of relatives."

"That covers a lot of people," he said, chuckling.

"We know that we're all related as God's children," I said, "but I believe there are unknown ties to more people than we can imagine, people we may only pass on the street."

I attempted to explain my compulsion to find some of the ties. I was still uneasy about others' reactions. My need for reassurance must have been evident.

"It's okay," Asia said. "I'm willing to tell you what I can."

I told him of examining census and tax rolls where I learned that Dumas families of North Carolina owned slaves. Records from the early days of the colony listed some of the slaves' given names. I'd searched bills of sale of slaves and found no purchases of slaves by the Dumas family. They undoubtedly moved with the family from Virginia, for they were slave-owners there, too. The slaves came here to North Carolina as an extension of the family. I told Asia of my direct line of ancestors who had lived nearby two hundred years earlier and of being disturbed when I found the list of slaves' names. "How does it come across to you?"

"All of that makes sense to me. But let me tell you about this Reverend Dumas I mentioned before. He said he traced his Dumases forward and back. He said there were some black Dumases that came over. So if we have a slave name, we didn't get it here. We had it before we came here."

"The French writer Alexandre Dumas was black, but that was his pen name, not his born name," I said. "However, he lived in France long after the time my family's Dumas ancestors had already settled here. I think it might help if I could locate the old Dumas cemetery. It might provide some clues about who was here and when—and maybe some relationships."

"Dumas cemetery? I've never heard about a Dumas cemetery."

"How far back have you traced your family tree? That might tell us a lot."

"My cousin Robert and I tried to figure out how far back we could go. I talked to some of the older folks to fill in what they could before they passed. The younger generations never really care much about their own history until the ones who could tell what they remember are gone. So you have to rely on what you can piece together and go with that."

Suddenly, Asia realized that he was going to be late. We hurriedly cleared the table, but Shirley objected when I began to rinse the dishes.

"Y'all go on. I know right where everything belongs."

Asia grabbed his jacket, and we rushed out the door. As I followed Asia's shiny white pickup to the African Methodist Episcopal Church, it dawned on me that I was probably dressed inappropriately. I'd never been to a regular church service at 2:00 p.m., so a rehearsal had come to mind when the gospel singing was mentioned. Suddenly, Asia's suit and tie made me apprehensive.

A few others were hurrying in as Asia and I approached. They laughingly warned, "The good seats at the back are all taken. We're going to have to sit on the front row."

Asia quickly introduced me to a woman named Katie who took me in tow while Asia joined his choir. Katie looked as though she had posed for the front page of Sunday's style section, complete with a dramatic wide-brimmed red hat. I suggested that perhaps I should take a seat in the rear of the sanctuary because I wasn't dressed suitably. Katie pointed a finger to the sky, saying, "He's the only one you need to please. What does He say?"

"He thinks I'll do," I replied, so Katie firmly took my arm and led me inside. Literally, the front row was all that was left, and the only route to the front row was right down the center aisle. This time I couldn't tell myself that no one was looking at me. With my white skin, hair permed to disarray, barefoot sandals, and hot pink slacks outfit, I felt as inconspicuous as Herschel Walker, the Dallas Cowboys' running back, dancing with the Texas Ballet Theatre.

Around me, the entire congregation was singing, clapping to the beat, tapping their feet, and joyously exclaiming a refrain saying, "feel at home." Various voices sounded in solo for a verse, then again came the rousing refrain. As the music ended, the words became clear, "I can't feel at home in this world anymore."

There was no director, no musical instrument, nor even songbooks. The music merely ebbed and flowed, then slowed softly, and died away. I saw or heard no cue, but after a moment of hushed silence, a powerful mezzo-soprano voice immediately behind me rang out, "I arose this morning..."

Rhythmical clapping brought the congregation into a melodic chant, "Ah-ah-nor, ah-ah-nor, Honor to the Father, Honor to the Son, Honor to the Holy Ghost." In natural breathing spots between phrases, solo voices rang in counterpoint, "ah, yes, ah, yes," and "believe it, brother."

The sanctuary seating was arranged like Sacred Harp singings, with four sections of rows facing the altar in the center. Asia and the rest of the choir sat directly behind the altar, dressed in scarlet robes and gold satin vestments. If Sacred Harp singers were correct regarding the best position for experiencing the exhilarating mix of sound, my default seat on the front row gave me the closest possible access to the heart of harmony. My vocal chords responded like a tuning fork, aching to know the words so I could join in.

And when the church body silenced as one, the guest preacher, pastor of a church in a neighboring town, came to the pulpit. Reverend Eric Leake appeared to be in his mid-twenties. His large frame was clad in a black velvet-trimmed clerical robe and as he turned, his voice reached out to include everyone in all directions, drawing all who were present to settle down and chuckle about being drowsy after a large noon meal, thus effectively preparing the "one body" for his message.

Upon his giving thanks for the opportunity to share, there was a round of anticipatory "amens." He prefaced his text by saying the scripture was a story that everyone had heard preached so many times that "every one of you could get up here and preach it yourself."

"My Lord," the woman seated next to me said aloud.

"It is found," he said, opening his bookmarked Bible, "in the fifteenth chapter of Luke: the story of 'The Prodigal Son.'"

The preacher's passionate retelling washed over the congregation, and as one body they worshiped and exclaimed together about God's everlasting love. I felt as though we in the congregation swayed in a boat together, riding out the rough waves of a storm with Reverend Leake as our captain. The congregation's momentum grew with each word and their thunderous sound reverberated off the church's smooth white walls and wooden pews.

"The son said, 'Daddy, I've sinned against Heaven and against Thee, and am no longer worthy to be called your son.' The daddy looked at the servant and said, 'My son is ragged. I want you to go and get the best robe and put it on him. Get shoes to put on his feet. Get a ring and put it on his finger. It looks like he's hungry. Kill the fatted calf. We will eat and be merry. For this my son was dead, and is alive!'"

The roar of the ensuing swell engulfed the congregation, and the reverend wiped his perspiring brow with a handkerchief.

"Isn't that like God? Oh, I don't care how long you've been in sin. I don't care what the sin is. The Lord will have forgiveness. You see, we've all sinned. And God so loved the world that He gave his only son that whosoever believeth in Him would have everlasting life! Jesus died for the sins of the entire world. He died for everybody."

"Oh, my Lord Jesus," a woman to my left exclaimed.

Reverend Leake's voice rang out, "Come on home. God is saying, with open arms, 'Come on home.'" He coaxed gently, "If you're weary, come on home. If you're lost, you don't have to stay lost. Jesus died for every one of us, that we might be saved."

Eric Leake's mighty baritone poured over the congregation that he had shown the windows to Heaven and to Hell, "Amazing Grace, how sweet the sound…"

I thought of John Newton, who penned the words to that beloved hymn, and wondered if they knew—these people whose ancestors were brought to this far country against their will—that the same John Newton had once been a slave trader. I wondered how many present were now Americans because of John Newton.

"…that saved a wretch like me…"

I, too, felt God's presence in this small North Carolina church, a ship on a brief, but memorable voyage. I was one with this body and would, from this day, remember them in sweet communion when I take the bread and the cup.

When the revival service had concluded, Katie introduced me to several worshipers who had gathered around us. A petite woman in her mid-fifties identified herself as "a MacAuley who had been a Dumas." Her welcome seemed genuinely warm, but she could not contain her curiosity.

"I want to hear how you have a Dumas ancestor," she said. "I had no idea there were any *white* Dumases."

"I didn't know about *black* Dumases," I responded, and Mrs. MacAuley burst into laughter.

While she acquainted me with other Dumases in the church membership, she said that her aunt, Annie Lee MacAuley, was the oldest Dumas living. She elaborated on the relationships of several local families of Dumases. "I guess you know that Eric is a Dumas, don't you?"

"Eric?"

"The preacher. His mama was a Dumas. She married a Leake."

Eric Leake and Asia were chatting near the pulpit and beckoned me to join them. In Asia's introduction, he said that Eric was working on his master's degree at the seminary in Salisbury and that he was interested in my research on Dumas families. Annie Lee MacAuley was again recommended as one most likely to have helpful family information. I began to make plans to return the next day.

"Why, I can call her from here," Asia said. "Maybe we can drop over to her place right now."

"Someone said she wasn't at church this morning. This might not be a good time," I said.

Asia insisted that it was as good a time as any, and he immediately phoned his aunt who said to come on over.

Annie Lee Dumas was born in Montgomery, meaning Montgomery County. "It was in April, so my Mama said." Annie Lee was reluctant to reveal the year.

I first asked, "Could you describe the most outstanding local, historical events as far back as you can remember?"

"Well, that ain't very far back. I didn't live far back."

"Oh, I mean when you were a girl. You remember back then, don't you?"

"Mmm-mmm," Annie Lee resisted, shaking her head.

"I remember many things from when I was a child better than I can remember last week," I insisted. "Didn't you ever ask your mama about the times when she was young?"

Annie Lee rocked side to side. "Well, no, honey child."

Asia attempted to smooth the difficulty. "We started having family reunions, Auntie. Now, that's true, isn't it, that we just recently started trying to put the families back together?"

Annie Lee agreed, and I asked, "How many children do you have?"

"I didn't have none."

"Only nieces and nephews?"

"I had stepchildren—four by my first husband."

"Was that before World War II?" I thought the question was safe enough, but Annie Lee continued to side-step attempts to tie down a time frame.

"I'm afraid you're not going to be able to tell me anything about the old times," I challenged.

"Not the old times, no. I done forgot 'em."

I conceded that Annie Lee didn't want to remember, and I laughed out of frustration.

Annie Lee looked sharply at Asia. "What do you two want to know this for?"

"It's about family history. Her family's name was Dumas, too," he told his aunt.

"Oh, is that right? And you're checking on it?" Annie Lee visibly relaxed. "Well, what about Reverend Dumas? Don't you know about all he has? About his checking?"

Asia turned to me. "Reverend Dumas was saying he thought some of his Dumas relatives stayed in North Carolina, and some went off down into Georgia."

My thoughts were racing in multiple directions. "Is he the one you said was from Alabama?"

"Yes. Yes, Alabama, I believe, but he lives near Salisbury now. That's here in North Carolina. He was trying to put some Dumas things together. I don't know if he has them all finished or not."

"Maybe I could get his name from you and go talk to him. How far is Salisbury from Raleigh? I'll be going back to Raleigh before going home to Atlanta."

Annie Lee attempted to recall details of their efforts to establish a link between the North Carolina Dumases and the family of Reverend Dumas in Georgia. Though she was more willing to help, her memory was too foggy for use.

"We claim Reverend Dumas as kin," Asia explained, "though we don't have exact proof. But his head looks just like mine." Asia grinned and rubbed his bald spot.

Annie Lee said, "I have a church association book. Here, Asia, look up Reverend Dumas' information in the directory for her. He's the presiding elder, so it'll be in the front."

Asia jotted down Reverend Dumas' address and phone number. As we rose to leave, I thanked Annie Lee for her time and apologized for barging in on her when she wasn't feeling her best. "I hope you'll feel like going to church next Sunday."

As we headed to separate cars, Asia said, "When you head back to Atlanta from Raleigh you could stop off and see Reverend Dumas. It'd save you making a special trip, and Salisbury is right on the interstate."

On my state map, Asia circled Granite Quarry, the small town near Salisbury where the reverend lived. While we examined the map, I commented on the close proximity of Mount Gilead to the nearby Town Creek Indian Mound, marked as a point of interest.

"Yeah, that reminds me of a story I've heard all my life," Asia said.

"Robert, a cousin of my mother, was plowing down in the field, and he plowed up a pot, all intact. He never looked in the pot, or even whether he could get into the pot. He was afraid to try. He carried the pot to Mr. Frutchey, the landlord, who traded him an iron bed for the pot. Robert—and maybe Mr. Frutchey, too—never found out what was in the pot, but soon after this happened, they started in earnest on archaeological digging in the area. The discovery proved that the spot right there at the forks of Town Creek and Little River was once an Indian village and a sacred burial site."

I told him of the exploring John Clark whose accounts of the deserted village had attracted the first Dumases to the then-unsettled region. I glanced at my watch and realized that I was going to be late in meeting Doug.

"Oh, yeah," Asia said. "You'll have to hurry to beat dark."

As I backed out of the driveway, another thought occurred to me. I rolled down my window and asked, "Asia, I loved your choir's music today. I sing some really old music. Is there a chance you might have ever sung fasola, or shape-note, music?"

Asia walked to the car window. "Shape-note? You mean like the old Do, Re, Mi shape-notes? Yeah, I heard it when I was still too little to sing in the choir. I remember the old folks used to sing it sometimes, and there was a man who came around teaching shape-notes in a singing school. But that old stuff died out a long, long time ago."

Brethren, we have met to worship, and adore the Lord our God;
Will you pray with all your power, while we try to preach the word?
All is vain unless the Spirit of the Holy One comes down;
Brethren, pray, and holy manna will be showered all around.

"Holy Manna" #59 in *The Sacred Harp*
Words, George Atkin, 1819; music, William Moore, 1825

CHAPTER 11

Unseen Epitaphs

"DOES it bother you that you met blacks named Dumas?" Doug asked.

I thought for a moment. "It was more of a surprise. Meeting Asia was a shock, like diving into cold water. But he's just a person, and when you're talking to someone, you aren't thinking of color. There is only one thing that disturbs me about Asia's family having the same name. I'm convinced there's a definite connection, but they don't seem to think that slavery was involved."

"You mean a blood connection?"

"That's certainly possible. But I think I've already worked through that aspect," I said. "The issue they seem to want to avoid is slavery, like it was shameful to be a slave. Shame belongs where the evil began—in the heart of the enslaver. Maybe Asia's Auntie Annie Lee knows best about the old times—just forget them."

"Can you do that?"

"I don't know. I don't know what I expected to find in Mount Gilead, North Carolina."

"I thought you wanted to find the old Dumas cemetery. Did you ask Asia about it?"

"He'd never even heard of a Dumas cemetery. Carine gave its exact location in her book, and she had an authoritative source. The day was gone before I knew it, and there was no more time to look."

"We have all day tomorrow," Doug suggested. "I wouldn't mind seeing some of the countryside myself."

We had an early breakfast the next morning and then leisurely drove south on Highway 109 toward the Peedee River. We suddenly realized we were already crossing the bridge, and there was no safe place to pull off the road. A dense forest of tall trees bordered both sides of the highway and continued on the other side of the river. Doug drove for a mile or more before he could find a spot to turn around. As we drove back across the bridge, he slowed to a crawl. The river was wide, and its rushing waters were as dark and forbidding as the wall of towering trees that lined its banks. I tried to picture the tavern and the ferry crossing, but the location was too heavily wooded to accommodate the mental image I'd constructed. The forest had swallowed all visible signs of habitation.

"We passed a stretch of farmland shortly before we got to the river," Doug said. "Maybe something there will give us a clue."

"Yes, and Carine listed the cemetery as a mile north of the river on the west side of the road."

We drove slowly north out of the trees, but for four miles we found only cotton fields. Doug turned around and repeated the route, but we were becoming resigned to a fruitless search. In a last ditch attempt, Doug turned east onto a dirt road toward the only house within sight. It was a turkey farm. As we neared the house, we met a young couple in a pickup truck heading back toward the highway. Doug stopped and lowered the car window.

The driver of the pickup was a bone-thin girl with a mane of dark hair haphazardly pulled into a ponytail.

"No, I haven't heard of an abandoned cemetery or any cemetery right around here," she said. "Sorry."

Her pickup roared and kicked up a cloud of dust but suddenly braked and backed up.

"I'm headed to Thomason's Store. Why don't you follow and ask Mr. Thomason? He's real old and has lived here all his life. He can tell you about a lost graveyard, if anybody can."

Doug had to wheel the car around hurriedly to catch the pickup. A short distance up the road, the pickup slowed to approach a nondescript frame building with peeling paint. It appeared to be a small barn. We turned into a graveled parking area alongside the pickup as the young woman entered the store alone.

An elderly man of slight build met us at the door. He appeared energetic and spry, though his skin was as transparent and colorless as the wisps of hair above his ears. "Name's Thomason," he said amiably, as he offered his hand to Doug.

Mr. Thomason operated a general store inside the box of a building, a true convenience store—his own, as well as that of his customers. He opened for business only when a customer called to say they needed something. And he had what I needed. Mr. Thomason knew exactly where to find the old Dumas cemetery.

"I used to play there as a child, but that was more than eighty years ago. We used to walk and run on the old rock wall that circled the cemetery. We boys thought it great fun to race around the top of the wall, and then we'd jump off." Mr. Thomason chuckled at an old recollection. "It was a nice rock wall, dressed out with a smooth ledge at the top to tempt a child's antics. The wall's gone now, though. It's been broken up for years. I think somebody used part of it to build the foundation of a house.

"Yes, it used to be a nice little cemetery, but eventually, there was nobody left to care for it. Now, the spot is mostly plowed up, out in the middle of a cotton field. There were some bigger markers in the center part. They're still there, I imagine. They'd be in that clump of trees and heavy brush on the rise, right there in the middle of the field.

"To find that cemetery you should go back toward the river. You'll pass the turkey farm on your left, but go slow. It's in sight of their place. You'll see an old ramshackle house on the left, way off the road. From right about that spot, look to the west of the highway and you'll see a field road—a dirt road going out in the cotton field. And from there, you'll see the rise with the clump of trees."

After paying for two soft drinks we followed Mr. Thomason's detailed directions leading to the cotton field. From the field road we saw a circle of trees on a knoll two or three hundred yards away. Doug stopped when we were even with the trees, and we stepped out onto the hardened surface of the trail. I started to walk between the rows of cotton plants toward the trees and found that my feet sank into soft, dusty sand where the field had been cultivated; my sandals filled with a gritty powder as fine as talc that found its way between my toes. Doug stood with his feet buried in sand also, and with his handy binoculars he saw that all the clump of trees concealed was made inaccessible by the tangle of wild underbrush.

"I'm sorry, honey," he said. "Even if we decided to trespass on this cotton field, we'd need boots and jeans and a machete to get through all of that brush. Then we'd have to cut away growth around each gravestone. The 'No Entry' sign of brambles and thorns is plenty clear. Judging from the years of neglect, I'd be surprised if we could read names on any of the tombstones, anyway."

I was heartsick to learn that the graveyard had been swallowed by time and neglect. Impulsively, I broke off a cotton boll to have a bit of tangible proof that we'd been there.

"Why? When do burial grounds cease to be sacred? Why did they not, at least, leave the stone surrounding wall intact? Who decides that a grave is no longer important?"

"The land was probably sold, and the new owners might not have had ties," Doug said. "Maybe they never knew anyone who had ties here. Most likely, they lost track of identities."

I had imagined turning back the blanket of time to uncover long forgotten memories of those whose lives bloomed and flourished in the river valley. "Now, we've lost track, too. We have no idea who is buried out there in the field. It could be Ben III, the Revolutionary soldier who lost his life for our freedom, and maybe his father and mother, David and Old Sarah. If Ben III is there, Susannah is probably there, too. I think most of the family is out there."

"It's near where they lived," Doug said. "If not this specific spot, they would logically be buried somewhere nearby."

I have an affinity for specific spots, like a kinship with the land, especially places where we say our final goodbyes. That's when I feel closest to those I never knew. It has a lot to do with re-living things that happened when they lived in a specific place. Izzie had told me about what happened in this valley. Then Ben III and Susannah's sons moved off to Georgia.

A dark foreboding gripped me. "You said they might have lost track of identities. Could it have been a case of mistaken identity? It was a surprise, only yesterday, to blacks who had lived here in North Carolina all their lives that whites with the same name were the first to settle along this river."

"You mean that the neglect might have a racial undercurrent?"

"That's exactly what I mean. Slaves were buried here, too. Did people come to think that this was a Negro cemetery? Could it be that breaking up the wall was a hateful, malicious act?"

"What was, is theirs. What is, is ours," Doug said. "And what is at the moment is a beautiful day stretching out into a few living hours of whatever we make of them. Let's go see that Indian Mound. I saw a sign pointing the way at the last crossroad."

I had imagined the Clark and Dumas venture into the wilderness to the village deserted long before the white man arrived as an idyllic return to Eden. Now I'd seen the land, some of which must bear a close resemblance to its native state, and could more fully comprehend the tremendous accomplishment of clearing fields so that crops could be planted.

"It makes you realize that the land was tamed by hard labor," Doug said. Hard slave labor, I thought.

A book of Anson County history referenced an article in the *Ashboro Courier* in describing what life was like for the slaves on one of the large plantations in the valley. It could as likely have been the Dumas plantation. The writer, Herbert C. Greene, had said slave owners didn't need wagons in those days because the slaves could move mountains. The landowner had a wheat field a mile away from the threshing machine, but the distance didn't matter because he had enough slaves to carry the wheat in hardly any time at all. They were said to look from the distance like a line of black sheep as they wended their way toward the threshing machine with shocks of wheat in their arms.

"The history book said this area was once teeming with slaves on plantations," I said. "But at the time the article was written, in October of 1929, there were only a few white families scattered about in the community. The only marks of slavery left were said to be a few slave owners' homes and a Negro cemetery or two."

"Meaning the Dumas cemetery?"

"I guess so. The slaves are buried there, too. Their contributions to taming the land still live in ways we don't recognize. The same article spoke of the valley which once rang with African folk songs of the slaves. I can almost hear echoes of their chanting while they heaved those shocks of wheat."

> *Our praying time will soon be o'er, Hallelujah,*
> *We'll join with those gone before, Hallelujah,*
> *Struggle on, struggle on, Hallelujah,*
> *Struggle on, for the work's most done, Hallelujah!*

"Struggle On" #400 in *The Sacred Harp*
Words and music, H.S. Reese, 1859

The rhythm helped the captive workers keep going. They sang their troubles out, like a prayer. The music was God's grace comforting them as they toiled in the fields. Someone heard them singing, and someone saw them and later wrote about it in the article.

Perhaps Edmund Dumas heard their songs and wrote new words to pair with their melodies. He lived here until he was six or seven years old, in this same river valley where slaves sang their rhythmical chants. Even as a small child, with music in his genes, he would have absorbed the melodies and retained them in his subconscious mind. Some of our older hymns give a tune source as an "American Folk Hymn" or a "southern" melody. Only God knows the true age and origin. I began humming:

> *I'm a long time trav'ling here below,*
> *I'm a long time trav'ling far from home,*
> *I'm a long time trav'ling here below to lay this body down.*

"White" #228 in *The Sacred Harp*
Words, *Dobell's New Selection*, 1810; music, Edmund Dumas, 1856

In Raleigh the next week, I skimmed countless books—histories of counties, towns, and families, scanning each index for names of people and places—and occasionally found nuggets of relevant information to add to my notebook. By connecting the dots, a picture gradually emerged of the Dumas family in North Carolina in the days of the Revolution. And Izzie had set the stage.

Ben III and his brother, Andrew, set up a mobile command post on the Dumas Island, which was situated in a pivotal position upriver from the ferry and tavern. The island, sometimes called Buffaloe Island, was located near the juncture of Rocky River and the Great Peedee River, and provided various options of access and safety. Because it was on the established trade route, the river crossing and tavern bustled with militia, couriers, and supplies passing back and forth.

Edmund Lilly, Ben III and Andrew's uncle, was brought to the island after he was injured in a revolutionary skirmish: they set up a hospital tent to care for him and, later, for others. Edmund Lilly had married David Dumas' sister, and so was a son-in-law of Benjamin Dumas I. Lilly was a plantation owner as well as a preacher but after his injuries in the American Revolution, he had to be "carried" to preach.

I'd found a link to their church. But what church? Edmund Lilly had originally been a Quaker, but he was excommunicated surprisingly not for carrying a gun but for marrying out of the faith.

Much general background information of the region supported Mabel's contention that the primary purpose for relocating the family from Virginia was to establish a sanctuary for displaced Huguenots. My research showed that the valley attracted a great number of religious refugees, an indication of its spiritual receptiveness.

The well-traveled Moravian route from Philadelphia went directly through the area. The Moravians were known for their music, which would have added another layer of influence to Edmund Dumas' musical and spiritual background.

Political and religious issues were so closely intertwined it was difficult for me to distinguish between the two. Of necessity, evidence of political resistance was hidden, other than the documented links with the Regulator movement. There was also a wide variety of connections of the North Carolina frontier with the city of Philadelphia. Philadelphia—specifically, Benjamin Franklin in Philadelphia—was Anson County's primary authority for political and religious thought.

According to the *Documents of the American Revolution 1774-1776*, Benjamin Franklin and other founding fathers frequently used codes in their correspondence, one of which, the Dumas' cipher, was devised by Charles

William Frederick Dumas, born in Germany of French Huguenot parents. Franklin's letters to C.W.F. Dumas were sent to The Hauge, a city in the Netherlands, which is today the *de facto* judicial capital of the United Nations.

Dumas genealogy books note that Franklin received money for the revolution from a man named Dumas in Hamburg, Germany, where some of the Huguenots had sought refuge after fleeing the massacres in France. Benjamin Dumas I's father escaped from France through Switzerland and Germany before arriving in England.

A couple of diplomatic exchanges were recorded officially in the office of the Governor of North Carolina. A letter from Governor Johnston to John Jay in the United States Office of Foreign Affairs noted correspondence with a Mr. Dumas and requested assistance. I made a copy of the reply to the governor:

Office of Foreign Affairs
26 May, 1788

Sir:
Mr. Dumas, agreeable to the request of the Envoy of his Swedish Majesty at The Hague, has transmitted to me a note he received from that Minister which I have now the honor of communicating to your Excellency in order that such measures may be taken on the Subject as Circumstances and the Laws of Nations may dictate.

With great respect,
JOHN JAY

It seemed plausible that the request might have been to admit additional Huguenot refugees, many of whom eventually came to settle near the tavern on the river. Because Susannah ordinarily handled both the business and personal correspondence for her father-in-law, David Dumas, the date of 1788 indicated that Susannah might have written the letters he dictated. I could hardly wait to tell Barbara that perhaps Susannah had been one of the earliest women in America involved in foreign diplomacy.

When I returned a book to the desk, the librarian spoke up. "I know of another avenue you might want to explore. We have some fairly large files of miscellaneous historical collections that have been donated to the archives—an assortment of documents, old letters, and such. There might be a reference to your family in one of the collections, and if so, it would be noted in the card catalog. You'll find them listed by box numbers, and I can pull the boxes. You might not find anything at all that interests you, but then, you never know."

The estate of Isaac S. London, editor of the newspaper in Rockingham, North Carolina, had given his collection of historical papers to the North Carolina State Library and Archives. I recognized London's name as the historian who had assisted Barbara's mother, Mabel, with genealogy research. After watching the librarian reappear silently from the dusty archive shelves, I sat at an empty table and lifted the box lid to leaf through London's papers. My eyes were drawn to a file labeled, "Mrs. Douglas Crenshaw." I tentatively opened the file and began to read London's typewritten side of the correspondence with Mabel.

Rockingham, N.C.
February 17, 1956
Dear Mrs. Crenshaw:

Received your check for $4 to the Post-Dispatch for a year's subscription. We are happy to have you on the lists.

In the 1770s and thereabouts, people lived mostly contiguous to the Peedee River—then the only source of navigation. . . . It is interesting to note that the two big ferries across the river many years ago were the DUMAS Ferry and the Hailey Ferry—these two ferries being about twenty-five miles apart.

Write me to look for anything else you can suggest. I want what I do to be of value to you, even though valueless parts entail much hunting.

ISL

The file continued with handwritten letters in a graceful, confident penmanship—responses from Mabel Crenshaw, Barbara's mother:

Feb. 22, 1956

Dear Mr. London,

Your outline sketch of the Dumas & Moorman families arrived last week. You've done an excellent job. I do appreciate all the research you have done, and I assure you that I am one person who knows how much time and work it takes. You have not stated in any letter how much money I owe you.

Following are a few comments and a question I would like to ask:

1. Susannah Dumas, widow—witnessed the deeds from David Dumas to his children. It was almost as if old David wanted her approval. Her land was next to their land. Susannah Dumas was the widow of the Benjamin III Dumas, who was a son of David and Sarah Dumas.

2. The Grant to Benjamin Dumas III (in 1787) and the Grant to Susannah Dumas (in 1794) seem to be the *same* land. I have been told that the powers that be were always good to Revolutionary War widows. Was it customary for the widow to be granted land that had already been granted to her husband?

3. Are there any records to indicate that Susannah Dumas might have remarried?

Thanks so very much for all you've done. In the future if you come across any interesting Dumas data I would appreciate it if you would pass it along to me. The work you have done is priceless, but do let me know how much I owe you.

Sincerely yours,
Mabel Dumas Crenshaw

March 25, 1957

Dear Mr. London,

Bless you! I don't know whether you realized it or not but you sure did hit the *Jack-Pot* in the Will of Arnold Thomason. "I lend to my son David thirty-three acres and a half of land lying on Peedee River, it being *Susannah Ryan's dower as the widow of her former husband Benjamin Dumas III, deceased.*"

So Susannah Dumas did re-marry, after all. One or two Dumas deeds mention land adjoining *Patrick Ryan*. This is probably the Ryan who married Susannah Dumas, Benjamin III's widow. Could it be that her new husband tried to take her land? There are family stories that Susannah's sons had difficulty claiming their inheritance.

Now, is there a will or administration papers for Susannah Ryan deceased about 1805? Susannah's three sons sold land jointly January 28, *1808* and February 17, *1808*.

July 13, 1807—Obediah Dumas (brother to Benjamin Dumas III) sells "land that was patented to Susannah Dumas, deceased." Part of the legal description of the land is *"Patrick Ryan's line* 120 acres." This deed proved that Susannah Dumas was deceased, but made me think she had not remarried. I guess they used the name Susannah *Dumas* because the land was patented to *her* in 1794 as Susannah Dumas, but sometime after 1796 Susannah, widow of Benjamin III Dumas, married a Ryan and probably Patrick Ryan.

I now feel that we are really getting somewhere—thanks to you.

Sincerely,
Mabel Crenshaw

Attached to Mabel's handwritten letters were some notes casually scrawled on discarded calendar pages for April 1 and 2, 1957:

1. Patrick Ryan, Grantor to Arnold Thomason 33 ½ acres

2. Will of Susannah Ryan, widow of Ben III Dumas. Susannah died 1805.

3. Deed Book I page 5—June 20, 1807—120 acres, formerly Ryan property, B.H. Covington, Sheriff to Sons of Susannah Dumas

4. B.H. Covington Sheriff to Arnold Thomason 33 ½ acres.

So the sheriff set the record straight. The three orphaned sons of Ben III and Susannah—one of whom was my great-great-grandfather, Benjamin Franklin Dumas—regained the land that had been awarded to their mother, Susannah Dumas, the Revolutionary War widow. This must certainly have been the source of funds for Benjamin Franklin and Martha Ussery Dumas to move their family from North Carolina to Georgia.

Mabel's incidental notes provided a relishing glimpse: somehow, Mr. Thomason even got the acreage he thought he'd already purchased from Patrick Ryan—perhaps the same land of the present-day Mr. Thomason's convenience store.

Mabel Dumas Crenshaw in middle-age, great-granddaughter of Edmund Dumas. (Photo courtesy of her descendants.)

April 10, 1957
Dear Mr. London,

Thanks so much for the data you have sent me.

Do you have a record of the Dumas Cemetery? It is in Richmond County. Colonel Stanback said the brush was so thick he couldn't get to all the tombstones. Is there any way to find out if Susannah is buried there? Or if her gravesite is with her second husband, Patrick Ryan? I will keep in mind your admonition regarding unmarked graves.

I noticed in your last issue of the paper that you stated that some of the tombstones were difficult to read. You may know this, but in case you don't—when you are going on a trip to some old cemetery to read tombstones, always carry with you a bag of *flour* and a *rag*. Dust the flour on the tombstone and wipe the surface smooth to make the carving reappear. You may then read names and dates that are otherwise unreadable.

Sincerely yours,
Mabel D. Crenshaw

I glanced at my watch and saw that it was almost time to meet Doug at the hotel. I leafed through the remainder of London's files and found no additional Dumas inquiries. As I straightened the letters in his file for Mabel

Crenshaw, a loose note fell out. It was printed in bold letters, "Rocky River Church—See Baptist collection at Wake Forest." I scribbled the information on my notepad and circled it to flag my attention.

When I descended the wide steps of the archives, going-home traffic had already reached a frantic pace. Everyone was rushing home to their own private lives, but I was reluctant to leave the solitude of the past and chose a route through a park to have a few blocks of reflective silence. I thought of the generations of my family who had invested hopes and dreams in the land along the river. They had lived their allotted morning and evening, and their children heard of a new land where the earth was yet unspoiled and even more plentiful. The few white Dumas families who chose to stay behind through the westward migrations were no longer here. After seasons of rain and drought, through centuries of summers and autumns and winters and springs, Susannah and Ben III Dumas' family was forgotten. A few markers covered by a clump of brush on a rise by the river are all that remain of their physical presence, and even those reminders are no longer visible. Their abandoned physical bodies have transformed into the dirt we walk on, the cotton we wear. Dust to dust to dust.

> *And am I born to die? To lay this body down!*
> *And must my trembling spirit fly into a world unknown?*
> *A land of deepest shade, Unpierced by human thought;*
> *The dreary regions of the dead, where all things are forgot!*
> *Waked by the trumpet sound, I from my grave shall rise;*
> *And see the Judge with glory crowned, and see the flaming skies!*

"Idumea" #47b in *The Sacred Harp*
Words, Charles Wesley, 1763; music, Ananias Davisson, 1816

A woman walked toward me on the path. I imagined it was Susannah. And as she approached, head held high, the woman smiled a greeting. Susannah lived in a different time than I, but I knew we shared the same human yearnings for love, for freedom, and for our families to live happy, productive lives. Our eyes met, and it seemed I could read her thoughts.

You breathe; I breathed. Can you say that my spirit is less real than your own? My love and my passions did not cease when my heart stopped beating. You know me. I am all women.

Ben III followed a few steps behind her, his presence saying, "We two are all humanity."

One family, we dwell in Him, one church above, beneath;
Though now divided by the stream, the narrow stream of death.
One army of the living God, to His command we bow;
Part of the host have crossed the flood, and part are crossing now.

"Arnold" #285 in *The Sacred Harp*
Word, Charles Wesley, 1759; music, L.P. Breedlove, 1850

CHAPTER 12

The Presiding Elder

THE hotel room's radio alarm, set earlier than usual, roused me fully awake. I peeked through the draperies for a hint of morning's mood and saw that it was still dark outside. From the seventeenth floor, I had a broad view of Raleigh's major traffic routes being mapped by the automobile headlights of early risers. The sky's faint glow became brighter, and I watched in fascination as the first red rays of sunlight teased the outer edge of a large cumulus cloud into a glowing pink reality. The sleeping city gradually took form as the office towers rose from the fog and stretched heavenward. A bright gleam in the distance grew vertically to reveal itself as the white spire of a church on the hillside. And squinting in the glare of a nearby building, its glass surface intensely reflecting the sun's piercing rays, I knew I now had to hurry.

I had arranged to meet Reverend Dumas at his home in Granite Quarry, near Salisbury. I would be driving to Atlanta alone because Doug still had unfinished business. He would fly home in the evening. Turning from the window, I saw that Doug had woken to the morning light.

"Are you going to try to have breakfast before you leave?" he asked with a yawn.

"I'd love to, if morning weren't in such an all-fired rushing hurry. I'd like to have a cup of coffee and glance at the newspaper with you, but I planned to be on the road by 7:00 a.m. I'm not sure how long it will take to reach Salisbury. And then I'll have to find the little town where Reverend Dumas lives."

As soon as I reached Interstate 85, I was in bumper-to-bumper traffic. People on the west side of town wanted to be on the east, and everyone on the east side wanted to be on the west. No one was in the place he wanted to be. There was no noticeable difference when I finally escaped the downtown area.

I turned on the radio for a traffic update. The clogged arteries were normal for the time of day, but my agitation increased when I heard news highlights dominated by the weekend's upcoming auto races. Don't they know about the World Series? We had tried to pick up a Braves' game over the previous weekend, and we found instead five different stations broadcasting auto races. How does one relate to a car race on the radio?

It was important not to be late for my 10:00 a.m. appointment with Reverend Dumas in Granite Quarry. I felt fortunate that he could arrange to see me as I returned to Atlanta from Raleigh. His official title listed in Asia's African Methodist Episcopal Church Association directory was "Presiding Elder, The Reverend Dr. O. C. Dumas, Sr., D.D." The initials, periods, commas, and abbreviations at first intimidated me, but in our phone conversation, Reverend Dumas' good-natured accommodation quickly brushed aside my uneasiness.

His deep, resonant voice rang out over the phone, "Oh, Granite Quarry (pronounced Queh-ry) isn't all that big. We don't have but one stop light. Call me when you get to town, and I'll come over and lead you towards my home."

I called the reverend from the Exxon station and waited at the window near the door. Checkered flags and large advertising posters of racecars and drivers were posted prominently around the station, so I wasn't surprised to hear a super-charged vehicle roar into the drive. I turned to take a look at what I expected to be a sleek, long-bodied racer, but the source of the commotion was an eye-popping Volkswagen Beetle.

Reverend Dumas had failed to tell me how to spot him, and I was astonished to see bounding from the brightly-painted, Funk Art Beetle a portly black man dressed in white from head to toe and wearing a clerical collar. He didn't try to speak over the roar of the car, but waved vigorously for me to follow.

The car's exuberant spirit was difficult for the reverend to rein in. I marveled at the power of the Volkswagen's engine and thought perhaps his son used it for weekend drag races. I followed hurriedly, trying to keep up with him, keeping my eyes on the "Jesus" and "Desert Storm" bumper stickers. We quickly made a right turn, crossed some railroad tracks, sped down another road, made a right turn onto Dumas Road and a left onto Joe Louis Drive and into a homey setting under enormous oak trees with broad, arching branches. I had expected Reverend Dumas to be somewhat reserved, like Asia, but he was in manner much like his Beetle. He was out of the car and opening a tall gate before I had come to a complete stop in the shade of a gigantic oak.

I had to listen as fast as I'd had to follow. He said they had just returned from a meeting in New Orleans, and he talked of preparing for the annual conference the following week in Greensboro. Reverend Dumas explained that in the United Methodist Church his position is called District Superintendent, but in the African Methodist Church, he is called the Presiding Elder. It is the Presiding Elder's responsibility to prepare reports of the work done throughout the year in all twenty-four churches in the association.

"I grant you that the duties are sometimes an overwhelming task, but it's something I do because I love the Lord and I love the work. So you see, it's not a chore; it's something I've been doing all my life.

"I've been a preacher ever since I was seven years old. I was a born preacher. Started out in a small town called Saint Elmo, near Chattanooga. When I was a young boy—a boy preacher they called me—I preached all over Tennessee. But Georgia, I think, is where I preached most—on Sunday evenings in 1935. And in 1944, when I became sixteen, I was ordained and had my first church to lead as a pastor."

Reverend Dumas talked without pausing. "I'm sorry I haven't had time to be fully prepared for you, because I guess I'm the only Dumas— except maybe Asia—now you say you've talked to Asia? You see the strong resemblance?"

I recalled Asia's receding hairline.

"You can see it, I'm sure. Everybody else does." He laughed heartily, as he rubbed his shining baldness.

In answer to my question of what kind of meeting they'd attended in New Orleans, he responded, "Oh, that was the Women's General Convention, the missionary ladies of the church. About three thousand women meet every four years. They have seven hundred voting delegates and they underwrite a massive missionary program. They take care of many schools and hospitals and bring some of the brighter students to America. These students are educated at Livingstone College, or, if they are going to be a doctor or something else advanced, they attend some other school. Then they send the students back home, so they can be helpful to their people."

Reverend Dumas' deep voice continued to roll without stopping, "And those three thousand women come from all over the world: from Africa, from the Virgin Islands, from London. Why, we've had some from India. We have churches in India now. The missionary department—the one that had the convention last week—they brought a young man from India over here to go to school. He finished at Livingstone, and then he finished the seminary, Hood Seminary, and when he went back home to India, he set up five or six churches. When they had the convention this year, he led his delegation to come to America. That must have been exciting for him, but the most outstanding highlight of that meeting, for me, was to hear the Africans sing, in their native language, the African songs."

"Could you recognize any of the melodies?" I asked.

"Oh, yes, yes. They had planned the event well. They had the African words printed on one side of the bulletin with the English translation on the other. Bishop Speake's wife—she was a missionary over there for years—put the music to it and directed it, and in just a little while, she had all of those women singing in the native tongue.

"It was an amazing thing to see the African ladies sing," he continued. "They don't do like we do, standing in one place to sing together as a choir. When the African women sing, they are *very* enthusiastic. They stomp and they move—all around the auditorium. But no matter how far they were away from one another—marching around that great auditorium with three thousand women all singing the African songs—they had it together. Oh, it was something to hear."

The exhilarating aural and visual sensations of my recent experience in a black church flashed in my mind. And now, Reverend Dumas described Asia's enthusiastic church as the restrained baseline in comparison to the conference's vitality and excitement. If Edmund Dumas' earliest memories of slave songs echoing in the river valley had inspired his Sacred Harp melodies, perhaps the strong, emphatic beat came not only, as I'd first suspected, from the rhythm of his horse's gait, but from far over the seas to a distant time in Africa.

Reverend Dumas stopped abruptly. "Now, let's talk about what you want to know about the Dumas family."

I recalled hearing that the reverend had met with Asia's family for one of their reunions in the past, though he had not been able to attend the last several homecomings. And the mention of Asia was all that Reverend Dumas needed to get started on a new subject.

"My oldest boy was here from Las Vegas a couple of weeks ago. He's like you; whenever he goes into any city, he looks in the phone book for anybody named Dumas. He calls, no matter who they are, and he does that everywhere. He wants to know about every Dumas, every Dumas family he can find."

I was surprised with a chance for a comment of my own. "It isn't a common name, but it has spread all over the world."

"That's true, that's true. It's certainly not a common name," he said. "But let me go back and tell you the beginning, like I told Asia Dumas and his folks when they was wondering about their grandfather and their great-grandfather, where they started. Now, my grandmother, who was white—I'll show you a picture of her directly, before you leave. She was a hundred and three years old when she passed. I think she passed—must have been about seven years ago.

"My grandmother was originally out of Rome, Georgia, in Floyd County. And when she was a young child, one of the Dumases left—either from Alabama or Georgia—and they went back *home* to the *Carolinas*. She wasn't sure whether it was South Carolina or North Carolina, but back there then, they called both of the places the Carolinas. I know now that it had to be North Carolina, because years later—oh, I'd say about thirty years later—I came to this part of the country. That's when I looked 'em up and found out about them. Then I knew what my grandmother was talking about.

"So," he said, "The Dumases that came this away to the Carolinas— those that broke off from the main stock of the Dumases in Alabama— are the ones that's responsible for all the Dumases in Asia's area, in Mount Gilead. There's no question about that."

Suddenly, the door opened, and an attractive, vibrant woman entered. She was dressed in a brilliant red-orange garment that could have been either a flowing long skirt or trousers. "Now here is Sister Dumas," the reverend said.

She extended her hand, smiling warmly. "Hello. I'm Clara. It's so nice to meet you."

Clara, who wanted to look at the familiar old photos, followed as Reverend Dumas led us into his study. On the wall were photos of milestones in his ministry—breaking ground on a new church building, gatherings of church people—and a large Dumas coat of arms that he'd ordered from a genealogical service.

"The same service sent the family history that I'm going to show you as soon as I can find it in one of these stacks of important papers on my desk." From the table, piled high with photo albums and scrapbooks of newspaper clippings, he selected an album that pictured his white grandmother.

"During my grandmother's time, when the segregation was so strong that the blacks had to be in the back and the whites in the front, she could go anywhere because of her light color. And when she would have *us* along, the white folks would say, 'Madam, who are those...'" Reverend Dumas paused, trying to think of the correct word to use. "'Who are those little children you got there?'"

Clara corrected, "*Pickaninnies* is what they said."

In an old black and white photo, he pointed out a lovely fair-skinned young girl. "Now that is my grandmother when she was young. And this is my grandmother when she was about a hundred, down in Rome, Georgia. Her maiden name was Battey, and then she married a Dumas, then an Osborne, and then a Muse."

"And this is my great-grandmother." His great-grandmother Battey, who appeared to be white, was also strikingly beautiful.

"Let me get on over to the oldest patriarch of the Dumas family." Pointing to another photograph of a black man, he said, "This is my grandfather, and this is my aunt, and these are some of my mother's family." All appeared to be perfectly black, with the exception of his white grandmother and great-grandmother, who had no black features. "But it's been so long, I don't know who they are. I believe I can figure them out if I use the lists of family names. I'm going to do that one of these days."

"You'd better get started right away then," Clara joked. "There's no one else who can."

Reverend Dumas led me from the study to another room—a second study, library, storeroom, or all of the above. Clara refused to enter and hummed as she headed towards the kitchen instead.

"My wife, she calls all this *junk*, but most of it belonged to my grandmother. And she was so old, she had a lot of accumulations. I saved all of it because I remember when all these precious things filled her home. My wife don't know it, but one of these days all of this will be valuable to other people too because they don't take time to make things the same way anymore."

The room was lined with shelves all the way to the tall ceiling, at least ten feet in height, and the shelves were full of books and knick-knacks. There were rows of tall freestanding units of additional bookshelves filling the center of the room, like a modern library. The space was even equipped with a ladder for the top reaches. Every wall area that was not covered with books was filled with framed photographs. There was a photo of Reverend Dumas with Richard Nixon, another with Jimmy Carter, and two large autographed photos of President and Mrs. George H. W. Bush, and of Jesse Jackson.

Suspended inside the tall, curtainless windows were frames of leaded stained glass salvaged from an older structure, possibly a church. The sun had begun to reach that side of the house, and as it shone through the glass, the windows glowed like jewels and cast a soft glow over the room.

I took an unsteady step to get a closer look at an autograph, and I almost stumbled. The carpeted floor was not smooth or level. Reverend Dumas reassuringly advised, "It might feel unstable, but it's rock solid." I suddenly realized that the several stone steps we descended into the room were not stones stacked in place, but instead, had been carved in place from granite that had always been there. And the entire back room addition of this house in Granite Quarry was built directly on an outcropping of stone.

"Here's a picture of my grandmother," Reverend Dumas said, "and this one's my great-grandmother. These are old-timey pictures, but you can see that they were both white. You couldn't tell them from you—with blue eyes and sandy hair."

The women were as white as anyone I knew. One of the men in an album in the other room looked white, too. I wanted to know about the racial mixing, but when I hesitated to ask, he had moved on to another topic, and I missed my chance.

I opened my notebook and brought out a chart of descendents of the white Benjamin Dumas I who moved to North Carolina from Virginia in 1750. I pointed out the sons, David Dumas (1730-1803), of my own family line—the one who operated the tavern and ferry, and his brother, Benjamin II, who operated the plantation. Under David's descendents, I pointed out the Benjamin III, who was married to Susannah and died fighting in the American Revolution.

"These are the Dumases who are my ancestors. They lived right here in North Carolina two hundred years ago."

He took the page and read off names of those who married Dumases. "I see you got DeBerrys. DeBerrys are some of our close friends. They live down there around—why, I see Lillys. The Lillys are highly concentrated in that area. And I see you got Pembertons."

His mind seemed to be racing as he lowered the page. "The old man—the patriarch at Mount Gilead—died about three years ago. His name was John DeBerry. And the Lillys and Pembertons—they are all concentrated in the area down near Brother Asia. So I'm wondering—did you miss anything down there? Because see, I've pastored there, and I know everybody. I *know* people with these same names."

"But this page is from way back in the 1700s, more than two hundred years ago," I protested.

"I understand that. But what I'm saying is—if they stayed down in that area—"

"Yes?"

"It's possible, you know, that they mixed and co-mingled, and that's how some of the folks got their names. And if that be the case, and since they are concentrated—the DeBerrys, the Lillys, the Pembertons—they're all in there."

Freed slaves had often taken names of their former owners. Reverend Dumas had been unaware that white slave owners named Dumas might have been the origin of his name. I was unaware that he might have had a darker meaning to the mixing and co-mingling, which spoke to me of an integrated society before the divisive wall of segregation in the aftermath of the Civil War. Church memberships had included both races. They shared the same scriptures and beliefs, and the same music. Evolving interpretations of spiritual or sacred music tell the stories of their evolving journeys.

"Well, let me leave this copy with you," I said. I realized he saw loose threads all over the page. "The name at the top, Benjamin Dumas I, is the first white Dumas male in this line who was born in America, about 1705."

I pulled out another page I'd copied from *The Heritage of Blacks in North Carolina* at the State Library in Raleigh. "This might be significant. This is about the slaves in Montgomery County back in 1763, back before the United States even existed as a country—"

"I understand. So down here we've got…"

Scanning the page for *Dumas*, we simultaneously spotted it: *David Dumas.*

"David Dumas. That's this one right here," I said as I referred to the chart. "It says that David Dumas and his brother, Benjamin II, were both here in North Carolina in 1763. They both fought in the Revolutionary War. I read that one of the sons of David Dumas—named Obadiah—sold his land in the early 1800s and took his family and slaves to Alabama. That's a tie-in with your grandmother's story of relatives who returned *home* to the Carolinas."

We located Obadiah's name on the chart. Then I pointed to his brother, Benjamin III, my ancestor. "The branch I'm descended from moved on to Georgia from North Carolina about 1815 or so. Some of the family stayed here for awhile. There's an old Dumas cemetery with a lot of the white Dumases just north of the river, not far from Mount Gilead. I guess they all died out or moved on somewhere else because no one knows of any white Dumases in recent years."

"Well, we were surprised about white Dumases at first," he said, "but I see you got their names."

"I'm going to send a copy to Asia," I said. "I don't want to force anything. I just want—"

"You just want to find out. There's nothing wrong in finding out the truth."

I explained that I was devastated when I realized that not so very long ago, my family was involved in slavery, that they thought they could *own* another person. And Reverend Dumas saw that I was revealing a painful experience. "But there's no wrong-doing for you; that was the way of life. It was just the way of life."

He sighed and shook his balding head. "But somehow, I feel that there's a connecting thread that runs right down through the whole thing. And when I find this other record of genealogy that I've been looking for to show you—it's already been documented—we can put the whole picture together.

It's got the names and the break-offs. I just put it away too good."

As I prepared to leave, Clara joined us. She had known the reverend's grandmother well and had many long talks with her when she was alive. The grandmother said that her grandfather had gone to work for a man named Battey, back about 1850.

"Her grandfather was not a slave. Mr. Battey told him, 'You won't be a slave at my place.' And the grandmother said they never were slaves at the Battey place. They came there to work. But then the Battey family comes into all of that," Clara said in a confidential tone. "You know, all of that mix-up. Did you see the pictures of our white relatives? Reverend Dumas' grandmother, Mama Muse—that's what we called her because her last husband's name was Muse—said her grandfather was General Lee."

Clara continued, "Nobody would believe my son when he told his class that he was descended from General Robert E. Lee. When the Confederate soldiers came to the Battey plantation down there in Georgia, they ordered all the girls together, and they took their pick. Mama Muse said they took her grandmother to the General. And she was just an innocent young girl! I used to do volunteer work at school, and they asked me if it was true about being descended from General Lee. I told them, 'Yes, we have the history written down.' But they didn't believe it because we're black."

Clara's voice took on an edge of suppressed rage. "But we're not black; we're *mixed*. Blacks in this country are mixed. I've seen true black Africans, and they are purple-black. When we get mixed, we don't have that same color. We're mixed with their lighter color, and it wasn't at our choice that we were mixed!"

The story of the brutal military rape left me stunned. I could not absorb the myriad implications of its repercussions. As I drove from Reverend Dumas' home in Granite Quarry, I was unaware of traffic or even whether the sun was shining. I remember nothing of my trip home other than passing at Gaffney, South Carolina, their million-gallon water tower shaped and painted like a peach. The light-hearted landmark offered timely reassurance that I was moving in the right direction.

When I arrived in Atlanta, I called Mother. The phone rang five times, then six. She might be rushing to answer, so I let it continue to ring. Finally, on the eleventh ring, she picked up the receiver.

"I was out on the patio," she said breathlessly, with the now-familiar wheeze as she spoke. "I was pinching back some spent chrysanthemums, and I can't run to answer the phone anymore. I figured it must be you. How was your visit with the preacher you wanted to see?"

I summarized the encounter and continued, "Clara looked up exact names and dates for me. Reverend Dumas' great-grandmother was Mary Dixon Battey, born October 18, 1863, the result of rape, in the thick of the war. This is the most troubling issue I've yet encountered. I can't seem to get away from the cruelty and abuse that blacks have suffered in this country. Doug knows a retired man in Arizona who is a Civil War expert. I'm going to phone him about major battles in Floyd County early in 1863 to see if I can learn any more about this."

The next day I phoned Dr. William L. Baran in Phoenix and briefly told him the story of Reverend Dumas' great-grandmother. I paused while he wrote the names *Mary Dixon Battey, Floyd County, Georgia,* and her birth date in 1863 to verify dates of battles in the relevant time frame.

"I know there were numerous battles all around that northwest corner of the state," Dr. Baran said, "but I can tell you right now that Robert E. Lee is not the villain in the story. You see, he was tied up at this specific time with the Army of Virginia in places like Fredericksburg, Gettysburg, and Appomattox."

The incendiary accusation against General Robert E. Lee, beloved military leader of the Confederacy, sent Dr. Baran immediately to his research books. A letter arrived in Wednesday's mail, stating that although a grievous wrong had been committed at the Battey plantation in January of 1863, the activities and location of General Lee in Virginia were well documented. He began a detailed chronology with Lee's assuming command of the Army of Northern Virginia on June 1, 1862. The Battle of Fredericksburg followed on December 13, 1862, stating that after the Confederate victory, the opposing armies went back to their entrenchments. Union General Ambrose Burnside made another troop movement against Lee to no avail. He was subsequently replaced by Major General Joseph Hooker, who crafted multi-pronged attacks against Lee's army, culminating in the Battle of Chancellorsville on May 1, 1863. Lee's location in Virginia is documented the entire time (and is easily verified today through Internet sources).

"This is not meant to diminish the gravity of the atrocity committed against the young mother of Mary Dixon Battey at the Battey plantation in Floyd County, Georgia. From the siege at Murphreesboro in the summer of 1862, through the Battle of Parker's Crossroads on December 31, and the Battle of Fort Donelson on February 3, 1863, the entire three-state border region of Tennessee, Alabama, and Georgia—and most notably Floyd County—was crawling with thousands of troops, under several generals. It could have been any of them. I could provide dates and locations of specific battles, although it would be impossible to establish paternity after such a passage of time."

I phoned Mother. I had no intention of trying to determine the father of Mary Battey's baby, although her family should have the right to know.

Mother suggested that we think about what the passage of years can tell us. "Jesus told us, 'By their fruit, ye shall know them.' Obviously, the child was accepted and loved by her mother's family. She grew up in an environment that was hostile to her race, yet she left a heritage of love that was passed down through the generations all the way to her great-grandson. His entire life has been devoted to following the principles of Jesus Christ. The family left spiritual tracks. They knew that our Lord God is working his purpose out. Love triumphed over evil, as in His time, it always will."

Yet there remains a deep discomfort in all of us, black and white alike, about race and the injustice of the past. Mother and Carine—and Reverend Dumas and Clara, too—because they'd dealt with the unresolved conflict longer or deeper than I, had managed to make a peace of sorts with our human limitations. Perhaps God, and time, will heal the conflict in us all.

> *O for a breeze of heav'nly love to waft my soul away*
> *To that celestial world above, where pleasures ne'er decay.*
> *Eternal Spirit, deign to be my pilot here below,*
> *To steer through life's tempestuous sea,*
> *Where stormy winds do blow.*

"Canaan's Land" #101 in *The Sacred Harp*
Arranged by E.J. King, 1844

Chapter 13

Carolina—the Spiritual Trail

WE'D been back in Atlanta only a few days when Doug told me apologetically that he would be returning to North Carolina frequently for awhile. He said he'd understand if I preferred to stay home much of the time.

He would be in Greensboro first. When I consulted maps to see where Greensboro was located, I was surprised to find it even closer than Raleigh to the Dumas family's former home. I, too, would be busy.

I had lunch with Barbara before we left. She was delighted with the new revelations, particularly her mother's correspondence with Isaac S. London, and was not at all surprised that I'd chosen to go back to North Carolina so soon.

"I dearly wish I could go with you," she said. "I feel certain there's a link of their Huguenot roots with early churches near their home. Benjamin I's father endured too much for the cause of his faith for his family to simply put it aside. I'd love to help you trace their spiritual tracks."

Their political trail had left behind a few legal recordings as evidence that the family had been there, and even that evidence was incomplete. I suspected it would be almost impossible to find spiritual tracks.

"Church records might tell you something." Barbara said. "They told you plenty here in Georgia."

"We don't even know the denomination of the church they attended," I said. "Carine wrote that they were Anglican in Virginia, but the family was Baptist by the time they came to Georgia. I wouldn't know where to begin to find out how their church membership evolved."

"When you say they were Anglican," Barbara said, "we have to remember that everyone had been Anglican because that was the official Church of England, so it was also official religion of the colonies. The Anglican Church was supported by the taxpayers. When the colonists overthrew the British, they wanted to be rid of everything British, which meant they dissolved the legal establishment of the Anglican Church. The Anglicans were left by the wayside, while the Baptists, Methodists, and Presbyterians found fields ripe for harvest; that was the beginning of the Bible Belt. I'm Episcopalian, but I like to think that all Christians are more alike than we differ. Families were likely to become associated with the denomination of the first preacher to reach their area."

I agreed to look first for the oldest churches in the county, especially the oldest Baptist churches. Maybe I would have some luck hunting down the Dumases in church records.

"I do hope you're keeping a detailed journal," Barbara said. "I find it very significant that you should find yourself in that specific area with nothing to distract you from finding answers to our questions."

Before the trip, I reviewed Carine's genealogy lists and my photocopied research pages telling of Benjamin Dumas I, who followed his brother-in-law John Clark from Virginia to North Carolina. His commitment was so strong that Benjamin I convinced his grown children and their spouses to leave everything behind and move to the western edge of civilization. Like Barbara and her mother, I was convinced that he had listened closely to his father, Jerome Dumas, the Huguenot refugee who came to Virginia seeking freedom to worship.

Benjamin I and his wife, Frances, shared a vision. I longed to sit down with them for a heart-to-heart talk.

What mattered most to you? What led to your commitment?

Frances died about 1753, only a few years after arriving in North Carolina. Benjamin I soon remarried. His second wife was a neighbor, Mrs. Martha McClendon Culpepper, a widow who had grown children of her own. And perhaps her presence in the wilderness area was an indication that she also supported the Dumas vision.

In the extensive library of our large home church in Atlanta, Second Ponce de Leon Baptist Church, I learned that Sandy Creek Baptist Church in North Carolina was acknowledged as the beginning of all Baptist churches in the South. When I pinpointed its location, I discovered that the Sandy Creek church was in the county just north of where the Dumas family settled in North Carolina. The church was organized in 1755, only a few years after the Dumases arrived.

A current map showed the town nearest the location of the Sandy Creek Baptist Church was Asheboro, no more than a half-hour drive south of Greensboro. Soon after we arrived in North Carolina, I drove through the town, hoping to spot a historical marker. As I passed a beautiful church building and noticed the name, Oakhurst Baptist Church, I turned around at the next opportunity.

After listening to my story the pastor, Dr. Randy Sherron, said "Yes, you are very near the site of Sandy Creek, the mother church. However, Rocky River Baptist Church is the oldest continuing congregation in this area. I have a little information about those churches here—I'd be happy to make you some photocopies—but you should really visit the extensive Baptist Historical Collection at Wake Forest University in Winston-Salem, where many original church records are kept." And I recalled the forgotten note also recommending the Wake Forest collection that had fallen from Isaac S. London's box of papers at the North Carolina State Library and Archives.

My map showed that Winston-Salem was only a short distance from Greensboro, in the opposite direction than I was headed. I would plan another day trip soon to Winston-Salem, a day more suitable for sitting in a library than this beautiful day. As I enjoyed the scenery of the road, I anticipated visiting the courthouses near the Dumas family's former home, beginning with Rockingham, about an hour farther south, and Wadesboro, twenty miles west of Rockingham.

At the Richmond County courthouse in Rockingham, a clerk glanced at the dates I was seeking and suggested that it would be more productive to look first in Anson County records. "You might as well start with the earliest settlers. If you find them there, it'll be easier to work forward."

I started to leave, and then turned to ask the clerk if she knew where the Rocky River Baptist Church was located.

"It sounds familiar, but I don't know of a church by that name around here. Maybe it's up on *Rocky River*. That's over in Anson County, too." She smiled tolerantly, and we both laughed.

I took the highway that led west, and in only brief minutes, I reached the Wadesboro city limits sign. I drove all the way through the small town on the main street, passed the high school, and had reached the western outskirts when I realized that I'd somehow missed the turn to the courthouse. I'd have to turn around and go back. I pulled into the next convenient turnoff, but as I turned into the drive, I saw a sign identifying the building as the Anson Baptist Association. The startling coincidence seemed like a generous gift of providence. Barbara would have smiled knowingly and simply said, "Interesting."

Taking advantage of the unexpected opportunity, I parked near the door and went inside. A woman seated at a desk raised an index finger to signal that she'd be off the phone soon. I examined a large map on the wall that displayed churches in the county, looking first for the river.

"Hello there," the woman said. "May I help you?"

"I'd like to find an old church—an old, old church called Rocky River Baptist. I don't even know what town it's in."

She smiled broadly before answering, "Why, Rocky River is the oldest church of any kind in the whole county. It isn't in a town at all, and it's actually no longer on the river, although the river is nearby." She wrote detailed directions to the church on a slip of paper and pointed out its location on the map, tracing the most direct route with her finger. Surprisingly, it was along the route I'd planned to take on my return to Greensboro.

I drove back into Wadesboro, retracing my route, and I watched closely for the turn to the Anson County courthouse. And this time I saw the prominent building and wondered how I could have missed it on my first drive through the small town.

The gray-haired man working behind the counter looked both intelligent and kind. He listened thoughtfully to my question and tapped his glasses as if the action might dislodge a knowledgeable answer.

"A lot of people come through here looking for old records. There would've been a wealth of recordings if we hadn't had to contend with war and fire. The worst fire was a long time ago, back in the Revolutionary War. Set the fire on purpose, you know. Then the courthouse has been moved several times, too, so the earliest records are kind of spotty. You should check first over at the annex and see if they have anything about your family. The oldest information is over there."

I had become accustomed to scavenging for overlooked scraps of information tucked away in backrooms and dusty courthouse basements, so I willingly climbed a ladder to retrieve the large volume of salvaged wills from the earliest days of Anson County from the top shelf. The book was labeled *Record of Wills, Volume I, 1751-1795*. An undetermined number of pages were missing from the damaged book, and some of the pages were charred beyond legibility. I wondered about the hands that had rescued its remains from certain destruction.

The large, battle-scarred book didn't include a Dumas will, but it did contain a record with information even more intriguing—an inventory of the estate of Benjamin Dumas I, signed by the administrator, his oldest son, David. I knew I'd found something important when I read his now familiar name. I knew these people. David was "Old" Sarah's husband. He was Ben III's father and later, Susannah's father-in-law.

The inventory was dated 1763. I quickly calculated that David was thirty-three years old, and his father, Benjamin I, who had established the tavern and ferry, had died at age fifty-eight. Susannah would not have been old enough to take dictation, for although she was probably already in the household, she and Ben III were still small children.

I skimmed the first page rapidly and took the hefty book to a table.

Benjamin Dumas I left a large estate. The inventory was lengthy—five pages, with several items listed on each line. Beneficiaries' names were not listed, thus it was not as informative as the 1852 record from the estate of Benjamin Franklin Dumas, this man's great-grandson. However, the inventory was surprisingly rich in detail. David Dumas painted a distinct picture of his father's home and physical world on the day he left it in 1763.

The Dumas Tavern and Ferry, in a strategic location below the point where the Rocky River runs into the Great Peedee, was the only ferry crossing for many miles. The ferry and tavern establishment was a hotel, a general store, a public gathering place, with something for everyone's wants or needs.

No timid beginning, the first line listed two thousand pounds of lead and seventy-five pounds of powder, a startling contrast to the next line that listed a pair of wool cards and two pairs of cotton cards.

Cards? Oh, for carding wool and cotton to make yarn. They grew cotton. Did they raise sheep? Sheep didn't adapt well, unless they were given special care, or so the history books had said. The tavern's activities encompassed a wider range than I had imagined. But it was also a general store.

"Eight thousand small pins...100 thimbles...3 dozen mettle buttons...84 Coat buttons...1 pr. Taylors sheers...3 setts of Knitting needles."

Separately listed and itemized were yards and yards of fabric—white sheeting, Irish linen, blue shalloon, brown Holland, calico, woolen cloth, and other less familiar textiles.

"Seven setts of Table Knives and forks...4 setts of tea cups."

"Two sifter bottoms...1 Earthen butter pot...4 punch bools."

"Seventy-seven gallons of Brandy...8 Juggs, also 2 gallons of Rum."

David must have reached the spirits cellar. The tavern seems to have been well supplied. He evidently had helpers bringing inventory totals from separate rooms and areas as they counted. The logic-defying order became more random. I searched for related items.

"Thirty-six Bushels of Wheet...882 Bushels of Indian corn...7 Head of Geese...12 ½ lb. of feathers...1 Pr. Candle moulds...455 lb. & 5 ounces of Tobacco."

"One hundred and twelve Head of Cattle...7 broke horses...1 Mare & Yearling...1 inglish horse...3 unbroke young horses."

There was a wide assortment of tools—from rasps and files to "hilling" hoes, "trowel" hoes, and "grubbing" hoes. He had broad axes and narrow axes, a "sett of wagon boxes" and a horse rake with iron teeth.

"Twelve Quires of writing paper...3 brass ink pots...3 spelling books."

We must have entered a room used for schoolwork. I pictured the young Ben III, about six or seven years old, his brother, Andrew, and the young

Susannah beginning their educations.

"Two Watts Psalm books...5 Psalters."

Oh, they sang. They sang!

"One Testament...1 Bible."

"One large old Trunk...1 pr. Candle snuffers...1 candle stick...3 beds and furniture."

"One Koon Hatt...2 canisters of Tobacco...6 pr. Shoes."

"One old brass kettle...4 water pails...1 washing tub."

"One small trunk...1 walnut chest...1 old canister & a few buttons with round tops...1 looking glass."

These are his personal belongings. We're in his bedchamber.

"One Virginia law book...1 book called *The Young Man's Companion*...1 book called *Duling Court*...1 Margent Bible."

"One large Gunbelt...2 pistoles...1 sword."

"One Beaver Hatt...2 Jackets...4 shirts...3 Coats...1 Razor...1 pair of spectacles."

The last item listed was Benjamin I's pocket knife. The picture in my mind was so real that I wanted to reach out and take the knife in my hand to feel for myself the object that I held. I imagined its solidity, its heft and the cold metal. If only I could see it and feel it, I could learn much about the man.

The long list of unfamiliar items made me wonder about their significance in the world as it existed in 1763. A knife was not likely to have been used for simply whittling. I wanted David to tell me more about these personal belongings, to help me know what Benjamin I was like.

As in a news story on television, my mind took me to the Dumas home and tavern on the river. I imagined walking across the floor of the bedchamber, my footsteps sounding resonantly on its wide wooden planks. I stood beside David Dumas as he itemized the objects on top of his father's walnut chest. I watched as he opened the old canister and shook out the few buttons with rounded tops. *Did David know the garment for which the buttons were intended? Did he wonder why his father saved a few special buttons in a safe place?*

The looking glass hung above the chest. What images had the mirror reflected? Considering the time and place in which he lived, Benjamin Dumas I was a gentleman, meticulous about his dress and grooming. I pictured him standing before the chest, watching his reflection closely in the mirror as he shaved. Then, he'd carefully apply a dab or two of sweet oyle before he reached for his spectacles. He'd adjust the spectacles, and— I caught my breath.

Did Benjamin secure the gun belt as he finished dressing? Did he adjust both pistols for ready action? Were they concealed beneath his coat?

Or were his eyeglasses merely reading glasses? Was he a sensitive, studious man? Perhaps his neck cloth was made of silk or soft wool, knit especially for him.

He lived in a different time, a time I didn't understand. Other than the Bible, the titles of his books were unfamiliar to me. I'd never heard of a Margent Bible. A reference librarian might help me determine the subject matter and gain insight into his mind.

Although his father came from France, Benjamin Dumas I was born in Virginia and was a British subject. The books of his personal library were listed as English books, not French. The Virginia Law book and the Bibles, psalters, psalms books, and testaments were important to him and gave revealing testimony about the focus of his thoughts. I didn't know whether Benjamin Dumas had elected to become a Baptist, Methodist, or any other denomination, but I was persuaded that he sought to know God. He was a man I would trust.

Before leaving the courthouse annex, I photocopied the inventory. Sitting in my warm car, I referred to the detailed county map I'd purchased my first week in Raleigh. Deciding on the route to take, I consulted the notes I'd received at the Baptist Association directing me to Rocky River Baptist Church and then started on down the road.

The sun was high overhead and gilded the leaves of the many trees that lined the road. The colors of autumn were reaching their full intensity. As I sped along the highway, it seemed that nature was performing a dress rehearsal for the third act of its grand ballet. A magnificent oak spun into center stage as the highway veered into a wide turn, and flashes of sunlight swept like a spotlight over crimson sumac that danced in and out of view.

I followed my directions, turning onto increasingly rustic roads that led through neatly fenced fields and pastures. I came to a crossroads with a stop sign and waited for a pickup, the only vehicle in sight, to slowly pass. As I crossed the road and continued on the country lane, it led me past cleared farmland and up a wooded hill. At the top of the hill, a prominent masonry sign set in a landscaped bed of flowers told me that I had finally found Rocky River Baptist Church.

I turned into the drive to see a white frame building with all the requisite features of a southern church—wide double-doors at the entry, tall windows on the sides, and its roof topped with a steeple. Despite similarities to other country churches, the distinctive bell in the steeple gave Rocky River Baptist Church its own unforgettable face. I marveled that a structure could so vividly project the spirit of its inhabitants. The building spoke of a straightforward and hardworking church body that appreciated the beauty of simplicity.

The building's placement on the hilltop assured its dominant presence in every direction. The peaked roof of the steeple's bell tower mimicked the roof on which it was positioned like a crown. A pair of seasonal wreaths on the entry doors repeated the curvilinear ornamentation in stained glass of the tall side windows, and iron handrails extended a welcoming assist for anyone who needed support to ascend the steps to the entry.

I searched in my deep purse for my camera and when I looked up, a young woman was walking toward a minivan parked near the rear of the building. I opened the car door and hurried to get her attention.

"Wait! Please wait," I called. The woman paused near the driver's door as she took keys from her purse.

"Hello. Is there anyone who would have membership rolls for the early days of this church? I'm most interested in finding a list of charter members."

The young woman considered the question, and then she shook her head negatively. "I'm only filling in for the church secretary, but I don't think we have anything like that."

"Do you know if you have any documentation about the church's beginnings?"

"Oh, yeah, sure. I remember seeing a booklet of church history written a long time ago. I think the pastor might have a copy. He's out of town for a few days, so you'll have to wait to talk to him. I can give you an Order of Worship from last Sunday that has addresses and phone numbers for the staff, in case you want to get in touch with him."

Abandoning the minivan, she turned and walked back to the church's rear entrance. I followed, hoping to see the interior of the church, and as she entered an office off the main hall I paused to look inside the sanctuary. My quick glance revealed that the interior was also well maintained, although updating for creature comforts through the years gave a more contemporary appearance than the picturesque old-fashioned exterior. I wondered how many buildings had housed the church body since its beginning in 1776. The courthouse and records had been destroyed or damaged, and I had learned that the heaviest fighting of the American Revolution in this area had occurred 1780-1782.

The young woman returned with the Order of Worship. "I'm sorry I won't have time to give you a tour. I have to be home when my children get off the school bus and they'll arrive any minute now. We'd love to have you worship with us on Sunday morning, any Sunday morning. And you're certainly welcome to come to prayer meeting tonight. It starts at 6:45."

I thanked her for the information and asked permission to take a few photos around the building. Snapping pictures of the building from several angles, I turned to judge the best view of the road heading purposefully up the hill. I was out of film, but the picture in my mind can take me there the rest of my life. The church, established so long ago, still makes its witnessing statement that believers continue to gather to worship on this hilltop in the Rocky River valley.

> *Sweet rivers of redeeming love lie just before mine eye,*
> *Had I the pinions of a dove, I'd to those rivers fly;*
> *I'd rise superior to my pain, with joy outstrip the wind,*
> *I'd cross o'er Jordan's stormy waves, and leave the world behind.*

"Sweet Rivers" #61 in *The Sacred Harp*
Words, John Adam Granade, 1803; music, William Moore, 1825

CHAPTER 14

Rocky River

THE trip to Winston-Salem was another brief and pleasant drive from Greensboro. I found the Wake Forest campus easily and was directed to the recently-completed library that housed the Baptist Historical Collection. I again followed the suggestion of the Richmond County courthouse clerk to begin with the earliest records and work forward.

Sandy Creek Baptist Church was the oldest church of any kind in the area. I only suspected a connection with Rocky River Baptist Church. The earliest information was in a book published in 1859, *History of the Sandy Creek Baptist Association,* by George W. Purefoy. He said the founding pastor of Sandy Creek Baptist Church was a fiery preacher named Shubal Stearns. Stearns had come to North Carolina in 1755 from New England with his brother-in-law, Daniel Marshall, and a band of followers who called themselves Separate Baptists, a name they chose because they wanted to separate themselves from the Congregational Church in Boston, which they believed could not be reformed from within. An oft-quoted bible verse was II Corinthians 6:17 (KJV), "Come out from among them and be ye separate, saith the Lord."

It was not until years after my excursions to Wake Forest that I learned of the important role that the Separatists played in the evolution and spread of the music included in *The Sacred Harp.* In her book, *Baptist Offspring, Southern Midwife—Jesse Mercer's Cluster of Spiritual Songs,* Kay Norton says, "The offer of 'free grace' in revival meetings of the Second Great Awakening opened the door for more inclusive Separate Baptists. . . . *The Sacred Harp* (1844) and *Social Harp* (1855) cited Mercer frequently as a text source."

Separate Baptists were known to be enthusiastic in their singing of a repertory made up mainly of hymns by Isaac Watts and folk hymn tunes. This "Sandy Creek tradition" is often contrasted with the more staid Regular Baptist tradition, as in the book *I Will Sing the Wondrous Story: A History of Baptist Hymnody in North America* by David W. Music and Paul A Richardson. Apparently, the music matched the style of Sandy Creek Baptist Church's firebrand preacher.

In the *History of Sandy Creek Baptist Association* that I continued to read at Wake Forest, Purefoy said Stearns and his group had first stopped in Virginia, but congregations of the churches already established there were too refined for the emotional style of preaching for which he was becoming famous (or infamous, depending on one's personal persuasion). Stearns and Marshall then heard of settlements in a "religious vacuum" on the western edge of North Carolina that might be more receptive to his rousing sermons—and probably, the lively music.

Stearns' reputation preceded him and drew large crowds, if for no other reason than to see the stirring preacher for themselves. He made direct, piercing eye contact with his audience and had a commanding voice that one observer said "made soft impressions on the heart and fetched tears from the eyes." The church that the New Englanders established in North Carolina, Sandy Creek Baptist Church, quickly grew from a membership of only sixteen to more than six hundred members, and soon established new churches, or "arms," in the surrounding area.

A name suddenly caught my eye. "Stearns and his company reached Granville County in November 1755. Here they fell in with the patriot and agitator Herman Husband, who acquired in the same month a large body of land cornering the site of the Sandy Creek Baptist Church location. The Baptists owned no lands of record at that date. Without a doubt, they settled under the design and leadership of Husband and probably built on his grounds, although his land was eventually confiscated."

Purefoy said Sandy Creek Baptist Church organized an association of nearby churches in 1758. At that time, the nearest arm to the Dumas family's land had no ordained ministers, but was represented by two "exhorters"—one of whom was Edmund Lilly. Edmund Lilly was the son-in-law of Benjamin Dumas I and husband of David Dumas' sister—the same Edmund Lilly who had been dismissed from his Quaker fellowship for marrying out of the faith. This was the same Edmund Lilly who was injured in the Revolutionary War and had to be *carried* to preach in his later years.

The church at Sandy Creek suddenly disappeared in 1771, but not for lack of interest. The land and homes of the church members had been taken from them and they were forced to move on. But the British effort to crush the protesters in the 1771 Regulator uprising in North Carolina had merely sent the church's seeds to more fertile ground.

Purefoy's *History of Sandy Creek Baptist Association* continued, "When Husband's land was confiscated after the Battle of Alamance in 1771, some of the displaced Baptists sought refuge along the Rocky River."

I had no doubt that one refuge destination was on or near the Dumas island, situated a short distance south of where the Rocky River flows into the Great Peedee River—and a short distance north of the Dumas Ferry and Tavern. Dumas men were known to be Regulators, inclined to break with the Church of England and likely to listen to what the Baptists had to say. The struggles for political freedom and religious freedom were inseparably connected.

I could have stopped reading, for I knew I'd found the family's church. But I'd read only one source. Perhaps I might find direct proof. If the substitute secretary at Rocky River Baptist Church had correctly known that someone had written an early history of their church, I should be able to find a copy in the Baptist Collection of the library at Wake Forest.

It was a small booklet, *History of Rocky River Baptist Church*, written in 1900 by its then-pastor, Blakely H. Mathews, forty years after Purefoy's association history and thus containing some repetition while providing new information. Mathews' history told that the church had been formed in 1776, five years after some of the displaced Baptists had taken refuge along the river. Edmund Lilly had been injured during the American Revolution and was taken to the island in the river to recover. Records in Raleigh had shown me that Benjamin Dumas I had deeded the island to his daughter, Sarah Dumas Lilly, and his son-in-law, Edmund Lilly. And as owners of the island, they knew its safe places of refuge well.

Mathews said Rocky River Baptist Church first built a brush arbor near the river for services and camp meetings. Later, the arbor was replaced with a traditional structure; an interior row of posts was built down the center of the church building, segregating the free and enslaved church members. The arbor remained for many years afterward and was used for special meetings or occasions.

I pictured a particularly special occasion under the Rocky River brush arbor when Ben III and Susannah were married. The preacher who tied the knot would naturally have been his uncle, Edmund Lilly. Within the next months, Ben III would follow his uncle's leadership into heated battles of the American Revolution. Edmund Lilly was his military leader as well as his pastor.

Mathews said Rocky River Baptist Church in 1790 was still under the care of Reverend Lilly, whom he described as "a distinguished patriot of the Revolutionary Period." Lilly continued to preach for another year, until John Culpepper assumed the pastoral duties in 1791.

Culpepper was pastor for the next fifty years. As I continued to read, I learned that Culpepper's father, Sampson, was a stepson of Benjamin Dumas I—the son of the widowed neighbor that Benjamin Dumas I had married after Frances died. This information pulled Culpepper into the Dumas family fold.

When John Culpepper was twelve years old, his father, Sampson, moved the family from Anson County, North Carolina, to Georgia. Mathews said, "When John was twenty, under the preaching of Dr. Silas Mercer, eminent early Baptist, he embraced the faith and entered the ministry almost immediately after his baptism. He returned to North Carolina and preached with great power."

Because of Mercer University in Macon, Georgia, I was aware that the name Mercer was prominent in Baptist history. I had not known, however, that Jesse Mercer, for whom the university is named, was Silas Mercer's son. John Culpepper had undoubtedly brought revival tunes from Mercer services to Rocky River Baptist Church and used them throughout his ministry—a fact that cast new light on the trail of their music and its connection to Sacred Harp music.

Jesse Mercer's early American text-only hymnbook, *The Cluster of Spiritual Songs*, published in 1810, was a forerunner of *The Sacred Harp* and contains many songs that Sacred Harp singers continue to sing. Among about two dozen hymns from Mercer's collections found in today's hymnals—and not limited to Baptist hymnbooks—are: "Come thou fount of every blessing," "What wondrous love is this," and "On Jordan's stormy banks I stand." A favorite text from Mercer's *Cluster* is "Lenox" #40 in *The Sacred Harp*:

> *Blow ye the trumpet, blow, the gladly solemn sound;*
> *Let all the nations know, to earth's remotest bound,*
> *The year of Jubilee is come; the year of Jubilee is come;*
> *Return, ye ransomed sinners, home.*

Words, Charles Wesley, 1750; music, Lewis Edson, 1782

Protestants of all denominations still sing some of the same songs Ben III and Susannah—and their young grandson, Edmund Dumas—sang at Rocky River Baptist Church.

Purefoy's Sandy Creek association history at Wake Forest included biographies of early preachers and revealed that John Culpepper was not only a preacher, but he also served six terms as U. S. Congressman from Montgomery County. Enthusiastic revivals accompanied his preaching wherever he went. "His popularity became so great that misguided friends urged him in 1806 to become a candidate for Congress because it was the only means of preventing the reelection of the incumbent, who was particularly disliked by voters in their part of the district."

When the returns came in, Culpepper took the district in a landslide. However, he didn't intend to remain in politics longer than to accomplish the defeat of the undesirable incumbent, and there is a gap after the first term. But whether by his own choice or at the urging of his supporters, he was returned to Washington in 1813 and remained until 1829.

At the same time, he continued to hold the title of pastor of the Rocky River Baptist Church. Culpepper himself made the selection of the substitute preacher for the time he was in Washington and trained him personally. And his choice was surprising; the name of his stand-in was Ralph *Freeman*. He had been a slave.

At the beginning of the nineteenth century, the membership of Rocky River Baptist Church included many slaves. One of the slaves, who belonged to an unidentified man, was named Ralph. Soon after professing his faith and being baptized, Ralph had the calling to preach.

Ralph, the preacher slave, attracted a great deal of attention in the years before the Civil War. He first preached in the Carolinas, then in Georgia and Virginia. His travels were watched closely by disapproving slave owners, and soon new laws prohibited slaves from holding public services.

The Rocky River Baptist Church congregation was determined to remedy the situation. The church members bought Ralph from his owner and gave him his new last name and his freedom.

Purefoy said Ralph Freeman baptized numerous plantation owners, and generations afterwards delighted in relating their personal accounts. Many slave owners who went to Ralph's meetings for the sole purpose of breaking up the service were won over through his ministry and became not only members of his congregation, but also life-long friends and supporters of the church.

Once, when a law officer was sent to stop Ralph's preaching, an ordained white Baptist minister introduced Ralph and remained silent except for an occasional loud "Amen" until Ralph had finished his sermon. Then the white minister immediately took charge, announced the benediction and declared the meeting closed.

His contemporaries described Ralph as an avid reader who was especially well read in the scriptures. He was known to be an eloquent preacher, was often requested for funerals, and was frequently selected as the Sabbath speaker at association meetings, the honored slot of the days-long schedule.

The Baptist Collection at Wake Forest was indeed a plentiful source of information. I returned to the file drawer of loose clippings and documents relating to Baptist preachers where I'd found additional background of John Culpepper from E. M. Brooks, who in 1928 was still another former pastor of Rocky River Baptist Church. I located a file labeled "Ralph Freeman."

A loose newspaper clipping from the *Baptist Messenger* of December 9, 1905, with an article by T. B. Ashcraft of Wake Forest College, was headlined, "Ralph: The Old Negro Preacher." He repeated earlier details of Ralph's life, then added, "Mr. A. Lowery of Anson County says that at an association convention at Elizabeth church, they were discussing as to who should preach the sermon on Sunday. A preacher from Charleston, South Carolina, rose and requested that Ralph preach it. He said he had often heard of him and had come to hear him.

"He preached on 'The Temptation of Christ.' The one expression that Mr. Lowery remembers from the sermon was when Ralph, in the middle of his sermon, read the passage, 'All these things I will give thee,' and then, with a smile that evoked laughter in response from his congregation, he said, 'Poor devil, he didn't have a foot of land in the world.'"

In describing Ralph's looks, a member of the church said that he was of average size and "perfectly" black. "He had a smiling countenance, especially while speaking in the pulpit. He was humble in his appearance at all times, even when conducting services. But great personal respect was always shown him by the brethren whom he visited in his preaching excursions."

A white Baptist minister, Elder Joseph Magee, became Ralph's close friend, and they traveled and preached together. The two made a pact that the survivor would preach the funeral of the one who died first. On his deathbed, Magee, who had in the meantime moved west to Tennessee, asked as his last request that his family send for Ralph to come and preach his funeral. He had willed to Ralph his riding horse, his overcoat, Bible, and fifty dollars in cash.

Accompanied by a white church member, Ralph went to "the West" to Tennessee and preached the funeral service from a text his friend had chosen. When they returned, Ralph's companion on the trip said that he had never before seen so large a gathering. At the end of the service, the brother of Elder Magee spoke to the congregation and revealed the bequest that Magee had made for Ralph. He added, "If any of you would like to give him any amount, it would be thankfully received." The congregation collected another fifty dollars.

Other church members gave their recollections of Ralph's substituting for John Culpepper during the years their pastor served in Congress. Ralph Freeman had a great many white converts under his preaching, and he personally baptized all the new believers, "both white and black."

A longtime member spoke fondly of Ralph's visits to their home, where he ate and sat with the family for Bible reading and prayer. "He then went to the Negro quarters and slept on a bed specially prepared for him."

A short time later, the Baptists in North Carolina became embroiled in an argument over missions that led to a deep division, the same division that had split the Baptists in Georgia. Churches who became known as Missionary Baptists wanted associations to pool their resources in efforts to spread the gospel. Those of the opposing view distrusted the authority of a higher association and sought to maintain their independence. They became known as Primitive (meaning "authentic") Baptists. The church where Ralph Freeman and his family then had their membership joined the anti-mission side, although he was in ill health at the time, and there was no evidence that he took that position.

In the 1830s, while the schism raged, Culpepper wrote to his trusted colleague, Elder Ralph Freeman:

I am old, and I have spent the present year almost entirely at home. Our English and American brethren have sent our preachers to Hindoston, to Burmah, [*sic*] and elsewhere, and they have translated the Scriptures into about thirty languages, now printing and circulating the Bible in many languages. The Missionary Baptists in America raised last year for printing and distributing the Bible, $35,714.66; for Foreign Missions, more than $63,000; for Home Missions, more than $15,000; and large sums for building Meeting Houses, Schools, and Colleges.

As we can now travel by railroads and steam boats and ships, so rapidly we hope the time is near when "the earth shall be filled with the knowledge of the Lord, as the waters cover the sea."

And now, my dear Brother, in view of these things, let me say to you, if through the want of information on these subjects, you or any member of your family have honestly opposed these benevolent plans and thought you were doing God's service, recollect that Saul of Tarsus once thought he ought to do many things contrary to the name of Jesus. If you are on the Lord's side, persevere, for as sure as God is in Heaven and His word is true, so sure the effort Baptists are doing is God's work. As I never expect to see you again in time, but shall surely meet you at the bar of God; till then, I bid you an affectionate farewell.

J. Culpepper

John Culpepper, at the age of seventy, traveled in his sulky through twenty-nine counties on a Mission tour, preaching 233 sermons. His son followed in his father's footsteps, and it was when the noted Baptist minister was visiting his preacher son in South Carolina that he became ill and died in January of 1841.

But what became of Ralph Freeman?

On July 27, 1941, a hundred years later, in a feature article under a headline "Slave Takes Pulpit When Owner Leaves" in the *Greensboro Daily News*, Paul Ader stated, "The brilliant career of Elder Ralph Freeman was darkened near its end by a law passed by the North Carolina legislature. The act forbade Negro preachers to speak in public in the service of any church. Ralph bore his humiliation with meekness, but his last days were shortened by the weight of his discouragement... Though he had the sympathy of many brethren, his great heart could bear no more. He lived only a short time after the enactment of the law."

The article continued that Ralph Freeman dropped out of sight at the passage of the law and left no further record in the church. His gravesite was marked by nothing more than a plain quarried stone. In 1907, the stone was replaced with a granite headstone inscribed simply, "Ralph."

I couldn't stop thinking about the extraordinary relationship between these two exceptional men, John Culpepper and Ralph Freeman. They were about the same age and had probably known each other all their lives. I read on in the 1941 newspaper article again from the beginning and realized that new information had been discovered in the century after the two had departed this life.

The writer said, "Mr. Culpepper acquired a slave named Ralph, who was born and raised on Culpepper's property in the shadow of Rocky River Baptist Church."

Culpepper himself had been Ralph's unidentified owner. In all likelihood, Culpepper acquired Ralph, a slave who belonged to his family, through inheritance. I imagined the two boys playing together as small children, even before they were aware of differences in their color and status. The accepted prejudice against color seems to have never made a difference in their esteem for each other. Culpepper addressed his former slave as, "My dear brother."

Ralph Freeman was not treated as most slaves as he made his preaching rounds. He was an avid reader in an age when it was unlawful for slaves to be allowed to read. But how did he learn to read?

I smiled as I pictured the young student, John Culpepper, taking his assignments from the old schoolhouse near the Rocky River Baptist Church brush arbor to the nearby hillside, as well-behaved schoolboys were allowed to do, according to Elder E. M. Brooks, where Culpepper was joined by his best friend and they jointly completed the work. The two great intellects continued to discuss issues close to their hearts all their lives.

The newspaper article said Ralph left a legacy that continues to touch North Carolinians, a legacy of the spirit. The beloved former-slave pastor of Rocky River Baptist Church preached from the Bible of Jesus' love and forgiveness. Lasting messages from his sermons were passed to new generations who continued to read the Bible and preach its lessons.

As I walked from the library, autumn was in its full glory on the Wake Forest campus. I sensed the spirit of Ralph Freeman and his converts, black and white, still alive on the grounds of the Baptist university and the surrounding North Carolina countryside. I was convinced that I, too, had been touched personally by Ralph's spiritual legacy. At Asia Dumas' small church in Mount Gilead, North Carolina, I had heard a message from Reverend Eric Leake, who, like Ralph, had grown up "in the shadow of Rocky River Baptist Church," and who was, if not a direct descendent of Ralph Freeman, as I imagined, certainly one of Ralph's spiritual descendents.

> *When the sun, or the light, or the moon, or the stars be not darkened,*
> *Or the clouds return after the rain, or the silver cord be loosed,*
> *Then shall the dust return to the earth as it was,*
> *And the spirit shall return unto God who gave it.*

"The Spirit Shall Return" #512 in *The Sacred Harp*
Words, Ecclesiastes 12:7; music, J.E. Kitchens, 1959

CHAPTER 15

Fasola and the Margent Bible

WHEN Doug and I returned to Atlanta, the phone recorder held only one message that required a quick response: Barbara needed to make reservations for an upcoming luncheon. She had assumed that I would also want to hear a speaker from the Huguenot Society, so she had sent in registration fees for both of us. The luncheon fell on a date when Mother was planning to visit and I knew she would want to go. Since the time Mother had first read in Carine's genealogy book, *Dumas Families of Union Parish, Louisiana,* that our ancestor Jerome Dumas had escaped France as a child, she had wanted to learn about the Huguenot roots of the Dumas family. Luckily, Barbara assured me it was not too late to add an additional name.

The next day, Sunday, I asked Betty Rose Colwell in my Bible study class if she could talk with me a few moments. I was not well-acquainted with Betty Rose, but I remembered hearing that she had written a dissertation on hymnology, so I was eager to talk with her about the psalters and Psalms books in the inventory of the estate of Benjamin Dumas I. To my surprise, Betty Rose was already aware that I'd been researching family history, and she asked if I'd discovered an old family Bible while in North Carolina.

"Unfortunately, no," I said, "but I did find a reference to such a Bible in the inventory of an estate back in 1763. There were several testaments and Bibles listed, although the one that has me stumped must have held special significance to this ancestor because it was grouped with his personal belongings. It was listed by a specific name—a *Margent* Bible."

"I've never heard of a Margent Bible, either," Betty Rose said. "You might look in the church library. Ours here at Second Ponce de Leon Baptist Church is one of the best anywhere."

"Along with the testaments and Bibles, the estate held a number of psalters and Psalms books," I said. "That's why I wanted to talk to you."

When I couldn't recall a publication date, I explained, "That particular line of items caught my attention because of the importance of psalters as they relate to art, which is my own special interest. As a student, I had trouble

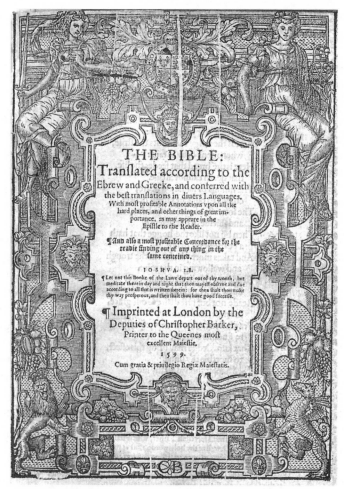

THE BIBLE:
Tranſlated according to the
Ebrew and Greeke, and conferred with
the beſt tranſlations in diuers Languages.
With moſt profitable Annotations vpon all the
hard places, and other things of great im-
portance, as may appeare in the
Epiſtle to the Reader.

¶ And alſo a moſt profitable Concordance for the
readie finding out of any thing in the
ſame conteined.

IOSHVA. 1.8.
¶ Let not this Booke of the Lawe depart out of thy mouth, but
meditate therein day and night that thou mayeſt obſerue and doe
according to all that is written therein: for then ſhalt thou make
thy way proſperous, and then ſhalt thou haue good ſucceſſe.

¶ Imprinted at London by the
Deputies of Chriſtopher Barker,
Printer to the Queenes moſt
excellent Maieſtie.
1 5 9 9.
Cum gratia & priuilegio Regiæ Maieſtatis.

Title page of my copy of the Geneva Bible, printed in 1599 in London.

grasping history in the broad context, and I still tend to put historical events in relation to art of the period. It gives me a familiar timeline to use as a crutch."

"That's an excellent way to paint the entire picture. The artist is the true historian," Betty Rose said. "But tell me what you know about psalters in relation to art."

In art history courses in college, I'd learned that psalters were important in the development of what's called illumination art, like illustrations painted in books to *illuminate* the story. Few people other than scholars could read, but anyone could read a picture. An early psalter was an illustrated prayer book, usually from the Psalms. Illumination art was typically pen-and-ink drawings in the margins that explained the written text.

Betty Rose continued my thought process, asserting that psalters were also important in the development of church music. "In the beginning song books were all text, and the harmonized parts, for two or three voices, first appeared in English psalters in the reign of Elizabeth I, in Shakespeare's time, in the mid-to-late 1500s. They used the syllables Fa-So-La-Mi in the musical scale to hear the tune of a song."

"That sounds like the four syllables used in Sacred Harp music," I said. "We sing Fa-So-La, Fa-So-La-Mi-Fa as the ascending notes of an octave, and we sing a song first in its fasola syllables to sound out its tune."

"It's exactly the same system," Betty Rose said. "The four-syllable, fasola solfège had been used in psalters since the earliest days of America. In the beginning, before our round music note heads, the syllables themselves were positioned on the appropriate line or space of written music. Assigning shapes to the syllables came even later, a major reason that tune books like *The Sacred Harp* became so popular. A seven-shape system was a later development that was immensely popular, although it was more difficult to learn. Singing schools lasting two or three weeks used a variety of different shape-note books."

Betty Rose explained that psalters were words-only hymnbooks to which various tunes could be sung by matching a text to the meter of a song. Any number of texts could be sung—or lined out—to only a handful of tunes. In lining out, a leader would sing a line, and the congregation would repeat it. Books were scarce in rural areas, and few settlers could even read text.

A press that could print musical notation was not available in the developing areas of the South. Their songs were sung to the same tunes—and the same fasola syllables—that had been used for years, long before the syllables were assigned their identifying shapes.

There was a wide exchange of music from one area to another within the colonies. The music was spread through revivals, camp meetings, and itinerant preachers making their rounds. Betty Rose said the Wesleys and Methodism were credited with the proliferation of circuit-riding preachers and that the Moravians also had a tremendous influence on early American religious music.

I'd been a Methodist much of my life, and I was aware that while John Wesley is known as the hymn-writing "Father" of Methodism, his brother Charles Wesley was the more prolific hymn composer and made a lasting impact on sacred music. I recalled hearing that the Moravians' singing had been an influence on the Wesleys' music.

"Not *an* influence," Betty Rose said. "They were *the* influence. Charles Wesley wrote over six thousand hymns, but he wasn't known to write a one before he encountered the Moravians. While Charles and John Wesley were on a voyage to Savannah, a storm came up that was so terrifying they were certain they would not survive. While everyone else was weeping or screaming, the group of Moravians on board gathered in a circle in pitch-black darkness to calmly sing hymns and pray. John Wesley later wrote that he, too, wanted that kind of inner peace and strength that he did not yet possess."

Betty Rose's description of singing in a circle reminded me of Sacred Harp singers' hollow square. I could easily imagine gathering with other singers in a square in the worst of a howling storm, absorbing powerful reassurance from singing a fugue repetitively together, our voices rising steadily in intensity to match the fury the of lightning, thunder, and pelting rain:

> *Through every age, eternal God, Thou art our rest, our safe abode.*
> *High was Thy throne, high was Thy throne, ere heav'n was made;*
> *Or earth Thy humble footstool laid.*

"Stratfield" #142 in *The Sacred Harp*
Words, Isaac Watts, 1719; music, Ezra Goff, 1786

I wondered if perhaps Edmund Dumas and his grandparents had sung that Isaac Watts song at Rocky River Baptist Church in North Carolina before the family followed the same path to Georgia that the music had taken. The family patriarch, Benjamin Dumas I, had owned Watts Psalm books when he died in 1763. I pictured him, with family and friends gathered round, singing Isaac Watts' words from the depths of his soul. Such a sight and rolling sound in the memory of a child would remain a lifetime.

Fasola Sacred Harp music had been sung in my family for centuries, and someone passed on the technique to build upon. But who? I pictured the first schoolroom in the Dumas Tavern, with Edmund's grandparents Susannah and Ben III singing as children from their psalters. Countless other singers—generations of singers—had lifted their voices and taught their children.

Isaac Watts was the most prolific writer of hymn texts. Watts Psalms books were published in England in the early 1700s and first published in America in 1729 by Benjamin Franklin. Benjamin Dumas I and his sons apparently soaked up every word that Franklin uttered. They would have been a ready market for Watts Psalm books.

Come, sound His praise abroad, and hymns of glory sing;
Jehovah is the sovereign God, the universal King.
He formed the deeps unknown, He gave the seas their bound;
The watery worlds are all His own, and all the solid ground.
Come, worship at His throne, come, bow before the Lord;
We are His works, and not our own; He formed us by His word.

"St. Thomas" #34b in *The Sacred Harp*
Words, Isaac Watts, 1719; music, Aaron Williams, 1770

There were other influences on their music. The family had maintained ties to their fellow Huguenots, or French Protestants. Clement Marot, a contemporary of Martin Luther, had translated the Psalms into French, and the Marot psalter was used in the French Reformed church until about 1700 when they added an appendix of hymns similar to those sung in the Lutheran church. No changes were made for another seventy-five years until a Jean Dumas published a large collection of French hymns at Leipzig.

It is not known if there might be a family connection to this Jean Dumas, though the possibility is intriguing. Franklin had received funds for the American Revolution from a man named Dumas in Germany. In escaping France, Dumas ancestors went first to Switzerland, then to Germany, and on to England. Once-strong ties have been lost over time, distance, politics, and wars. The trail has grown cold, but the music goes on.

"I've been thinking," Doug said, as we drove home from church, "when you were discussing illumination art, you mentioned that the drawings were in the margins of the books. And when you look at early American spellings, you have to consider the phonetic sound of the word because their spellings were not the same as our modern spellings. I think *Margent* might have been a *margined* Bible, or a Bible with a margin column for interpretive notes.

"The Margent Bible your ancestor owned may be similar to the Geneva Bible we've been researching in my Bible study; it dates back to the Protestant Reformation and was banned by Queen Mary I, 'Bloody Mary,' who re-established Roman Catholicism in England.

"The most significant distinction of the Geneva Bible is its margin notes that interpret the scripture. The most prominent leaders and scholars of the Protestant Reformation—Calvin, Knox, Coverdale—wrote the margin notes. They are said to comprise the most complete writings of Protestant thought, and it's very possible that Benjamin I's Margent Bible was a Geneva Bible."

"But how did the Geneva Bible get back to the English people if it had been banned?" I asked with interest.

"It was first smuggled in bales of hay and sacks of flour. Then, after Elizabeth became queen, the Anglican Church reluctantly allowed the Geneva version to be printed in England. Elizabeth was interested in the Renaissance, not the Reformation. But the Geneva Bible was immensely popular with the people. The Bible scholar who spoke to our Bible study said it was the Bible of choice for the thinkers of the day. Shakespeare quoted from the Geneva Bible thousands of times."

I objected that the King James Version was the official Anglican version in the colonies and would have been the version a colonist of 1763 would, or should, have owned.

"Yes, you're right. And that's a critical point," Doug said. "From the time it was published, the King James was the official Anglican version, period. It was the only officially acceptable version. That was the case in England and also in the colonies."

The King James version came about as a direct result of the Geneva Bible, or rather, as a result of its infamous margin notes. The clergy was enraged that the notes argued against the practices of the institutional church, while King James had his own disagreement with the notes. His primary objection was to the interpretation that kings, even tyrannical kings, could be overthrown. So, he authorized a version that basically accepted the accuracy of the Geneva's translation, but which deleted the troublesome margin notes.

I assumed that when the King James version became available, the Geneva Bible would not be as sought after among the public. Doug said that was not exactly the case. King James made it a felony to *own* one. Most of the Geneva Bibles were burned—those that were found—and it became known as the "forbidden Bible." Anyone who was found with one in his possession was in grave danger. To minimize the heresy charges, the Bishop of London tried to buy up all of outlawed books himself to burn to assure they were in fact destroyed.

The margin notes provided an explanation of the meanings of translated text as it compared with the original text. The notes were intended to clarify shadings of words that had no direct English equivalent or had more than one meaning. The scripture itself was not altered in the Geneva version; the information was purposely put into the margin to show that it was simply an explanation.

"We'd think of them as footnotes," Doug said, "only they were placed in the margins—like the illumination art."

The church was furious that the notes said the act of confession to men, meaning to the Catholic bishops, was not based on scripture. The marginal notes asserted that the Bible says man should confess directly to God, that an intercessor is not necessary. The relationship is between any individual person and God.

A page in my copy of the Geneva Bible. King James I of England vehemently objected to the controversial margin notes of the Geneva Bible, such as this note for Exodus 1:19, which excused disobedience to the Egyptian king and thus was interpreted as scriptural basis for revolution.

For the rest of the day, I was distracted by the ideas I'd heard. It was as if I had been groping my way through a dark, unfamiliar room, and someone suddenly switched on the lights. If King James had been angry because the Bible's margin notes said rulers could be overthrown, he knew that he, too, could be eliminated. There was no way he could overlook that kind of rebellious, treasonable thought.

A hundred years later, it was still dangerous for Benjamin Dumas I to possess such a book—the illegal, forbidden Margent Bible. One would have to either accept its teachings or reject them. Owning this book required making that determination. The information in its margin notes was vitally important to Dumas. He had found scriptural basis for revolution, the American Revolution.

> *No more beneath th' oppressive hand of tyranny we groan.*
> *Behold the smiling, happy land, behold the smiling, happy land,*
> *That freedom calls her own, that freedom calls her own.*

"Liberty" #137 in *The Sacred Harp*
Words and music, Stephen Jenks, 1800

PART THREE

THE FRENCH PROTESTANTS

Manakin Episcopal Church, established 1700, near present-day Midlothian, Virginia, is marked with a monument to the church's Huguenot (French Protestant) founders. This 1895 structure, the church's fourth, has elements of the earlier church buildings.

THE FRENCH PROTESTANTS

ca.1680
JEROME (JEROMAY) DUMAS born in the province of
Saintonge in southwestern France;
1685 escaped with relatives after the Revocation of the
Edict of Nantes; was educated in London;
July 31, 1700, arrived in Jamestown with other
Huguenot (French Protestant) refugees;
ca. 1702 married Unity Smith, a colonial heiress;
October 10, 1703 their first child was baptized at
St. Peter's Church, New Kent County, Virginia.
Children: Mathen, Benjamin (I), Jeremiah, Sarah, Temperance.

CHAPTER 16

The Huguenots of Saintonge

WITH an eye on the clock before leaving to pick up Mother at the airport, I sat down to read the summary of Huguenot history that Barbara had sent. It was a small booklet prepared by the National Huguenot Society and meant to serve as preparation for the Huguenot Society lecture and luncheon on Saturday. I scanned the beginning pages searching for names or dates that could establish a benchmark. I saw references to Calvin, the Reformation, the Renaissance, Catherine de Medici, Henry IV, and Louis XIV. A few evocative facts flashed across my mind: the Medici family, bankers to all of Europe, was said to have funded the Renaissance, and Louis XIV built the Palace of Versailles to house ten thousand people.

The summary said Renaissance ideas came across the Alps and found fertile ground at the University of Paris where Calvin was studying. Margaret of Navarre, sister of King Francis I of France, supported the movement and was in sympathy with the views of Martin Luther at the time his writings were condemned by the French Parliament. All other books and writings that Parliament thought contained heresy were forbidden, and they subsequently gave orders that all heretical material must be sought out and destroyed.

The Bible was one of the outlawed books. The same fears that obsessed the king and the clergy in England equally disturbed the court and the church in France. When it was translated into French, even the bourgeoisie could read the scriptures in their spoken language. For the first time, the Bible was understood as the instruction book to form a personal relationship with God.

An anti-Catholic pamphlet printed in Switzerland and distributed in France alarmed the king to the point that he felt the reform movement had to be crushed. Many of the reformers, derisively called Huguenots (from a German word *eidgenossen*, or *eidgenots*, meaning rebels or confederates) were executed. Others were exiled from France.

Despite persecution and political rulings against the Protestant Huguenots, the reform movement grew. Parliament then passed an edict decreeing that anyone who gave solace, support, or refuge to a member of the Reformed religion was guilty of high treason.

The booklet from Barbara continued with Catherine de Medici and the Massacre of Saint Bartholomew's Day to the coming to the throne of Henry of Navarre, who, as Henry IV of France, issued the Edict of Nantes, which gave the Protestants protection from persecution. Times of peace and prosperity blossomed under Henry IV and continued into the reigns of the Bourbon kings. It was Henry's grandson, Louis XIV, who revoked the Edict of Nantes on the crucial day of October 22, 1685.

At that point on the page, Barbara had placed a yellow stick-on note that said, "Read to the date 1685." According to John Wilson's and Carine's Dumas genealogy book, it was in the autumn of 1685 that our Dumas ancestor had escaped France; the stage was set to hear the rest of the story at the lecture on Saturday.

Mother and I waited to meet Barbara at our assigned table. On the customary name tags, the guests were asked to write the surname of his or her ancestry. I looked in vain for another Dumas descendant and noticed that some had written two or more names. A middle-aged couple seated at our table explained that when they found records of marriages and baptisms, they'd established kinship to several families.

"I ran into someone I know, a neighbor with Huguenot roots." Barbara said as she sat down at our filling table. "She said her mother's name had been Dabney. It originally had a French spelling, *D*-apostrophe-*a*-*u*-something or other... the Americans made some changes."

"That's happened to all of us," said a woman seated next to her. "The English mangled the French pronunciations, spelling the names on legal documents as they sounded in English. We had a speaker a number of years ago who handed out a lengthy list of name derivations. The list is probably still available. You might find you have more French connections than you would imagine, and you'd have to add an extra name tag."

"We should add the name Faure along with Dumas," Mother said. "Our Dumas family genealogy says that Faure was the maiden name of the mother of our first Huguenot ancestor in America."

The woman nodded knowledgeably. "*Faure* was given a spelling of *F-o-r-e* and sometimes became *Ford* because of the rolled *r*," she said. "I remember the speaker used that example because Gerald Ford was president at the time."

"I read an interesting book called simply, *The Huguenot*, about a Huguenot refugee named Apollos Riviore," her husband said. "His was a fascinating story about how he came to America and worked as an indentured servant to a silversmith to pay off the debt for his passage. His name was eventually altered, and we know of his son as Paul Revere."

A gavel sounded at the podium and the chairman called the meeting to order, introducing the speaker as a respected genealogist and historian from Virginia. Dr. Brian Armstrong's subject was the vast "Cousinhood of Huguenots." He reminded the audience that they should think of themselves not as an exclusive group, but rather as inclusive, for the Huguenots were scattered so thoroughly throughout the world that in nearly every corner, a kinsman can be found.

Dr. Armstrong briefly summarized the background history and the Italian influence through the Borgia and Medici families as well as Pope Leo X.

"The state church, the Catholic Church in Rome, had become corrupt to the core. Here we have the origins of the Mafia." The speaker suddenly had our rapt attention. "No writer, however imaginative, could fabricate more salacious tales of murderous intrigue than his contemporaries told of Pope Alexander VI, who died of poison he'd intended for his guest, a cardinal."

Europe was ripe for reform. The speaker led his listeners quickly to the predicament of the Huguenots escaping France after the revocation of the Edict of Nantes. Protestants were given a choice of abjuring—renouncing their faith and all they believed—or immediately being put to death. They were forbidden to assemble for worship, and their churches and libraries were destroyed. Leaving the country was not an option either; coastlines and French borders were guarded to intercept anyone attempting to escape.

Violence erupted immediately and the pent-up hostility was spewed out on the Huguenots. The hatred and barbarity of the St. Bartholomew's Day Massacre again swept over the country in waves of crazed, sanctioned killings and torture. The enmity came more from the king's court and the state clergy than from the Protestants' Catholic neighbors, and official armed troops, called *dragoons*, were sent village to village to occupy the homes of Huguenots to force them to abjure, proclaim themselves as Catholics, and sign documents denouncing the doctrines of Calvin and Luther.

Some did convert to Catholicism, but despite the king's barriers, countless numbers of Huguenots fled to England, to the Netherlands, and on to South Africa, Germany, Switzerland, and eventually America. There was no time to make elaborate exit plans. The Huguenots escaped in haste in any direction and in any way they could devise: by horse, by boat, or by their own feet. The only area of France where a significant number of Huguenots remained was in the Cevennes, a mountainous region in the south-central part of the country.

The safe haven of Switzerland was overwhelmed with daily increasing numbers of new arrivals. Each of the newcomers had a personal drama to relate.

"Each safe arrival was a personal miracle, and we each have a link to a miracle of survival," Dr. Armstrong said. "Look again at your ancestor's name on your name tag and think upon the miracle it represents."

He related stories of hazardous journeys over mountains or sea to reach safety beyond the French borders. He recited French surnames and the specific regions in France that had once been their homes.

"The Huguenots were a tremendous loss to France—the cream of intellect and creativity. They were industrious tradesmen, and many held high positions in the private court of the king. The countries of the world that welcomed these refugees at a substantial economic burden were in the long run enriched, both financially and spiritually. France had not only spilled its blood, it had spent it."

The refugees who went in such great numbers to Switzerland were dispersed as soon as host countries could take them. Initially, there was no organized aid, but the Huguenots' European neighbors were sympathetic with their plight and assisted generously when donations were solicited. A great many of the Frenchmen went to England, and because it was natural that the Protestants band together, a large community of Huguenots sprang up in London.

Dumas genealogy books said that Jerome Dumas, who was then five or six years old, had escaped with relatives in the Faure family along a mountainous route to Lausanne from their home in Saintonge. They arrived in Lausanne in 1686, soon after the revocation of the Edict of Nantes. Genealogists learned that later in the year, Jerome was with his brother in Frankfort, Germany, for a short while before their eventual arrival in London by unknown means.

As the speaker enumerated surprising destinations around the world, my thoughts remained with the child, Jerome Dumas. I imagined a frightened little boy traveling by foot over the mountains. He had likely seen the same sort of horror that was being chillingly described now. I wondered about Jerome's parents; had they rushed their son out of Saintonge in the nick of time? Had his parents survived?

Dr. Armstrong told of two young sisters who'd been sent to Holland and the coded letter they wrote to their father when they were safe. Only their parents would know that when they asked for the "little Nightcap" they'd left behind, they meant that it was time to send the last daughter. In back-against-the-wall desperation, the parents stowed their youngest child in a barrel and put her on a cargo boat to get her out of the country.

"How amazing," he said, "that the same little girl eventually found her way to Virginia."

The previous Sunday, my Bible study leader, Joann Bunch, had asked about Mother, and I told her of the coming visit and the planned luncheon and lecture. She said her husband had Huguenot ancestors who had also come from France around 1700 and made a dramatic and miraculous escape, a story that had been passed down in the family through the centuries. His ancestor, whose name was Dupuy, had been a royal guardsman in the court of the king. He escaped in full uniform, accompanied by his wife disguised as a boy, in the costume of a page.

After the lecture we lingered to talk while the crowd thinned. Barbara said, "I always think of historical events in relation to adults. The leaders do the deeds, but everyone, from the youngest to the oldest, bears the consequences. Jerome Dumas must have been a tough little kid to run for his life over the mountains."

Mother responded, "Children and teenagers probably fared better with such hardships than older people, but all the Huguenots had to do the best they could. They were going about everyday life, and suddenly, they had to leave with only what little they could carry. Think of the plight of the women. Imagine what they were enduring; they married young and were always either pregnant or nursing a child."

"And men were expected to protect the women and children as much as possible, regardless of whether they were young or old," Barbara said, "There was also the matter of food. What could they find for survival in the mountains in winter?"

I wondered how they kept from freezing and how many of Jerome's companions did not survive the harsh journey. The Dumas genealogy book revealed that, fifteen years later, when Jerome arrived in Jamestown on the ship *Mary and Ann* with other French refugees, he was with a cousin named Faure. By that time, he was a young man. His older brother had married and stayed behind in London. A "Widow Faure" and her four children were with the group that sailed to Virginia. We don't know what might have happened to her husband since leaving their home in France.

How firm a foundation, ye saints of the Lord,
Is laid for your faith in His excellent word,
What more can He say than to you He hath said,
Ye who unto Jesus for refuge have fled.
Fear not, I am with thee, O be not dismayed! I,
I am thy God, and will still give thee aid;
I'll strengthen thee, help thee, and cause thee to stand,
Upheld by my righteous, omnipotent hand.

"Bellevue" #72b in *The Sacred Harp*
Words, *Rippon's Selection,* 1787; music arr., Z. Chambless, 1844

"I wonder what our own family went through to get here," Barbara said. "Don't you wish we could find an Izzie who could tell us the inside story?"

As I walked to the car, I saw the woman from our table across the parking lot, the one with numerous French surnames on her name tag. She had found a wealth of information at the Huguenot library at the Manakintown settlement in Virginia, where the colonists put the French refugees when they arrived from London. And the young Jerome Dumas was with them when they reached Jamestown. Perhaps I could find information about him there. It might help almost as much as finding a knowledgeable aunt.

"Where is Manakintown?" Mother asked when I told her.

"According to the woman at the Huguenot luncheon, it isn't far from Richmond, and that's not far from Washington, DC. It isn't like it's on the other side of the world. Doug goes to Washington fairly often. He'll be going again soon and I want to go, too."

Doug had serious questions when I said I wanted to accompany him to Washington. I'd decided to drive to Richmond daily while he was in meetings.

"Have you checked to see how far it is from Richmond to DC?"

"Not much more than a hundred miles," I said confidently. "Manakintown must be nearby."

"A hundred miles!" He tried to sound calm. "I don't know, honey. Driving from city to city on the East Coast isn't like zipping along a straight and lonesome Texas highway. Let's think about it."

Manakin Episcopal Church, established 1700. A monument to the church's Huguenot (French Protestant) founders is in the foreground.

174

I knew he was evading the issue, but the evening after Mother returned to Texas, Doug arrived home from work with a thoughtful expression on his face. While loosening his tie, he walked to the windows and sat down on the sofa to talk.

"Looks like I'll be spending most of my time on another out of town project for awhile. I'll have to be there for possibly six months or more, so I'm thinking of getting a corporate apartment for the duration. Do you think you might like to go along—at least, some of the time?"

"Probably," I said. "Where?"

"How does Richmond, Virginia, sound?"

Doug and I arrived in Richmond in early January and I quickly mapped out locations of the Virginia State Library and Archives, various libraries, and historical collections. The noted library of the Huguenot Society of the Founders of Manakin in the Colony of Virginia was first on my list, but when I drove to "Manakin" as listed on my state map, on the *north* side of the James River, I found nothing related to the Huguenots. I eventually learned that the original village that had been abandoned by the Manakin Indians and later settled by the French Protestants was on the *south* side of the James.

When I finally located the site of the Huguenot settlement near present-day Midlothian, I encountered another roadblock. To visit the library of the Huguenot Society of Founders of Manakin in the Colony of Virginia, a visitor must first obtain an appointment and be accompanied by a society member at all times to read and research. Many books and documents in the collection are not simply rare, but are frequently the original and only documents. I began arrangements for my first visit and decided that the wait would allow me time to gather more background information.

My next venture was to the Virginia State Library and Archives. Again, strict security measures were in force. After registering, I was given a locker for my personal belongings, and as I entered the archives, I was allowed only a pencil and a tablet of writing paper. After a week of jotting down disconnected facts, I knew I needed some outside guidance.

"My word," Carine said, "You do manage to pluck the strangest questions out of the air. I have no idea how old Jerome Dumas acquired his four plantations in Virginia. I only wrote up the specifics of when, where, and how many acres. You sound like you work for the government."

"I'm just confused. A plot of land might have been purchased in one county, and if the original county had divided, it would look as though the same plot of land was located in a different county. I want to be sure we're talking about the same man. How did a refugee who came here with little or nothing get enough money to own four plantations?"

"Well, most of the early history I used for my book came from John Wilson out in Fort Worth, Texas, a Dumas descendant who had researched the family for years—even looked up records in France personally. He eventually hired a big-shot genealogist in Virginia to research Unity Smith Dumas' line."

The big-shot genealogist, Dr. John Manahan, had determined that Unity was descended from some of the earliest settlers of the colony. He traced the ownership of the land that she and Jerome owned and followed it all the way back to the original owners from whom it had been inherited.

"So Jerome Dumas most likely acquired the land through his wife, as Unity's dowry. You could get in touch with John Wilson, or while you're in Virginia, talk to his expert in that neck of the woods. You keep on checking those records, and I'll bet you a sugar cookie that's what you'll find."

I was satisfied with Carine's answer, but on the chance that they might supply additional background, I jotted a note to contact John Wilson in Fort Worth and Dr. John Manahan at the University of Virginia at Charlottesville.

Moving from the archives to the library, security was every bit as stringent. As a visitor I signed in, passed through an alarm device, and could still only access the reading room; the staff retrieved and returned books to the out-of-sight shelves. The precautions enhanced my feeling of time warp, and as I submitted request slips for books about the Manakin settlement, I imagined literally retracing the family's path as they moved into a new world. Every volume was tracked continuously. The books' apparent value enhanced the significance of the information they held.

Passenger lists of four ships of Huguenot refugees that arrived in Jamestown on July 31, 1700, revealed that Jerome Dumas was one of 207 passengers aboard the *Mary and Ann*. Taking myself back to 1700 in my mind to see what my ancestors saw on arriving in Virginia, I imagined the settlement of Frenchmen at the Manakin tribe's deserted village, the largest group of Huguenot refugees in Virginia and in America. The English never referred to the refugees as Huguenots, however; they were always called French Protestants. The settlers began with little more than their faith and hope for a bright future, as well as the generosity of the English, who provided beginning help, but expected the Frenchmen to pull their own weight to sustain themselves.

Benjamin Dumas I, the first Dumas son born in America, would have become well-acquainted with the Manakin settlement in Virginia while growing up nearby. Although he lived with his parents in the English settlement, his Faure cousins were in Manakin. When he began to see the need for an additional home for more religious refugees, the prospective use of another village left behind by Indians would have been a natural inspiration. It's easy to imagine what he thought when he heard his brother-in-law, John Clark, describe the long-deserted native American site at the Forks of Little River in North Carolina.

According to R. A. Brock in *Huguenot Emigration to Virginia,* the placement of the Huguenots' settlement in Virginia had been in itself a contentious issue. The Frenchmen had understood, or misunderstood, that they would arrive in the New World to find a French-speaking colony "betwixt Virginia and Carolina." Instead, in a political maneuver, Lieutenant Governor Francis Nicholson and the powerful colonist Colonel William Byrd I arranged for them to be placed farther west, up the James. Their intentions might have truly been to avoid sending the Frenchmen to low, swampy land with "moist and unhealthful" air, where they would meet an almost certain death. Still, the assigned substitute location, which was conveniently situated like a protecting buffer between the English settlement and the natives, hardly seemed any safer. The Frenchmen were even less pleased when they learned that Colonel Byrd profited handsomely by putting them on land that he himself owned.

The divisive issue of whether they were a distinct and separate colony was soon settled by an order of King William III that prohibited the refugees from using the term "colony." The Huguenots were also instructed to use only the English language in official business, and eventually, they were forbidden to conduct church services in their native French tongue.

Regardless of the disagreements, most of the French settlers, especially the young people, were eager from the beginning to become integrated into the English colony, and many of them, such as Jerome Dumas, found a marriage partner among the English.

One of the titles I requested in the library was an article from an old issue of *Harper's Magazine* that had a reference to a settler at Manakin who was from Saintonge, the province where Jerome Dumas' family had lived. When I went to the desk to pick up my selections, I noticed that the publication date was indeed April 1857, and not a misprint as I'd supposed. The personal account, passed down through descendants of a French family, had taken place nearly two hundred years before the issue of the magazine was published.

"The Story of a Huguenot's Sword" story began in Saintonge, the province of my ancestor, and I imagined it could have been near the actual Dumas home.

On the evening of Palm Sunday of 1684, the year preceding the revocation of the Edict of Nantes, about a dozen men had gathered in the province of Saintonge for a religious service conducted by Jacques de la

Fontaine, a young minister. Beside him stood his friend, Barthelemi Dupuy, in the uniform of an officer in the Royal Guardsmen of his Majesty Louis XIV.

A short time after the meeting, on information supplied by a man named Agoust, Fontaine was arrested and thrown into prison for heresy.

After numerous delays, Fontaine's trial finally came before the Seneschal of Saintonge, whose justice regarding Huguenots was less than evenhanded. The story became a battle between Fontaine's advocate, or attorney, and the accuser Agoust. Fontaine's advocate, who was sympathetic to the Huguenot cause, a dangerous position for an attorney to take, finally arranged for Fontaine's case to be presented to Parliament, a more impartial court. On hearing the advocate's compelling arguments, Parliament ordered Fontaine's release.

Fontaine's friend, Dupuy, waited at the gate with inside information that Louis XIV had decided to repeal the Edict of Nantes. The dragonnades began immediately, and the first targets were provinces of Huguenot strongholds.

The troops descended like an avalanche on the province of Saintonge. As the company of dragoons burst into the courtyard of his home, Dupuy pushed Fontaine into a hidden closet. The dragoons had broken down the entrance and the captain was shouting that he had come to arrest Dupuy as a heretic.

"You will do nothing of the sort," said Dupuy, reaching for his sword. He held a strip of parchment toward the officer. It contained this message:

These to our well-beloved guardsman, Barthelemi Dupuy, who has an amnesty granted him, with all his household, until the first day of December; any annoyance of Seigneur Dupuy will be at the peril of the officer who commands it. Such is our royal will, and, moreover, we pray our trusted friend Dupuy to abjure his heresy, and return to the bosom of the Holy Church, in which alone is rest.

Done at Versailles this 30th October, in the year 1685.
LOUIS

When the captain's eyes reached the signature and seal, he angrily handed the paper back to Dupuy and reluctantly ordered the dragoons to leave. Dupuy bolted the door and rushed up the stairs to release Fontaine, who would go at nightfall for his fiancée and his orphaned niece.

At twilight on the next evening, Fontaine, with his niece in front of him on the saddle, clasped the hand of his fiancée on her own horse; they bowed their heads in prayer and headed into the darkness.

On the afternoon of November 30, 1685, the last day of his amnesty, Dupuy sent for Agoust, Fontaine's accuser. Dupuy proposed to sell his home at a quarter of its value. Agoust agreed immediately, knowing that if he informed on Dupuy's plans to escape, the fine chateau would be escheated to the crown and out of his grasp. Agoust returned in an hour with a heavy bag of gold. As soon as Agoust departed, it was time for the village tailor to arrive. Dupuy had ordered him to have readied in six hours the complete costume of a gentleman's page.

When the tailor disappeared at the gate, Dupuy called urgently for his wife, Susanne.

"Quickly! Take your jewels, your Bible and psalms book, while I arm myself. We must be far away before morning if we would escape with our lives!"

Dupuy took a last look at the portraits of his ancestors before lifting his wife, disguised as his page, into the saddle and vaulting onto his own horse. In another instant, they had disappeared into the forest toward the border.

The captain of the dragoons followed them in rapid pursuit, taking a shortcut to the path he knew they must take. As he met them, their horses at full gallop, he drew his pistol and fired at Dupuy. The shot missed Dupuy and struck Susanne full in the breast. She reeled in the saddle and fell forward on her horse's mane.

With the power of anger and adrenaline, Dupuy leveled his pistol at the captain, striking him in the heart. Dupuy grabbed her horse's bridle with his left hand, drew his sword, and passed through the dragoons.

Susanne raised herself erect and took from her bosom the last item she'd grabbed on their rushed departure—her psalms book. The bullet had struck the book, and she was unhurt.

They faced a hard ride to the border, leaving behind their homeland, never to see Saintonge again.

Saintonge. The same province the Dumas family had called home. The boy Jerome Dumas had escaped from this same place at the same time, at the revocation of the Edict of Nantes in 1685. Their hoped-for destination, Switzerland, would have been the same. All who made the desperate dash for freedom breathed the same air fraught with danger.

When through the deep waters I call thee to go,
The rivers of sorrow shall not overflow;
For I will be with thee, thy troubles to bless,
And sanctify to thee thy deepest distress.
The soul that on Jesus hath leaned for repose,
I will not, I will not desert to his foes.
The soul, though all hell should endeavor to shake,
I'll never, no never, no never forsake.

"Bellevue" #72b in *The Sacred Harp*
Words, *Rippon's Selection*, 1787; music arr., Z. Chambless, 1844

CHAPTER 17

The Advocate

EARLY on a Wednesday morning, long before the appointed time with my Huguenot Society sponsor, Miss Elizabeth Salle, I arrived at the Manakin church with my camera and extra rolls of film. I turned into a wide drive at a sign that said, "Manakin Episcopal Church, established 1700." The Earth had not yet thrown off its blanket of fog and frost covered the ground in a cold winter scene of dormant grass and leafless trees.

After parking my car out of camera range, I walked back toward the road, the lawn's icy surface crunching softly beneath my feet. The present-day Manakin church was housed in a graceful red brick building tucked in a clearing of heavily wooded bottomland near the James River. To the right of the main entrance, a covered walk led through a courtyard and under a series of arches to classrooms, offices, and the parish house. The deep green foliage of a large magnolia complemented the warmth of the brick, and a tall bell shelter at the entrance to the walled garden of gravestones stood like a shepherding pastor with his flock.

A car drove into the parking area near the entrance and blocked my composition. A man got out, waved a greeting and paused to wait as I walked toward him. I introduced myself and said I was to meet Miss Elizabeth Salle in a short while.

"I know. I'm James Salle, Miss Salle's nephew. We've been looking forward to meeting you. I'm early, too. I came to show you around. You don't want to miss seeing—well, I won't say any more. You must see. I'll go get the keys."

I took pictures in the walled enclosure until James returned. We walked along the path past the main entrance where the sun shone its early rays on the east wall, defining a crisp, bright line at the corner of the building. We paused at the large monument commemorating the Huguenots' settlement and contribution to religious freedom, then continued on a path through the forest of slender tree trunks until we approached a remarkable white frame structure. James identified it as the church's earliest building that was still standing.

A front extension of the small building was three-sided and was roofed with three peaks beneath the taller roof of the main structure. The sun reflected brightly off an angled front wall, accentuating the building's unique architecture. As we stepped into the reverent silence of the sanctuary, intense early morning sunlight streamed through the arched windows and the glowing hues brought to life a stained glass scene behind the altar. Its message was direct and gripping. This was what James had wanted me to see.

"It's called, 'The Sower,'" he said, "and it honors our first pastor."

In the depiction, the sower's robe and head covering followed a sweeping gesture of his arm as he cast seeds from a wide, flat basket. On his left, birds descended to devour seeds on rocky ground, while the path continued past stones and thorns to an open, level field.

"God answered our prayers and led us to the good soil," James said. "We are the seeds."

Absorbing the meaning of Jesus' parable, I walked to kneel at the altar. My heart was full of gratitude for the blessings I'd received from the sower's seeds. I prayed for spiritual growth and guidance, that I, too, might be fruitful. When I rose, I saw that James had knelt at my side.

I followed James back up the aisle and further up the shallow treads of a steep staircase. "Slaves were admitted as members, too, but they were made to sit here in the balcony."

James stopped at an old, but sturdy, straight-backed wooden pew placed against the rear wall. "This is the only pew that remains from our original church building. You've said you have ancestors from the beginning days of Manakin. Go ahead and take a seat. It might be the same pew where they once sat."

On our way back to the library, we entered the beautiful sanctuary of the present church. Walking down the center aisle, James pointed out small brass inscription plates on some of the pews. He stopped at the second row.

"Read it," he said.

The pew was dedicated to the memory of Jerome and Unity Dumas, a gift of Dr. John E. Manahan, the genealogist from the University of Virginia who had traced the family line.

Leaving the sanctuary, we walked past classrooms and parish offices to the section of the complex that housed the rare books and documents of the Huguenot Society of the Founders of Manakin in the Colony of Virginia. We were greeted at the door.

Miss Elizabeth Salle, petite and pleasantly soft-spoken, appeared to be about seventy-five or eighty years old. She understood that I wanted to make the most of our time in the library and promptly showed me to a modestly sized room—modest for a library, that is—which housed the prized collection. No one else was in the room. Miss Salle took a seat and pulled a needlework project from a large bag.

"Please ask me, if you need any help," she said.

I took a volume from the shelf, *Huguenot Emigration to America,* by Charles W. Baird. He said the Huguenots loved to sing. Shortly before the revocation of the Edict of Nantes in 1685, two of their temples—the term church was reserved for the Catholic majority—were destroyed because of their music. A house of worship was demolished in 1682 because some of the Huguenots, on their way by boat to the service, had sung songs aloud. Another in the same province was destroyed in 1676 because the Protestant temple was too near the church of the sanctioned religion, and their psalm-singing disturbed the service of the mass.

As I continued scanning the shelves, a name beneath a title caught my eye. *Tale of the Huguenots, Memoirs of a French Refugee Family—from the original manuscript of James Fontaine, transcribed by one of his descendants.* I opened the small volume to see if there might be a Fontaine-Dupuy connection and read the introduction:

> Among the private documents of the family of this present writer, there has long been preserved with pious care a manuscript autobiography of one of its ancestors, who, as a persecuted Huguenot, endured much for his faith. The original work, which extended to several hundred pages, was written in the French language, without any view to publication. . .

I turned to the table of contents. Each chapter was summarized with generous detail and read like an outline, an easy way to read the whole story. Fontaine's personal account in chapter one painted an informative picture of the history of Protestantism. I watched for an indication that the writer might be an ancestor of Jacques de la Fontaine.

> Chapter II. James Fontaine—Called to the churches of Vaux and Royan…Summoned to appear before the governor for preaching on the ruins of the Church—A second summons—his Death.
>
> Chapter III. …In my father's steps—Schooling—My mother's death—Division of property.
>
> Chapter IV. …Protestants assemble in the woods—A spy watches—Warrants issued—Warrant against me.

Now I had no doubt. The writer could be none other than Jacques de la Fontaine himself. My eyes raced over the next lines.

Chapter V. ...Indictment against me—Examination of witnesses—Agoust...

I tensed when I read the name of the traitorous Agoust, the man who had betrayed the worshipers in Saintonge. The picture was eerily realistic, a picture sketched by another eyewitness, Jacques de la Fontaine, told in his own words. It was his personal testimony of the same events that Dupuy had passed on to his children. The same time, the same place, the same actors in the drama. I quickly found the nearest chair and skimmed the rest of the summary. The likelihood that I would find the particular volume I'd selected at random was too great to comprehend. I wanted to read the entire book immediately. I turned a few pages for a glimpse of this latest version of the disastrous event as it unfolded.

The church at Vaux was levelled with the ground, and most of the churches in our Province shared the same fate; thus my neighbors could not reach a place of worship without great fatigue; and feeling compassion for them as sheep without a shepherd, I felt myself called upon to invite them to join in my devotions.

Jacques said his neighbors came eagerly. They continued without interruption during the entire winter, "till Palm Sunday, 1684."

A miserable pettifogging [abjurer] named Agoust...lived within four hundred paces of a high road by which some of the men returned home from the meeting...It was impossible for him to recognize individuals at that distance, the service having continued till after dusk. Nevertheless, he made out a list of names, putting down some who were and some who were not there...and I [was] at the head...On the deposition of a single witness (a man of indifferent character at best) before the Seneschal of Saintes, warrants were issued against [me].

I was reluctant to put the book aside, and I turned a group of pages at once to see how the story advanced. A name jumped from the text: *Dumas. Jeremie Dumas, Advocate.*

This is a brief statement of facts, and the said Fontaine now proceeds to justify his appeal. In the first place, the testimony of a single witness is not sufficient under any circumstances, and the witness in question merely testified to seeing him on the highway, and not at the place of meeting, and confessed afterwards that he only thought he had seen him. A witness to be depended upon should speak with certainty, and not by *credit vel non credit* any more than hearsay. . . . The said Fontaine concludes that having made this just appeal, the former decision will be declared null and void.

Dumas, Advocate
Presented 6th August, 1684

Jeremie Dumas was the Huguenot attorney for Jacques de la Fontaine! I searched carefully for another reference to Jerome Dumas' father, but I found no other direct reference to his name, only to the "Huguenot advocate." The number of books in the library suddenly seemed overwhelming.

I was amazed and grateful for the discovery of a concrete moment in this family's life. I could see them caught up in issues of tremendous importance for the future—a future that would include our present generations—my own, as well as their own. It was like seeing this man's image flash briefly in a preview on a movie screen. Now I wanted to see the whole film.

After showing the book and what it held to Miss Salle, she said, "There are quite a number of these inspiring personal accounts," Miss Salle said. "But unless the writer was from the same town or village, as you happened to find, you would have less chance of locating your family before they left France. I seem to recall reading of a Dumas in Switzerland. You might take a look at some of the more general accounts in their destination city."

She helped me pinpoint on a map the town of Saintes in the province of Saintonge and of Lausanne in Switzerland, Jerome's first destination.

The books were old and typically lacked an index. In *History of the French Protestant Refugees,* translated from the French in 1854, I was reading of a fund to aid French Protestants that was set up in Switzerland by a Frenchman when Miss Salle walked to the section next to me and pulled a book off the shelf. She thumbed a few pages, closed the book, and replaced it in the slot. She frowned studiously, bent to the next shelf, and selected another book.

She read quietly for a moment, then placed the open book on the table before me. My eyes met her intent gaze that shifted to the open book, *The Huguenots in France after the Revocation of the Edict of Nantes,* by Samuel Smiles. Abandoning the French Fund, I began reading from the new-found text. Miss Salle returned to her needlework without a word.

The writer's words looked backward from a safer place in time. Smiles' book was published in 1874, more than two hundred years after the revocation that caused the Huguenot diaspora, yet accounts had endured of families caught in the dilemma. The Dumas home in Saintonge was near the sea and because sailing was a common mode of transportation, it was a natural avenue to safety. It was impossible to escape in a sizeable group, so the family developed plans with goals of mutual destinations, regardless of the route taken to get there. Even the best-laid plans held an unstated acknowledgement that any such attempt to escape was a no-alternative gamble to survive.

However, despite pre-arranged plans and contingencies, the Dumases had waited perilously long. Protestant advocates had been forbidden to practice law for some time. The sympathetic advocate, Jeremie Dumas, had long aided Huguenots caught in legal difficulties and had frequently defended Protestant pastors. He had contested measures that suppressed their congregations. For those reasons, he was suspected of being more than simply a sympathizer, and he was constantly watched for a betraying clue.

In early autumn of 1685, Jeremie Dumas, the advocate, and his wife agreed that the wilderness was a safer place for the children than the village. The dragonnades had already begun in the neighboring province of Poitou.

Their sons were to flee with their cousins, who were only a few years older, through the forests to the mountains, using streams as their guide. After quickly gathering the barest of essentials, the parents knelt with the boys between their embracing arms and asked for God's care and mercy to guide them to safety and eventual reunion with them. Jeremie had friends in Lausanne, Switzerland, the interim destination. They were to meet there as soon as possible.

He hurriedly led the children along the river Charente to the forest and past the most imminent danger. When Jeremie was finally assured that they had eluded pursuit and were headed in the right direction, he instructed them how to best move on unobserved, spending daylight hours in barns or haystacks or forest caves. He cautioned them to stay out of sight and concentrate on survival. The boys were full of excitement and adrenaline, anxious to get on with their adventure.

Fontaine had mentioned "difficulties and dangers" of his escape, but the difficulties he encountered on the sea would have been far different than those that the boys, Jerome and Jean Dumas, and their Faure cousins would have faced. The children had fled through the mountains of the Cevennes with winter approaching. It was indeed a miracle that they survived and eventually reached Lausanne.

Jeremie Dumas, the advocate, returned home to unimagined horror. He found his wife and family murdered in the smoldering ashes of their home. He turned immediately to retrace his steps to overtake his young sons.

They were among a seemingly endless flow of refugees. The number of new arrivals in Lausanne increased daily, and many of the new arrivals were preachers who took to the streets with impassioned speeches. Lausanne was overwhelmed.

Jeremie Dumas thought first of attempting to work and provide in the only way he knew how, as an attorney. But he soon gave up that objective and devoted himself to the more immediate needs of the Huguenots. He served on a committee that facilitated the settlement of the refugees or helped them proceed to another destination.

I had just finished reading that the French Fund was depleted and money was scarce. Most of the refugees came with nothing but the clothes on their backs, and no one could have imagined the sheer number of refugees. According to John H. Wilson's research in *The Dumas Families, Volume I, Jerome (Jeremiah) Dumas,* this was the time when Jeremie Dumas, who was immersed in working to aid the refugees, traveled to Frankfort to solicit funds, and his sons went with their Faure cousins from Frankfort to London.

In the book Miss Salle had handed me, Smiles said that an unsigned letter was made public in Lausanne that stated positions critical of the pastors who had deserted their flocks:

If instead of retreating from your persecutors, you had remained in [France]; if you had risked your lives to instruct and lead the people; if you had exposed yourselves to martyrdom— as in fact those have done who have endeavored to perform your duties in your absence—perhaps the examples of constancy, or zeal, or piety you have discovered might have invigorated your disciples, renewed their courage, and arrested the fury of your enemies.

The pastors protested. If they were to take this advice, they would return to be executed. The letter writer was not a pastor; it was easy enough for him to be bold. A minister wrote in his own defense, "You who condemn the pastors for not returning to France at the risk of their lives, why do you not first return to France yourself?"

Jeremie Dumas, the advocate, knew the issue would never leave him. The letter's reproach spoke directly to him and he vowed to devote himself to God's path for his life, dedicating the remainder of his days to the consolation of the Shepherd's wandering sheep. Jeremie Dumas answered his high calling, continually tracked by spies of his enemies. He was hunted from place to place by the troops of the King Louis XIV, who followed him into the most remote and inaccessible places. According to Samuel Smiles in *Huguenots in France after the Revocation of the Edict of Nantes:*

> In the year of 1690, Dumas was apprehended in the Cevennes, thrown on his back across a horse, and fastened by the troopers to be taken to Montpelier to be executed. His bowels were so injured and his body so crushed by the manner in which he was conveyed that he died before he was half way to the customary place of martyrdom.

By the year 1700, Jerome, the younger Dumas son, and his cousin, Jean Faure, had become as English as any two boys in London's community of French Protestants could become. The two cousins were both still unmarried, and their education and training had recently been completed. Their hazardous journey as children from their home in France had given them sufficient confidence and experience to join the group of Huguenots being assembled to emigrate to the Virginia Colony in America. Their ship, the *Mary and Ann*, sailed under the Marquis de la Muce and arrived in Jamestown on July 31, 1700.

Following the account, Smiles stated that the French Protestants were given land for a settlement along the James River at a location that had once been an Indian village, long since deserted by the Manakin Tribe. "Among the settlers at Manakintowne were Barthelemi Dupuy and his wife (his one-time page), and Abraham Michaux and his wife, she being the former Susannah Rochette, who had made her first voyage in a barrel."

The Frenchmen brought with them their psalms books, psalters, and melodies to join other voices and sing a new song in a new land.

There is a land of pure delight, where saints immortal reign,
Infinite day excludes the night, and pleasures banish pain.
Could we but climb where Moses stood, and view the landscape o'er,
Not Jordan's stream, nor death's cold flood, should fright us from the shore.

"Jordan" #66 in *The Sacred Harp*
Words, Isaac Watts, 1707; music, William Billings, 1786

PART FOUR

■

EARLY JAMESTOWN COLONISTS

The tower entrance to the church at Jamestown
was added between 1639 and 1647.
The tower is the oldest portion of the present
church. (1991 photograph by the author.)

EARLY JAMESTOWN COLONISTS

ca. 1680
UNITY SMITH DUMAS born in Jamestown, Virginia; ca. 1702 married
Jerome Dumas in Virginia, who had arrived in Jamestown from
London in 1700 with other Huguenot refugees; October 10, 1703,
their first child was baptized in St. Peter's Church, New Kent
County, Virginia; died between 1628 and 1634
Children: Mathen, Benjamin (I), Jeremiah, Sarah, Temperance.

ca. 1660
MARY WHITE SMITH born in Jamestown, Virginia; ca. 1679 married
George Smith in Virginia; died before 1691
Children: Unity, Esther

ca. 1640
MARY CROSHAW WHITE born in Jamestown, Virginia; ca. 1658
married Henry White in Virginia; died after 1671
Children: William, Mary, Unity, Rebecca

1619
ELIZABETH YEARDLEY CROSHAW born in Jamestown, Virginia; ca.
1637 married Joseph Croshaw, son of Captain Raleigh Croshaw/
Crashaw (pronounced "Crah-shaw") in Virginia; died prior to 1660
Children: Mary, Unity, Rachel, Benjamin, Joseph

1588
LADY TEMPERANCE FLOWERDEW YEARDLEY born in Norfolk County,
England; 1618 married Sir George Yeardley in London
shortly after he was knighted by King James (I) and appointed
governor of Virginia Colony; died in 1628 in Jamestown, Virginia,
surviving her husband by only one year
Children: Elizabeth, Argoll, Francis

CHAPTER 18

Stranger in a Foreign Land

MOTHER had noticed another change in her vision. Because she had no sight in her left eye, the progression of macular degeneration in the right eye demanded immediate attention. She was referred to a specialist in Dallas for laser surgery to save any peripheral vision, and in the aftermath she retained only a sliver of sight in the right eye. Changes must be made. I considered how to approach the subject, but Mother's thinking was always a step ahead.

"Now, don't you start on me, too. I know what I can and what I can't do," Mother said. "What I can do is get around in this old house. We've lived here since Eisenhower was president, and if I don't know every nook and cranny by now, it isn't going to be known. There's still a little bit of sight, enough to get around when I already know exactly where to put my foot."

Mother was unwavering. "This home holds a lifetime of memories, everything that's good about living. Please don't ask me to leave. I can't drive. I can't read. I can't watch television anymore. I can't cook or do my gardening or my housework. I can't even do my handwork." A deep cough threatened to take control.

"Oh, Mother, you can still knit. I've seen you knit without looking at your stitches."

"Not knitting. I could once crochet without watching, but I haven't done any crocheting in years." She had left open a window of possibility.

The adjustment would be less stressful if Mother could stay at home. A companion was the most acceptable option. Louise, a longtime close friend, would help find someone to come, or she might stay occasionally herself. Mother's friends promised that her daily needs would be met. An agent of the Texas Society for the Blind brought advice for simplifying routine tasks and Mother would soon be receiving audio books through the mail. I understood why she wanted to stay; despite the tobacco smoke that permeated every room and triggered my allergies, I loved this house too. I had insisted that her smoking was the cause of her persistent cough, but she was unyielding in that it would clear up with first cool spell.

As I returned home, first to Atlanta and then to Richmond, I phoned Mother almost daily, always thinking of her seated for sightless hours in her chair by the window. She could no longer enjoy many pastimes including the window's pleasant view, so her interest in my historical searches had increased.

"It's like one of my soap operas," she said as she recapped the dramas of the multiple Jeremiahs and Benjamins. "Your centuries-old stories might even move a bit faster." She was eager to hear of each new revelation.

The Richmond winter seemed especially cold and long to a southerner who thought of Virginia as "up north." It would be a late Easter, well into April, and as Palm Sunday approached I looked forward to returning to warm Georgia and later to the unpredictable weather of the Texas Panhandle.

We arrived in Atlanta late Thursday night and had been home only seconds when the phone rang. I was surprised to hear my brother's voice. John cautioned me to not be frightened, but he had to deliver some unwelcome news. Mother was all right, for the time being.

It was her lungs. The doctor had carefully outlined the treatment options. She had adamantly refused to go through chemotherapy and radiation. John said frankly that she couldn't survive the ordeal. The doctor gave a time frame of approximately three to five years.

The next week was brimful of necessary chores and errands in Atlanta; the must-do aspect was a blessing, for my mind needed rigid structure. As I tossed newspapers onto the recycling stack near the elevator, a headline caught my eye. An underprivileged area near downtown was being displaced by plans for the Olympics, and a group of residents was protesting. A face came to my mind, the young woman who had worked at the hotel down the street when we first moved to Atlanta. Arlette, I remembered. Could that be where she lived? I identified with the hardworking woman who had to support her young children alone. I, too, had been a divorced mother with two young children and, although my family and friends were supportive, I had experienced fears like Arlette in trying to provide a home. The world had problems. Atlanta, my community, had problems. I had problems. How could God hear all of us crying out at once?

The sun shone brightly on Easter Sunday, both in Atlanta and in Amarillo. When I arrived, Mother pointed to lilies on the dining table and the buffet. I was too distracted to give them more than a passing glance. Mother's oxygen tank was large and noisy, but she exclaimed again and again that it brought indescribable relief. It was placed in her bedroom between the closet door and the hallway. The oxygen line was long enough to provide access to the entire downstairs.

"We never did get around to closing off that hallway to enlarge the bath," Mother said. "I guess the good Lord knew we'd need it set up exactly this way."

I felt guilty for my years of complaints about her smoking. I recalled one particularly vitriolic outburst after my eyes began to water and itch immediately upon arrival at her house. In the smoke, my eyes soon began to swell painfully, and when they were almost swollen shut, I cursed angrily and slammed the back door as I retreated to the backyard. She would have seen me from her favorite window, and I wondered how deeply my angry words had hurt her. She forgave me quickly, but the words had been said and could not be erased from my memory. Now, my anger was no longer directed at her, but at the tobacco industry.

Mother could disconnect the oxygen line for brief periods and she had a small tank for outings to the grocery store or salon. Within a few days, I was comforted to see that she had managed to continue her life in much the same long-established order. The changes that now seemed so rapid had progressed gradually and subtly. Doug had recommended that I stay in Texas as long as I was needed, but Mother insisted she didn't need the help yet.

"You'll be back in a few weeks. You have to get to the bottom of those stories you've been tracking. I want you to get busy and write all this history down. That's what you can do for me. I'd like for you to read it to me before the Lord calls me home."

Doug had been out of town all week and arrived in Atlanta a short while after I returned. We felt a great need to be home for the weekend, to be in our church on Sunday morning to drop anchor and feel safe. As we sat quietly listening to the prelude music, I longed to be more completely part of Second Ponce de Leon Baptist Church and our still-new community. I glanced through the printed announcements and saw a notice for an upcoming prayer breakfast. Former President Carter would address poverty-related problems in Atlanta. I looked at Doug and pointed to the item. He nodded his head, which I knew was agreement for me to make reservations.

He planned to tie up loose ends in Richmond over the next several weeks. I would go with him, for I knew it might be my last opportunity to have direct access to the rare books and historical documents relating to the early years in Jamestown.

On reporting the latest findings to Carine, she said, "You've learned only half of the story. Yes, Jerome came to an English world, but what about our English ancestors? Have you talked to John Wilson or the Virginia genealogist?"

When I phoned Mr. Wilson in Texas, he said he'd be happy to go over his research material with me the next time I planned to visit my daughter Elise in Fort Worth, which would not occur for several months.

I tried to phone Dr. Manahan on Monday after we returned to Richmond. There was no residential listing in his name in Charlottesville. When I called the University of Virginia campus, I was transferred several times as they sought information about him. Finally, I reached someone in the history department who had known the eccentric former professor. She told me regretfully that Dr. Manahan had been deceased for more than two years, since March of 1990. My questions came too late. But the work he'd left behind was invaluable.

When I'd made my most recent visit to the Huguenot Society of Founders of Manakin in the Colony of Virginia's library, I had returned to Richmond by a route through Goochland County, where Jerome Dumas' estate had been recorded after his death in 1734. Because he had owned a plantation in Goochland County when he died, it seemed logical that it had been the place of Jerome's last residence. A day trip to search recorded deeds in Goochland County might unearth fresh details.

I located the department at the Goochland County courthouse that housed the oldest records. Prior research cited in John Wilson's Dumas genealogy book had revealed that Jerome Dumas sold land there in 1729. The immense record book detailing the transaction, a typically cumbersome volume of its day, was in surprisingly good condition.

The first sentence threw me off track. Jerome was identified as "Jeromiah Dumas of the Parish of Saint Paul in the County of Hanover." Apparently, Jerome Dumas owned land in Hanover County, too; I would go there next. Jerome's signature on the Goochland County deed was recorded on the following page, although his own spelling of his name was, "Jeromay," indicating he used a French pronunciation of "Jerome." The deed of sale was for three-hundred-twenty-five acres. In the legal description of the Dumas property, one of the boundaries was worded, "parting this Survey and the Land of Captain Jefferson." As I continued reading the florid script, my eyes fixed on one word, a word Carine had used: *dower*. I read, "Unity, wife of the said Jeromiah (she being first privately examined) relinquished her *right of Dower* in the land by this deed . . ." Jerome Dumas' personally signed signature was again spelled, "Jeromay." But he was not the original owner of the land; it had belonged to his wife, Unity.

When I went to the copy machine, I asked the clerk if the Captain Jefferson mentioned as owner of the adjoining land might be related to Thomas Jefferson.

"Oh, but of course. Captain Peter Jefferson was the father of President Jefferson. You'll find other references to both of them here."

She took the book from me, referred to an index, and turned to page 142.

"Here's a recording giving power of attorney for Captain Peter Jefferson to William Randolph in 1735."

She then turned to one of the last pages in the book.

"On the fifth of August, 1799, Thomas Jefferson of Monticello in the county of Albemarle sold two tracts of land in Goochland County."

I made copies and took the book to a work table to examine it more fully and search for other Dumas deeds. I found that on the third of November 1744, *Benjamin Dumas* sold two tracts of land in Goochland County, 150 acres and 400 acres. The sale of the two plots of land provided at least part of the funds to begin the Huguenot refuge in North Carolina.

In skimming through the Dumas deeds and property boundaries, I found references to the name Clark, the maiden name of Benjamin I's wife, Frances. There was also a reference to a Moorman, the family name of their daughter-in-law, David Dumas' wife—the same "Old" Sarah who was Susannah's mother-in-law in Izzie's story.

The pieces dovetailed together nicely. These were ordinary people who were characters in factual history. Major events or shifts in direction are recorded as the work of a country's people as a whole, while the necessary contributions of individual citizens remain anonymous. The Dumases were neighbors on the James River with the Jefferson family. This was how President Thomas Jefferson had known from an early age of the Clarks' affinity for exploration.

Jerome Dumas owned four additional 400-hundred-acre tracts each in Hanover County and still more land in Louisa and New Kent counties. It was possible that some tracts were one and the same if the county had been divided. The parishes of the church also experienced divisions due to growth, which added another layer of confusion, but I felt more confident after seeing the actual Goochland County courthouse records. The Church of England, the Anglican Church, was the established state church and its parishes functioned much like our present day counties. The parishes were responsible for surveying land and collecting taxes, or tithes. Unfortunately for my searching purposes, the parishes and the counties did not divide simultaneously as they experienced growth. In 1729, Jerome Dumas lived in "the Parish of Saint Paul in the County of Hanover."

Hanover County was nearby, inviting another day trip, and when I went to look for the county's oldest recordings, I asked a clerk to also direct me to someone knowledgeable about history of the county.

"Mrs. Wickham is the one you need to see, Mrs. Lois Wingfield Wickham. She is the undisputed historical authority and knows everything there is to know about Hanover County."

I phoned Mrs. Wickham, expecting to make a weeks-off appointment. To my surprise, she spoke familiarly, as if she'd been expecting my call. She asked for the name of the ancestor I was tracing, and the dates that he lived in Hanover County.

She said, "I have to leave in a few moments to drop off some papers near the courthouse anyway, so go ahead with your search. I'll find you there. We'll verify your ancestor's location on the map, and then I'll give you a brief tour of Hanover County as we head towards your ancestor's land."

Mrs. Wickham breezed in like a fairy godmother, with county reference books in hand. She was blessed with an abundance of southern charm, and her enthusiasm for her chosen role as historical ambassador for the county was equally delightful. We stopped at a courtroom, where I listened in rapt attention to descriptions of Patrick Henry's rousing speeches. Mrs. Wickham's impassioned voice resounded in the empty courtroom, "Give me liberty or give me death!"

Her manner and voice suddenly changed. "I realize this was after the time you're interested in, but I want to point out that Studley, Henry's home, is right close to where the Dumas land was located, over by Polegreen's Field. We'll take my car, since I know the turns."

Mrs. Wickham knew the precise locations we were to go and she took the books with us only to jog her memory and verify dates.

"Now here's an entry where Jerome Dumas sent some corn to the church for the preacher's house. And he had an account for keeping somebody. You see, if they didn't put the unfortunate in the poor farm, they'd let them stay out with someone who could care for them, and the church would pay for their upkeep. The church was responsible for welfare in those days."

As we drove along, Mrs. Wickham's nonstop spiel contained more historical tidbits than I could absorb. "See that enormous tree? It was a sapling that served as a tent post for Tarleton's men. It still produces walnuts—two bushels last fall."

She changed subjects and time periods without warning. "The stream under this Totopotomoy Creek bridge we're crossing used to be a navigable river. Too much farming of tobacco filled up the river with sandy topsoil. The planters rolled their round hogsheads of tobacco to market at the wharf. The land sloped down to the river so it was easy to roll the heavy weight with gravity on their side. The trouble was that all that rolling to the river took the soil along with it, and the boats could no longer get to the wharf. Page's Wharf, later known as Hanovertown, was near the Dumas land. Page's would've been the capitol, but it lost out to Richmond when the ships couldn't come up here anymore."

"I don't know that the Dumas family actually lived on this plantation," I began, "Not always, anyway. I'm not sure where they lived. Jerome Dumas owned several parcels of land."

"Why, planters didn't generally *live* out where the planting was going on. The plantations were strictly business ventures. They cultivated as many tracts of land as possible. The planters carried on their business away from their homes—much like businesses have branch offices now. The families lived near each other in small settlements. That practice began for protection, of course, but everyone likes to socialize." Mrs. Wickham flashed an enchanting smile before quickly pointing out the distinctive peaked roof of a typical Virginia barn, somewhat like a capital *A*, with the legs of its lower portion widely splayed.

"Right in here is where marl was first put on fields to increase the yield— not only of tobacco, but of anything else they raised."

"Marl?"

"You've heard *Marlboro* I'm sure; it's a place with a certain type of rich soil. Marl is a type of fertilizer, something like peat moss, that has nutrients from blue-gray clays and fragments of old shells. Tobacco could deplete the soil rapidly. Growing tobacco was like growing money, but it demanded a lot of land and slaves, as well as a strong overseer for such a time and labor-intensive crop."

"It's hard to imagine Jerome Dumas owning slaves," I said.

"I can assure you, if he owned a plantation, he owned slaves."

A cloud suddenly darkened the bright mood of the day. Patrick Henry had been a slave owner. His inspiring quotes were overshadowed with visions of long hot days spent toiling in a tobacco field, overseen by a harsh task master.

I had trouble accepting Jerome Dumas as a slave owner, particularly an absentee owner on a *tobacco* plantation. To me, it was if he'd been growing opium. What kind of world was this in which he found himself? Resentment of tobacco and slavery again filled my mind and mood.

I intended to concentrate on positive aspects when I phoned Mother, but I couldn't avoid discussing the conflict Jerome must have faced when he arrived in Virginia.

When he married Unity, Jerome apparently married into considerable wealth. Miss Elizabeth Salle, my sponsor at the Manakin Huguenot library, had told me that the unmarried of the French new arrivals—both young men and young women—were highly sought after, and some of the country's greatest fortunes bear Huguenot names, such as Dupont, that began with such marriages. The Frenchmen, most of whom, like Jerome, had recently completed their educations in London and possessed more refined European manners than was customary in early Jamestown, were very attractive to the Virginians. To an heir or heiress, a lack of money was unimportant.

I found it hard to believe that Jerome would marry for money.

"How do you know that he did?" Mother asked. "You don't know anything about what made up Unity Smith Dumas. You need to learn her family's story."

It would be pointless to phone Carine. She would only advise me to look for church records. One of Mrs. Wickham's random facts occurred to me— that Saint Paul's parish was formed when Saint Peter's parish was divided in 1704. Jerome and Unity's first child was baptized at Saint Peter's in 1703, and they were in Saint Paul's parish the next year, a parish which later lost its records to fire. Still, I might find Unity's family in the old parish. Mr. Wilson and Dr. Manahan had said her father's name was George Smith.

I dug tediously the next weeks through records at the Virginia State Library and Archives and at Saint Peter's vestry books. After chronologically arranging known information, I was finally able to place real people in a related time line.

George Smith, Unity's father, was indeed in Saint Peter's parish of New Kent County. He was in Virginia as early as 1652, when he received land from the Indians. He was consistently involved as a vestryman in the parish until notes of the vestry meeting of November 1691 recorded that he had died.

Unity, the young daughter he left behind, inherited tracts of land from both her father's and her mother's families. As she approached adulthood, her circumstances were far different from those of the man she was to marry. In 1691, Jerome Dumas had been an orphaned refugee with many other French Protestants in London. How challenging it must have been for Jerome and Unity to see heart to heart.

Unity had grown up as a member of the church of St. Peter's parish, where she and Jerome were married in 1702. St. Peter's might also have been the church of William Byrd II, son of the powerful William Byrd who placed the Huguenots at the deserted Manakin Indian village, who mentioned a singing school at the church in his diary in 1710. He gave few details of the music, other than learning to sing psalms, but we may safely assume that Unity and Jerome might also have found a mutual interest in singing psalms. Their son, Benjamin Dumas I, took English psalters and psalms books with him to North Carolina. English psalms tunes had been greatly influenced by the French from the time that congregations were first allowed to sing. A tune originally used for the French version of Psalm 134 did not fit English words for that psalm, but instead, became the

This Indenture made the fourteenth day of May MDCCXXIX between Jeremiah Dumas of the parish of Saint Paul In the county of Hanover on the one part and Thomas Prosser of the same parish and County on the other part Witnesseth that the said Jeremiah Dumas for and in consideration of five shillings sterling to him in hand paid by the said Thomas Prosser the Receipt whereof he doth hereby Acknowledge hath bargained and Sold and Doth hereby bargain and Sell unto the said Thomas Prosser all that his Tract of Land of Three hundred and Twenty two Acres Situate lying and being in the parish of King William in the County of Goochland bounded as followeth (to wit) begining at a black Oak thence Running thence North West Thirty six poles to a corner Hickory on the line of John pleasants Thence on his lines West Sixty poles to a black Oak thence South fourty poles to a White oak, thence West one hundred and Ten poles to a black oak Thence South Eighty poles to a white Oak thence West one hundred fifty Eight poles to a black Oak Thence North West by North Thirty six poles to a corner Seadar on the upper broad fork of fine Creek thence up that Creek as it Coudeth to the mouth of a Meodow branch parting this Survey and the land of Capt. Jeffersons thence up that branch as it Coudeth to a corner black Oak Thence on Jeffersons line South Twenty six poles to a black Oak Thence South Sixty seven Degrees East fifty Eight poles to a black Oak thence North Seventy Two Degrees East Two hundred and Eighty Eight poles to a Thence North one hundred and Twenty poles to the begining and the Reversion and Reversions Remainder and Remainders together with ye Rents and profits of the premisses and Every part and parcel thereof to have and to hold the said Three hundred and Twenty two Acres of Land and all and Singular other the premisses and Every of their Apurtenances unto the said Thomas Prosser his Executors and Assigns from the day next before the date hereof for and During the Term of one whole year from thence Next Insuing and fully to be Compleated and Ended yeilding and paying therefore the Yearly Rent of one graine of Indian Corn at the feast of Saint Michael the Arch angel only if the same be demanded to the Intent that by vertue of these presents and of the Statute for Transferring Uses into possession the said Thomas Prosser may be in the Actuall possession of the premisses and be Enabled to accept a grant of the

Goochland County deed showing Jerome Dumas land sharing a boundary with Captain Peter Jefferson, father of Thomas Jefferson. The Dumas children grew up in the same social and political climate, struggling with the same issues, as the future president.

Distinctive music notation from the Marot Psalter of 1681 showing the original French tune for Psalm 134, the same tune of the English "Old 100th" tune, which most of us know as the "Doxology." The size of this psalter book is approximately 5" x 6.5". Its hefty thickness of three inches or more gives credence to the story of a similar psalter stopping a pistol shot. (Photo courtesy of Bowld Music Library, Southwestern Baptist Theological Seminary, Fort Worth, Texas.)

"Psalm C" ("Old Hundred") in English language for four voice parts. Music notation is from Book of Psalmody, ninth revision, 1792; collected by Rev. John Chetham. (Photo courtesy of Bowld Music Library, Southwestern Baptist Theological Seminary, Fort Worth, Texas.)

tune for the English Psalm 100—"Old Hundred" #49t in *The Sacred Harp*. To this day, we continue to sing the same French tune known widely as the Doxology.

The plantations that Unity inherited were already productively established, and institutions were already entrenched. I wondered what, or if, Unity thought of slavery. Her earliest memories would have been that she was cared for by slaves. That was the world into which she had been born.

Unity and her new husband shared a land boundary on the James with Peter Jefferson, the father of the author of our Declaration of Independence. They raised their children in the same environment that influenced Jefferson as he first began to contemplate freedom, justice, and equality for all. He became known as the foremost advocate of liberty. Yet he owned slaves. How could the lofty ideals that make America great co-exist with an economic system that denied basic freedoms to the laborers who sustained that economy?

In an effort to understand the conundrum, I turned to Jefferson himself. Interestingly, at that moment more than two hundred years after he'd penned the immortal document, Jefferson's thoughts on slavery and his private double life in fathering children by a slave were being heatedly debated. I read numerous books about Jefferson and listened to arguments from those who viewed him as near a god and from those who would judge an entire life on the lapses in judgment of a man with feet of clay.

Thomas Jefferson first mentioned "equality of all men" in his defense of a mulatto slave who sued for his freedom in the 1770 case of *Howell v. Netherland*. The mother was white and free; the father was a black slave. At the time, Virginia law said that a child would have the same status as his mother.

His wife's inheritance made Jefferson the wealthy owner of land and slaves, some of whom were Mrs. Jefferson's half-sisters and half-brothers. Thomas Jefferson's slaves were part of the family. Did that affect his attitude toward miscegenation?

Why did he—and Jerome Dumas—not set his slaves free and treat them as ordinary servants? After months of reading books about Jefferson and slavery, I eventually accepted that slavery in his time was an issue over which he had little or no control. The slaves at Monticello did not belong to him alone. Because the slaves had been inherited by their wives, neither Jefferson nor Dumas had sole ownership or sole control. Slaves were wealth. Jefferson and Dumas lacked the right to dispose of family property.

However, they were responsible for the slaves and responsible to God. To a man of conscience, responsibility could be a heavy burden. There seemed to be no satisfactory answer for Jefferson or the rest of the world to the thorny question of slavery. If he hoped that as president he could make slavery illegal within the Louisiana Purchase, the entire economic system would have to be changed.

As the reason for not selling his slaves, Jefferson said it was "for their sake, not my own . . . [I] shall try some plan of making their situation happier." He called the issue a "wolf by the ears." To release the grip would mean to be devoured. It was an issue he was never able to resolve.

Jefferson counted the abolishment of the slave trade from outside the borders of the United States as one of the major achievements of his presidency. He renounced slavery as an institution, yet he continued to be a slaveholder all his life.

But what were the views of Jerome Dumas regarding slavery? Mother reminded me to look to the evidence Jerome left behind. His son's life demonstrated what Jerome had taught him. His lessons were personal and urgent.

Benjamin Dumas I, first son of the Dumas family line born in the New World, had doubtless heard from his father's lips the first-person account of his escape from France as a child from the massacres after the revocation of the Edict of Nantes. Jerome Dumas would have surely related the story of how his mother and siblings lost their lives and of his father's subsequent martyr's death. He would have stressed to his son the plight of fellow Frenchmen who would never again see their homeland.

Jerome's son, Benjamin Dumas I, also listened to a call to go to a foreign land, a village long deserted by Native Americans at the fork of two rivers. He sold his Virginia plantations, gathered his Margent Bible, his psalms books and psalters of fasola music, and moved his entire family to North Carolina and a new beginning.

> *On Jordan's stormy banks I stand, And cast a wishful eye*
> *To Canaan's fair and happy land Where my possessions lie.*

"The Heavenly Port" #378 in *The Sacred Harp*
Words, Samuel Stennet, 1787; music, Edmund Dumas, 1859

CHAPTER 19

The Sea Venture

AFTER absorbing the story of Jerome Dumas and the families of his son and grandsons, I was ready to address Carine's challenge to learn the other half of the story—Unity Smith Dumas' family. I expected to find very little information from the seventeenth century, certainly no personal details, about ordinary people. However, the will of Unity's grandfather, Henry White, recorded in York County, January 10, 1672, provided a glimpse of a man who seemed to possess a sense of humor.

Among the unquestionably valuable goods and property bequeathed to Henry White's beneficiaries was a gift to Major John West—"five pounds sterling to buy him a beaver hat." John West, White's brother-in-law, was one of the wealthiest men in Virginia.

White was apparently wealthy, too, and owned "branch office" plantations. He left the majority of his land holdings and a mill to his eldest son, Joseph, who was expected to provide for his widowed mother, Mary Croshaw White. The other four children were each given three-hundred-acre parcels of land. Henry White's will also granted early release to a young—though we don't know *how* young—indentured servant: "Whereas Mary Woods is bound for one and twenty yeares, that she be free at Eighteen."

At least part of White's land holdings were received at his marriage to Mary Croshaw from her father, Joseph Croshaw (sometimes spelled Crashaw; pronounced Crah-shaw). A deed in York County, dated 22 March 1659, but recorded on 10 September 1660, describes two parcels of land—two hundred acres and three hundred acres—given to Henry White and Mary Croshaw White, "providing Croshaw in his lifetime may build a mill on the three hundred acres, and after his death, the mill to revert to said Henry White."

Joseph Croshaw's father, Captain Raleigh Croshaw, came to Jamestown in September of 1608. He wrote an effusive poem in honor of his good friend, Captain John Smith, which Smith attached to his *General History of Virginia, Third Book.* Smith had great respect for Croshaw's knowledge of

Indian customs and warfare. He said Croshaw was on a trading mission on the Potomac in 1622 when he learned of the massacres that were meant to wipe out the colony, and almost did. Croshaw immediately challenged Opechancanough, chief of the Powhatan tribe, who was known to be a giant of a man, to fight him naked. The offer was not accepted, however.

Joseph Croshaw, who was first married to Elizabeth Yeardley and then four other wives, left a lengthy trail through courts of law, exchanging land and many hundred-pound units of tobacco. Educated in England, Croshaw was an attorney who was given to filing or being charged in one lawsuit after another. The second generation of colonists had already established a very litigious society.

I finally remembered the good advice to search the earliest records first. Over the next weeks, I read continuously in the Virginia Historical Society's collection of manuscripts and rare books searching for the earliest accounts of Unity's ancestors, Sir George Yeardley and Temperance Flowerdew. I found accounts of the same events from various people in the time of occurrence as well as from historical viewpoints. All the while, I tried to keep my mind focused on how George and Temperance were affected and what their perspectives might be.

The first mention of George Yeardley was about 1600 as a young Lieutenant Captain with England's troops in the Netherlands, as they fought against their mutual enemy, Spain and its king, Philip III. After Pope Alexander VI had in 1493 given the entire New World to Spain because of Columbus' discovery, England and most of the rest of Protestant Europe had thought there was surely enough land and trade to be shared. A major part of the competition for the New World was a religious struggle. With the Treaty of 1604-1605, England and Spain agreed to a tentative peace—peace on land, if not on the seas—and the soldiers came home from war.

James I had come to the throne after the death of Queen Elizabeth in 1603. The new peace with Spain and increasing world trade had built up a group of wealthy London merchants. In 1606, King James granted a charter to establish the Virginia Company of London with the intent of founding a colony in the New World. We know the story of the first settlers who left England in three small ships under the first charter of the Virginia Company of London in December of 1606, and we know of problems they faced. I'd essentially thought of the events as happening to storybook characters and failed to consider the basic reasons why they had come to the New World in the first place.

Trade and conquests of land were of primary interest to the stockholders of the Virginia Company of London, as well as the idealistic aim of planting

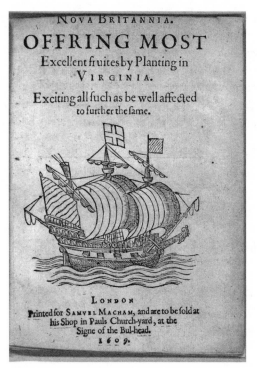

NOVA BRITANNIA.

OFFRING MOST

Excellent fruites by Planting in
VIRGINIA.

Exciting all fuch as be well affeǎed
to further the fame.

LONDON
Printed for SAMVEL MACHAM, and are to be fold at
his Shop in Pauls Church-yard, at the
Signe of the Bul-head.
1609.

"Nova Britannia" advertising poster of 1609. King James I of England granted a charter in 1606 to establish "The Virginia Company of London" allowing the sale of shares in a venture to found a colony in the New World. Investors' enthusiasm grew as the public saw advertisements such as this posted all over London and throughout England. (Photo of woodcut courtesy of Special Collections Research Center, Earl Gregg Swem Library, College of William and Mary, Williamsburg, Virginia.)

the principles of English thought and government in the new land. From the beginning, however, turning a profit, the foundation of capitalism, was the ultimate goal.

Enthusiasm grew as the public saw advertisements posted all over London praising "Nova Britannia." The Virginia Company of London's venture was widely promoted as an economic boon, and investors were so eager to buy into the opportunity that a second charter was soon necessary. The lure of easy money appealed to most young men who had no obligations to hold them back. Wealthy gentlemen simply bought their way onto the first voyages to Jamestown, but a crew of rougher, stronger seamen was also needed. We like to think of them as adventurous, and they were, but many were undisciplined, ruthless, and motivated only by greed and desperation.

George Yeardley was chosen by Sir Thomas Gates, his former commander in the Netherlands, to be captain of the military troops on the voyage under the second charter that was to take Gates, who was to be the new governor of the colony, to Virginia. Gates had seen his young captain in battle and was confident that Yeardley could command not only the company of soldiers, but also the unruly seamen who had signed on for the endeavor.

Yeardley was too young to have made a fortune of his own when he joined the Virginia Company of London. His father was a simple tailor and it was in that London tailor shop that George Yeardley, barely in his teens, first met Sir Thomas Gates. Yeardley was impressed with the military leader, and apparently Gates was also impressed with young George; Gates saw in him the potential for a great soldier. Yeardley had a naturally commanding appearance, a person whose presence was noticed upon entering a room.

With gloomy horrors overspread, though in the paths of death I tread,

My steadfast heart shall fear no ill, for Thou, O Lord, art with me still;

My noon-day walks He shall attend and all my midnight hours defend.

"Protection" #402 in *The Sacred Harp*
Words, Joseph Addison, 1712; music, C.F. Letson, 1869

But in 1609 the war with Spain was over, and a young man who had seen battle was likely to be ready for a new challenge. George Yeardley was naturally intrigued by the voyage to Virginia. The idea of sailing across the Atlantic to Jamestown was as exhilarating as an early space launch was in our time.

A few husbands brought their wives and children, but the majority of those who applied to go were unattached young men. An unattached young woman must have aroused a great deal of attention. Any young woman who would choose to take such a daring journey would be remarkable, but Temperance Flowerdew was not an ordinary young woman. She was the high-born, well-educated daughter of Anthony Flowerdew, whose grandmother was a half-sister to Amy Robsart, the ill-fated wife of Robert Dudley, Earl of Leicester, and intimate friend of Queen Elizabeth. Temperance's mother, Martha Stanley Flowerdew Garrett, was an investor in the Virginia Company of London, who could likely be seen at the theater waving her fan of white feathers and wearing the black velvet cape she bequeathed in her will to a prominent kinswoman in London.

Temperance sailed on the *Faulcon,* along with her older brother, Stanley Flowerdew. Stanley's presence would not be surprising, but curious onlookers might have wondered why Temperance was on the passenger list. However, if we were to observe Temperance and the young military captain, George Yeardley, I think we'd know why. He had duties to perform on the voyage, but they would be together when they reached Jamestown. Though the circumstances regarding when George and Temperance's relationship began and the specific date they married are unclear, my conclusions are based on facts and logic, based on their chidren's birthdates. It is reasonable to assume that Temperance did not go to Virginia to dig for gold.

The fleet of nine vessels consisted of the *Sea Venture,* the flagship carrying the new governor and his troops, and eight smaller ships—one of which carried, other than the crew, only livestock and pigs. They set sail from England with "the better part of five hundred people" in early June 1609, all well aware of danger if they confronted Spanish ships on the open sea. But the disaster they actually encountered was far worse than a threat of coming upon a Spanish ship.

The fleet kept together for fifty-two days, and they were within only seven or eight days of reaching Jamestown when they ran into a hurricane of historic force. The ships were separated. For five black days and nights, "in a hell of darkness," the crew on the ship carrying Temperance worked frantically in relays around the clock, pumping and bailing, while the water seemed to be gaining on them. Everything possible was thrown overboard to lighten the weight. They even considered cutting down the main mast. Many passengers despaired and turned to rum, drinking their last toast to one another until their reunion in a "more blessed" world.

Only seven of the original nine ships made it to Jamestown, and the crippled craft that did eventually limp into port brought none of the provisions that were desperately needed. They simply dumped on the struggling settlers their weak, hungry passengers, who possessed only tattered shreds on their backs. This was to have been the third supply voyage bound for the colony. To those in Jamestown, the arrival of more out-of-place "gentlemen" meant only more problems, more mouths to feed. What must they have thought when they saw the beautiful, disheveled Temperance walk down the gangplank?

Two ships were presumed to have gone down, including the largest in the fleet, the *Sea Venture,* which carried the new governor of the colony, Sir Thomas Gates, as well as the captain of his troops, George Yeardley.

I pictured Temperance waiting daily at the bleak shore, watching intently for a ship to appear that would bring George Yeardley to her. She had endured the hurricane and survived. All of her clothing and chests of household goods for setting up a new home, so carefully and lovingly packed for the voyage, had been thrown overboard. With each day's setting sun, her hopes and dreams slipped farther from any chance of fulfillment. The last two ships were finally given up as lost at sea.

When through the torn sail the wild tempest is streaming,
When o'er the dark wave the red lightning is gleaming,
Nor hope lends a ray the poor seaman to cherish,
We fly to our Maker, Save, Lord, or we perish.

"Save, Lord, or We Perish" #224 in *The Sacred Harp*
Words, Reginald Heber, 1827; music, M. Mark Wynn, 1869

We cannot know if Temperance believed in her heart that George Yeardley was still alive somewhere in the world, but we may safely assume that without him there was nothing of importance left for her in Jamestown. The colony had no food or warm clothes to face the approaching winter. Why would she—an attractive, young unmarried woman in a sea of virile men she didn't want—stay in the chaotic outpost? Under the circumstances, I am convinced that she would want to return home at the next opportunity, which did not come for months.

In early fall, while Captain John Smith was searching for a better site than the low marshland for the colony through the coming winter, a spark from a tobacco pipe ignited a bag of gunpowder in his boat. He was injured in the explosion so seriously that he was unable to move. He needed surgery, surgery that could not be performed in Virginia. Three ships were already making preparations to sail for England. He would go in one of them.

This had been the first opportunity for the distraught Temperance and her brother to return home. They most certainly would have taken it. I searched without success through every source available in Richmond for proof that they had been on the voyage with Smith. The staff at the Virginia Historical Society referred me to the library at the Maritime Museum in Newport News where the most extensive logs of ships were available. There, I confirmed that three ships made the voyage on which John Smith returned to England, but there was no individual listing for the passengers aboard. However, Stanley Flowerdew's will, written and probated in Scottowe, Norfolk County, in 1620 proved that Stanley had returned to England and died there, so we may safely assume that the siblings sailed together.

For months, nothing more was known of the fate of the *Sea Venture*. But because of a letter written by the secretary of the voyage, William Strachey, the world came to know what really happened. Strachey prefaced his letter to the Virginia Company of London: "A true repertory of the wreck and redemption of Sir Thomas Gates, Knight, upon and from the islands of the Bermudas, his coming to Virginia, and the estate of the colony then and after under the government of the Lord La Warre, July 15, 1610."

One ship did go down, the ship with the cargo of livestock. But the *Sea Venture* slammed aground onto the coral reefs near present day Bermuda. Gates, Yeardley, and the other men were marooned in alien waters, not on a regular British route, not even a route of the feared Spanish ships. There was no hope of rescue.

William Strachey had heard bizarre stories of the *Bermoothes*—tales of cannibals and ghoulish orgies. There is still an aura of mystery about the treacherous waters we know as the Bermuda Triangle where, into the present day, many ships and planes have disappeared. Their rescuers also have sometimes vanished without a trace. It is one of two places on Earth where a magnetic compass reads True North, not Magnetic North. The only other place where this occurs is the strangely similar Devil's Sea off Japan, which has likewise developed mysterious legends.

Fortunately, Gates and his shipmates found the "Isles of Demons" far more pleasant than their reputation, for they were forced to stay there nearly ten months. There was plenty of seafood, and they found wild hogs on the island. The spooky sound of "ka-hoo" was identified as coming from cahow pigeons, which were much larger than the rock pigeons of Europe and were found to be delicious when roasted or made into stew. For some strange reason, the cahows prowled at night and chanted their weird choruses only in the dark.

Through the fall and winter, the survivors built two smaller ships with bolts and beams and anything else they could salvage from the wreckage of the *Sea Venture* and with timber they cut from cedar which was plentiful on the island. They named the two new ships *Patience* and *Deliverance*. In the spring of 1610, they loaded ample stores of salted fish and pork, and crossed the seven hundred miles of ocean in two weeks to arrive in Jamestown on the tenth of May, almost a year after their departure from England.

The island survivors were shocked with the conditions they found in the colony. Despite being shipwrecked, the *Sea Venture* had fared far better than her sister ships. Since the incoming governor and official documents were in the missing ship, there had been no one among the newcomers to take over when Captain John Smith left for needed surgery. Confusion and dissension erupted. Until his injury, Smith had managed to hold the colonists in check for awhile, but when Gates and his company arrived no one was in charge.

Instead of an anticipated reunion with his beloved, George Yeardley's disappointment could only be assuaged with the comfort that she had not had to endure the winter called "the starving time" in Jamestown. When Smith left the colony in October, it had numbered about five hundred. When Gates arrived from Bermuda in May, he found only sixty survivors, who were scarcely able to move about the ruined village. The *Patience* and *Deliverance* brought food for their immediate short-term relief, but a rational appraisal of the situation brought a realization that there was no use in trying to get through the summer. The provisions would not last a month. With hearts heavy with discouragement and despair, they decided that Virginia must be abandoned.

On Thursday June 7, 1610, the cabins were stripped of everything that could be taken with them, a task left to Yeardley and his troops. His men were the last among the grief-stricken company to board the ships and return in utter failure to England. They weighed anchor and started down the river, stopping that night at Mulberry Island.

The next morning, they resumed making their way down the ever-widening James, but toward noon someone spotted a black speck on the eastern horizon. It was not an Indian canoe, as they first supposed. It was a longboat with a message that Lord Delaware was approaching with three well-stocked ships!

Lord Delaware and his fleet had already passed Point Comfort. After receiving the news from Captain John Smith that the *Sea Venture* was lost at sea, the Virginia Company of London had appointed Sir Thomas West, Lord Delaware, to be the new governor and to take replenishing supplies to Jamestown. On Sunday, Delaware stepped onto the shore, fell on his knees, and lifted his hands in prayer, thanking God that he had come in time to save Virginia. This date is the true first Thanksgiving in America, a full ten years before the landing of the Mayflower in 1620.

Because of his duties, George Yeardley was forced to remain behind in Virginia when Gates sailed back to England in the summer for a fresh supply of cattle. Accompanying Gates was William Strachey, secretary of the voyage, taking with them the first news that they had survived the hurricane and of their subsequent shipwreck.

A year had passed since Temperance had returned to her mother's home. George Yeardley must surely have wondered if, thinking he was dead, she had married another. He must have written to her, but if he did, his letter was for her alone.

William Strachey wrote the official report—and another letter, a personal letter. All England was fascinated with the story, and before the year was out, two narratives were printed, one of which was the official report published by the Virginia Company of London's council. William Shakespeare must have read these. King James himself was in the audience—perhaps on opening night on All Hallows Evening of 1611—of a new play by Master Will Shakespeare, *The Tempest*. It was most appropriate to the season. The plot concerned a shipwreck on a haunted island.

The similarities in some details of *The Tempest* and the published narratives have long been recognized. However, scholars believe that Shakespeare's most probable source of detail and inspiration was not just the official report, but Strachey's personal letter, which was not made public until fourteen years after the first performance of the play. Many words and incidents of the play that are also found in the letter do not appear in either of the earlier published versions, such as the parallel treatment of the apparition.

Because the letter was personal, it was seen only by an intimate circle. It was written to an unnamed "excellent lady," said to be an investor of the Virginia Company of London. It was likely that she attended Shakespeare's plays and/or was a confidante of Henry Wriothesley, Earl of Southampton, well-known as Shakespeare's principal patron.

No one knows the identity of the mysterious recipient, although Temperance's mother, Martha Stanley Flowerdew, fits the description. Because she had both a daughter and a son on the voyage, Martha might likely have received personal news. And because of the relationship of the daughter to the captain of the governor's troops, the letter was personally important to Martha and to Temperance.

We know that the unnamed lady showed the letter to some influential members of the Virginia Company of London's council because parts of it were incorporated into the company's official report. The Strachey letter was carefully guarded by the council, which means that the great playwright must have been on close personal terms with at least one of the councilors who had access to it.

Henry Wriothesley, Earl of Southampton, well-known as Shakespeare's patron, was on the council and was eventually elected treasurer, or chief executive officer, of the Virginia Company in 1620, replacing his friend and ally Edwin Sandys, who was George Yeardley's mentor. Hampton and Southampton are familiar place names in Virginia to this day. How could Shakespeare not have heard of the investor's daughter, a female survivor of the horrific storm? Perhaps he, as well as Southampton, talked to Temperance in person.

Temperance would have had much to relate.

> *There's nothing ill can dwell in such a temple.*
> *If the ill spirit have so fair a house,*
> *Good things will strive to dwell with't.*

William Shakespeare, *The Tempest* (1.2.457-459)

CHAPTER 20

The Year 1619

WHEN George Yeardley finally sailed into Jamestown harbor aboard the *Deliverance,* he learned from the remnant of Jamestown settlers that Temperance Flowerdew had miraculously survived the hurricane, but he had no way of knowing what had happened in her life since she'd returned to England. Regardless of the inclinations of his heart, Yeardley was a young soldier who couldn't desert his command and go chasing after his love.

Over the course of the next few years, Captain Yeardley impressed his commander and his employer, the Virginia Company of London. His future depended on the success of the Jamestown Colony. He could hope that Temperance would wait for him, but we have no way of knowing of personal correspondence between them or of what she said or did when she learned he was alive.

Yeardley made close friends among the Indians, particularly the Accomacks of the eastern shore along the Atlantic coast; theirs was an isolated region located on a peninsula that is separated from the rest of Virginia by Chesapeake Bay. Yeardley's friendship with Chief Debedevon, the "Laughing King" of the Accomacks, would later prove most fortuitous. Yeardley led a scouting party charged with determining whether gold or other precious metals might be mined in the New World. It was vital for the colony to find some way of supporting itself. The investors demanded a payoff. At the end of the first decade of settlement in Virginia, the colony was struggling and the Virginia Company of London was on the brink of bankruptcy.

After many trials and failures, the colonists eventually found a commodity that could be sold profitably in Europe, a crop that thrived in the virgin soil—tobacco. For the colony, it was a lifeline.

Tobacco. Like the apple in Eden, its choking, deadly roots were present from the beginning.

I was dismayed to learn how deeply George Yeardley was involved with encouraging his friend, John Rolfe, a fellow passenger aboard the *Sea Venture,* as he experimented with planting different varieties of tobacco, hoping to find a milder version than the harsh-tasting native tobacco the Indians smoked. Sir Walter Raleigh had introduced smoking in England on his return from the unsuccessful attempt at New World colonization during the reign of Elizabeth I, and although King James was disgusted with the "loathsome, filthie" habit, the fad had swept the country.

A supply ship arrived in January of 1614 with a report that tobacco shipped from Virginia the previous year had sold for an excellent price. The next crop was ready to load on the returning ship. The Jamestown Colony prospered by meeting the ever-growing demand, and Yeardley prospered handsomely as well. Tobacco was the key to riches, so it was the crop that every colonist wanted to plant—even to the neglect of their food supplies.

George Yeardley was appointed acting governor, and Virginia's tobacco exports went from 2,500 pounds in 1616 to 18,839 pounds in 1617. When his duties finally called him back to England in 1617, Yeardley was a celebrity. He was the hero of the investors, who credited him with multiplying their wealth enormously. He also found favor with King James, who knighted him in November of 1618 as Sir George and, with great fanfare and festivities, named him the new governor of Jamestown Colony.

However wildly exciting it was, there were protests in the opposition party within the Virginia Company of London. They thought that the king had lavished too much honor on the new knight, with fourteen or fifteen "fair liveries" following him in the streets. The core issue was that Yeardley had leaned suspiciously close to the political views of Sir Edwin Sandys, the treasurer, or president of the Virginia Company, who espoused policies that would have the colony become a republic.

By the end of November of 1618, the month Sir George had been knighted, he and Temperance were married. There has been speculation regarding the date of their marriage, but based on the dates their children were born, I conclude that it was near the time of his knighthood. On the Jamestown muster of 1624/25, the first comprehensive account of households in English North America, their daughter Elizabeth was six years old, so she was born sometime in 1619. Two younger sons were born in fairly rapid succession.

The couple had been separated by an ocean until Yeardley returned to England in 1617. And by January of 1619, the new Governor and Lady Temperance prepared to sail for Virginia, only a few weeks after the wedding that had been delayed almost a decade.

Lady Temperance had been to Virginia and would certainly have had her own thoughts about what to expect. Her new husband must have convinced her that Jamestown had changed and become a worthy home. However, when a comet appeared in the sky before they were to leave, their disastrous first voyage to Virginia could not have been far from their minds. Some took its appearance as a foreboding omen. The departure was delayed a week until it was decided that an omen does not necessarily portend evil. Perhaps it was a good omen. The comet stayed with them as they crossed the ocean and they arrived safely at Jamestown on April 19, 1619.

The new governor carried with him two of the most important documents in early American history. First was the "greate Charter," a commission of privileges, orders, and laws which was the earliest written constitution associated with the United States; and secondly, a commission to establish the General Assembly of Virginia, which became the first popularly elected legislative body in the New World. The colonists were being allowed a hand in governing themselves. The Great Charter commission, sometimes described as the real Magna Charta of Virginia, was issued November 28, 1618, purportedly the night a comet appeared in the sky.

> *Fair science her gate to thy sons shall unbar,*
> *And the east see the morn hide the beams of her star;*
> *New bards and new sages unrivaled shall soar*
> *To fame unextinguished when time is no more.*

"Murillo's Lesson" #358 in *The Sacred Harp*
Words, *Sacred Melodeon;* 1848; music, Morelli

Yeardley's first act as governor was to issue a proclamation calling for Virginia's first general assembly. It would consist of two representatives, or *burgesses,* from each hundred, or plantation, to be elected by its inhabitants to the House of Burgesses. This was the very first American election, and the two burgesses elected to represent Flowerdew Hundred were John Jefferson, an ancestor of Thomas Jefferson, and Edmund Rossingham, a nephew of Lady Temperance.

On the memorable morning of July 30, 1619, the burgesses assembled in the "quire" of the old church at Jamestown, an acknowledgement that music was a part of worship from the beginning. They bowed their heads while a prayer was said by the Reverend Richard Buck "that it would please God to guide and sanctifie the proceedings to His owne glory," and after each took the oath of supremacy, representative government in America was accomplished.

The year 1619 was a momentous year. Yeardley's administration was notable for three major achievements: the establishment of representative government, which was the foundation for our present-day democratic system; the establishment of the census and system for reporting births, deaths, and marriages; and finally, setting the monetary standard.

The standard was not based on gold, as I'd expected; *tobacco* was the currency.

Everyone wanted a money bush at the doorway. In every likely or unlikely place a tobacco plant sprouted. Smoking was seen as the height of sophistication, and a pipe was the indispensable fashion accessory for everyone. Small pipes were even made especially for children.

As my mother lay dying of lung cancer, I had to continually remind myself that the colonists did not know of tobacco's harmful effects. The seeds of addiction were sown with the seeds of freedom. The serpent's fangs sank deep into the flesh, and as I read on with a bitter taste in my mouth, I thought the irony could surely get no worse.

In less than a month after the historic elected assembly, a Dutch trading ship that had been ravaging the West Indies appeared at the mouth of the Jamestown harbor. It sent a messenger in a small boat asking permission to dock. They were short of supplies. After intense deliberations, Governor Yeardley accepted the ship's cargo—twenty starving Africans.

It is said that the Africans were accepted as indentured servants and that they were treated in the same manner as the indentured servants from England. The insidious difference was that the English servants came owing a debt for their passage to be paid with a term of service agreed upon in their indenture, but because the Africans had no indenture, their term of service had no end. Thus, Jamestown gave birth to the beginning of slavery in America—*when George Yeardley was in charge.*

The realization washed over me like burning acid. With my late-twentieth century hindsight, I could see that my task of following the Dumas family's journey was complete. I felt sick. There was no magic wand to whisk from my mind the bitter legacies of bondage brought by slavery and by tobacco. I'd lost sight of the good seeds.

In my stack of index cards, a single card remained with a notation from a footnote referring to a court case and a scandal regarding Lady Temperance. How much more degradation could be revealed? What difference could it make? I might as well look up the referenced source. It would be my last day at the library in Richmond.

The charge of slander in the court case was made in a diatribe against George and Temperance's son, Argall Yeardley. "His father did worke upon a Taylors Stall in London and his mother was but a common midwife—not to honourable women, but to *bye-blows.*"

Lady Temperance had defenders who vouched that she was a respected gentlewoman. I sought assistance at the research librarian's desk for the seventeenth-century definition of the word "bye-blow." I organized my notes until my name was called.

Lady Temperance had delivered bastards.

Time was brushed aside, and I saw Temperance as a woman who empathized with human misery. She was no longer the fair-haired, out-of-place maiden who walked proudly though unkempt down the gangway at Jamestown, a survivor of the tempest. She'd left England with the determined face of youth eagerly racing to live life to the fullest, and she'd returned to a subdued existence in her flamboyant mother's home.

The library had told me nothing about the lost years between Temperance's brief sojourn in Virginia and her marriage to George Yeardley. Almost a decade had passed since they'd first sailed from England with hopes of a bright future together. What had filled her time? Why would she become a midwife? And why would she reach out her ministering hands to only *illegitimate* children?

Temperance understood the plight of an unmarried mother. Suddenly, the puzzle pieces slipped into place, and the research librarians around me agreed. There might have been a reason we'd heard nothing of Temperance in the lost years after her return from Virginia. Perhaps Temperance had a long-kept secret—a baby of her own, a baby she'd been forced to give up.

Was George Yeardley the father? Or was she, when her betrothed was given up for dead, seen as fair game, the victim of unwanted sexual aggression? Could it be that she feared either was possible? Was Temperance unsure of the father's identity? Did it matter an iota in England's rigid religious climate? Did she even have the option of keeping her baby?

She would be safe in her mother's home while she recovered from the ordeal of the ocean disaster. A period of mourning the loss of her beloved would explain a withdrawal from the eyes of society. I imagined that Martha might also take the newborn, her own grandchild, to leave in the dark of night on the steps of the monastery or convent.

I saw Temperance as a loving, caring person, an instrument of God's mercy serving helpless castoffs. She did what she knew she must, regardless of malicious taunts. From the moment that she had been the first to see innocent eyes—straight from the presence of God—blink open to behold life with all its possibilities, she could not have done otherwise. My cynicism of an hour earlier began to melt away.

Temperance could not have foreseen the disastrous outcome of the Africans' involuntary servitude. Attention was focused on the present and on the vision of a noble experiment with self-government. She would know that although her husband might be part of the birth of democracy that would make its mark in history, her anonymous deeds, too, were worthy and lasting. Jesus said in Matthew 25:40 (American KJV), "and the King shall answer and say to them, Truly I say to you, inasmuch as you have done it to one of the least of these my brothers, you have done it to me."

How could I not admire her and love her for caring for the *least of these?* She offered hope, reminding me that Jamestown was not made entirely of those who were only looking out for their own gain as they—knowingly or unknowingly—trampled on the rights and lives of others.

Temperance's actions exhibited her concern for generations to follow. I pictured their rustic home in Jamestown and mentally compared it to regal dwellings in England. Mothers have sung lullabies in every corner of the world from the beginning of time. Why would she not sing to her own children and teach them the best of all she knew? Since Shakespeare himself expected his audiences to be familiar with fasola solfège music—I'd seen a reference to Shakespeare's use of the music system in his play, *King Lear*—we may naturally assume that Sir George and Lady Temperance were familiar with it. Perhaps her cradle songs were in fasola syllables.

At that moment, I felt that I knew Lady Temperance. I could feel her presence, reaching past the years. As Sacred Harp singers glimpse in one another's eyes across the hollow square a recognition that transcends all racial, sexual, economic, political, or religious differences, I saw Temperance Yeardley beyond the bounds of time and life, and I loved her everlasting soul. In the language of our sacred harps, I could sing Edmund Dumas' song with her:

When for eternal worlds we steer, and seas are calm and skies are clear,
And faith in lively exercise, and distant hills of Canaan rise,
The soul for joy then claps her wings and loud her hallelujah sings.
Adieu, vain world, adieu.

"Vain World Adieu," #329 in *The Sacred Harp*
Words, *Seaman's Devotional Assistant*, 1830;
music, Edmund Dumas, 1856

Southern face of the Old Church; the entrance tower is at the opposite end of this 2007 view. The brick church building, a 300th anniversary memorial gift in 1907 from the National Society of Colonial Dames, was reconstructed on the ruins of the original seventeenth-century church, retaining two tombs in the floor of the chancel (immediately behind the railing). The palisade wall seen behind the church stands on the same fort boundary that the first colonists constructed in 1607. (2007 photograph by the author.)

Interior view of the Old Church. Reverend Richard
Buck is buried to the left of the altar. The tomb to
the right of the altar is that of Governor Sir George
Yeardley, who died in 1627. Thin brass plates were
recessed in the stone slab over his tomb. As far as
is known, this tombstone is the only one in colonial
America with such engraved brass plates. In this very
room, in the "quire" of the church, Governor Yeardley
convened the first elected-representative body in the
New World on July 30, 1619.

CHAPTER 21

Homecoming

WE left Richmond early on Saturday morning, wearily facing a long drive back to Atlanta. The road trip was like a time travel journey from the days of our nation's beginning, through the interim years, and into the present. My mind dwelt on the significance of Sir George Yeardley's contributions as governor of Jamestown Colony and the far-reaching consequences of his actions. The overriding message of love came from Lady Temperance.

With the changing Virginia scenery, other faces came to mind, others I also knew well though we'd never met—Phil and Caroline; Reverend Dumas' white grandmother; Grandma's grandfather, Jeremiah Dumas; and his gold-seeking brother, Davie. They appeared to be as helpless as the bye-blows Lady Temperance had assisted. Mother had warned me about digging in the past. Carine had cautioned of problems left unsolved in a lifetime. When I pondered the sum of their lives, I was reminded that though we are known by our deeds only God can see into our hearts.

Of some hearts, I had no question. I saw Ralph Freeman, the freed-slave preacher; Reverend Eric Leake and Reverend Dumas; Jeremie Dumas, the martyred Huguenot advocate; and his grandson, Benjamin Dumas I, reading his Margent Bible in a new land. I saw Edmund Dumas and Grandma singing their unending, eternal Sacred Harp songs.

Doug and I stopped for a quick lunch in Greensboro, North Carolina, and opened the map to review the remainder of our trip. I recognized the line of a bold green marker that had plotted my route the day I talked with Reverend Dumas, a journey only an hour farther down the road from Greensboro. How pleasant it would be to pull off the road, introduce Doug, and enjoy a nice, long chat. But we had many miles ahead of us.

I felt a pang of sorrow as we passed the exit to Granite Quarry. I pictured the welcoming branches of Reverend Dumas' great oak tree and imagined his greeting with outstretched arms at the gate. My thoughts flew like a bird a few miles farther south to the driveway of Asia's cheerful home in Mount Gilead. We might never prove a bloodline, but a love-line is even stronger. I wondered if I would ever pass this way again.

Suddenly I thought of the imagined bye-blow baby, born in Temperance's young lost years. I asked Doug what he thought might have happened to such an infant. "Don't you know a mother would have been tormented in wondering about that little one?"

"I thought of that when you told me," he said. "A child abandoned in England in those ocean-going days could have ended up anywhere in the world."

Only God knows where such an infant might find a home. The child could be anyone's ancestor, any one of us. None of us knows our full ancestry. We're all illegitimate, and everyone is our brother.

It was raining when we arrived in Atlanta, but on Saturday morning, the sun was breaking through clouds as we left for the almost-forgotten prayer breakfast, scheduled weeks before, which was held at an old depot building near Underground Atlanta. We recognized no one from our church. But folks from all over the city were there, and admittedly, we could hardly lay claim to being frequent church-goers. The occasion offered a chance to become involved in the fabric of our home community, which we'd missed since leaving Dallas.

I greeted one familiar face who turned out to be our congressman, Representative John Lewis, someone whose picture I'd seen in the news. He had worked on a bipartisan measure with our former congressman in Texas, Steve Bartlett, a personal friend.

President Carter spoke in heartfelt terms of the bleak prospects for even a minimum standard of living for many of the most vulnerable in our community. I'd expected him to be a good speaker. But I'd not expected his proposal for a workable solution to the problem. It had imaginative, feasible possibilities.

There was a front-page story in Sunday's *Journal-Constitution* about President Carter's proposal for a broad volunteer program that would be called "The Atlanta Project" or "TAP." He described an amazing amount of work that is routinely done by volunteers. The objection that most people voice to becoming a volunteer is lack of time. Even the busiest people, however, usually agreed that they could spare an hour or two a week. An hour a week could be a good use of one's lunch hour—especially if an employer agreed to help facilitate the trade-off. Many companies had already agreed to include the hour as company-paid time off.

The next segment of the plan was to group the many single volunteer hours into an organized effort. Some gifted minds had designed a program through the Carter Center to accomplish that goal. Each volunteer would be a partner in a job-sharing endeavor. If forty hours were needed to do a job, forty volunteers with an hour to spare could complete the task.

When I phoned Mother, I expected to hear a variation of my own usually conservative viewpoint. She surprised me by saying she had no doubt that committed volunteers could do any job that was put before them, but that it would take someone like a Jimmy Carter or a Billy Graham to get such a project started.

"That puts the ball in your court," she said. "You don't seem to settle anywhere long enough to volunteer an hour anymore."

I'd already filled out the registration form and planned to be at the organizational meeting six weeks later. Doug would be spending more time in the Atlanta office and would be making numerous short trips as he finalized a number of cases throughout the Southeast. We had decided that I should spend more time at home in Atlanta in the future to be available on short notice if Mother should need me. Summer also meant an abundance of Sacred Harp singings, which were numerous in Georgia and Alabama, to choose from each weekend.

In the meantime, I would stretch our long-planned trip to Texas into a lengthier visit. Because I'd be in Fort Worth, as well as the Panhandle, I phoned the Dumas family historian, Mr. John Wilson, and planned a meeting with him while I'd be visiting Elise. Most of my genealogy questions were now answered, but I wanted to meet him. We could compare notes. I wished that Carine could join us.

Mother's voice was getting weaker, but her outlook remained positive. She was pleased with the wide variety and availability of audio books that allowed her to remain well-read, saying she had finally found a way to read and do handwork simultaneously. Since renewing her crocheting skills, she had completed afghans for most of the grandchildren. Louise saw to it that she was well-supplied with yarn. She fretted over mistakes she could feel in the stitches, but to the rest of us, her work was more beautiful than ever.

I wanted to go to the farmers market and cook big meals as we'd done before, but Mother insisted she wanted me to limit my time in the kitchen. She preferred to sit and chat. A single chore of cleaning the closet had been saved for me. We gathered a large box of usable clothing to donate and discarded old snow-damaged house shoes that even the dog rejected, but only after pulling out new ones still tucked in their Christmas gift boxes.

On my return home, while in Fort Worth for the stop-over visit, I phoned Mr. Wilson to confirm our meeting. I was asked to hold for a moment. Shortly, a young woman's voice came on the line and told me politely that Mr. Wilson had passed away the previous week. The timing of my call was awkward. I could only say that the legacy he left behind was invaluable to an appreciative family.

In early August, I went to the organizational meeting of The Atlanta Project, where I chose the project that touched me most. In the past in Dallas, I had picked paintbrush projects, but this time, I wanted to work with kids. I would be a tutor. I missed our grandchildren. If I could not be with them to help with school projects or attend recitals or ball games, I could help someone else's grandchild. God was speaking to me through what I'd seen Temperance do. The tasks I'd chosen were small and insignificant in the grand scheme of things, but a child learns to walk only one step at a time. A teacher is a midwife to education.

Tawanda, a second-grader with a heart-stopping smile, tripped on trailing shoelaces as she came into the library. As I tied them for her, she confided that she didn't know how to do it for herself. When we tried it a few times, she grew frustrated. But I'd noticed something. I asked her to write her name. She was left-handed. I'd been unable to teach my left-handed son to tie his shoestrings. The task had fallen to my ambidextrous brother. We found a leftie classmate to be Tawanda's instructor, and the next day, she was happily tying her own shoes.

Latrell was a worldly-wise fifth-grader who was shocked to learn that Martin Luther King was from Atlanta. "Here? The same Auburn Avenue?" Her response to the realization that historical figures were real people, not storybook characters, reminded me of myself when I began my Dumas family search.

When we returned from Christmas in Texas, Doug sorted through the mail and set aside a sizeable stack of recognizable Christmas cards that we would read together. I opened a large envelope from Granite Quarry and pulled out an impressive brochure with Reverend Dumas' photo centered on the front page.

"Oh, look. He's received an honor," I said.

Then I dropped the page and covered my face. Doug picked it up and read, "Victorious Homecoming Celebration for Reverend Dr. O. C. Dumas, Sr., Saturday, November 9." He reached for his glasses. "Eleven o'clock a.m., Varick Auditorium, Livingstone College, Salisbury, North Carolina."

I went to the kitchen to make coffee and try to regain my composure. Doug came to the doorway after reading some of the eulogy tributes. "He was quite a man," he said. "I'm sorry I didn't get to meet him."

We returned to the stack of Christmas cards to read in a single sitting with cups of coffee and in a more relaxed frame of mind. Opening the greetings a short time later, we read of weddings, new babies, graduations, new homes, and new jobs. Most told of only happy, pleasurable events or trips, although an occasional setback in health or job loss was mentioned, its very inclusion highlighting the pain it caused, knowing that we would sympathize.

Near the bottom of the stack, an indication that it had arrived weeks earlier, a card from Carine's sister held an obituary notice. A card; no phone call. But Carine's family had not known how close we had become. Perhaps they had tried unsuccessfully to reach Mother. And Carine had never phoned me; I had done the calling. With Mother's illness, I had not phoned her recently. I was now still shaken by waves of unexpected sorrowful news. My impulse was to cry out, "Wait, wait! I need to talk to you one more time."

Carine had died within days of Reverend Dumas. The accompanying note told of a brief illness, leaving bewilderment that death could strike so suddenly. They could not know which of death's thousand doors would open for them, nor could they know the hour.

Yes, death could strike unexpectedly, but it could also prolong its torture. Mother sat tethered to a hissing oxygen tank, sightlessly crocheting afghans for her great-grandchildren, and waited. What more could God require of her? Thinking of Arlette, the hotel maid, who questioned God, "Why me, O Lord, why me?" I could only ask God, "Why my mother, Lord? Why? What more must you require of my precious Mother?"

My visits to Texas to be with Mother became increasingly more frequent, and months became years before Mother finally agreed that she could no longer stay at home. We knew that she was often in terrible pain, yet until she moved to an assisted living apartment and entered hospice care, she refused anything stronger than Tylenol for relief. Her fear of the serpent of addiction was stronger than her fear of pain.

Once, as I was leaving, she said softly, "Honey, you do know that this old body isn't going to make it, don't you? No, no, don't cry. It's all right. Everything is right, in God's time."

I began to see that she was teaching me a last lesson. She lived out, minute by agonizing minute, her unwavering faith that God would help her conquer death itself. She met it gracefully. God's time for her was September 15, 1998. She, like Reverend Dumas, had a victorious homecoming.

For a long time after her passing, I had impulses to pick up the phone and call her about everyday happenings. Elapsed time was elongated, as in a Salvador Dali painting. Minutes differ significantly from moments. Moments have their own identity, not limited or defined by measured units, and live forever in our minds. Yet I would cling to familiar increments of hours and days—*she's been gone forty-eight hours now*, and then, *a week*—in an attempt to hold her human form close to me, like listening to the soothing lingering vibrations of a clock's chime.

I continue to feel Mother near me and sense her presence around me, as though she's just left the room and will soon reappear. She will always be with me. I know she's in our heavenly home, waiting for me. She's there with Grandma and Lady Temperance, there with all the saints I met along the path as I retraced my family's personal journey.

I never sang Grandma's Sacred Harp songs with her while she lived out her mortal life, but I can sing with her now as I gather with others, some new to the old music and many who've sung it all their lives.

Give joy or grief, give ease or pain, take life or friends away.
But let me find them all again in that eternal day.
And I'll sing Hallelujah, and you'll sing Hallelujah,
And we'll all sing Hallelujah when we arrive at Home.

"Hallelujah" # 146 in *The Sacred Harp*
Words, Charles Wesley, 1759; music, William Walker, 1835

EPILOGUE

THE next years passed as rapidly as if a steady breeze were turning pages of the calendar. Doug's work took us from Georgia to California before we built a home in Arizona to retire. To be near grandchildren, we eventually returned home to Texas, only minutes from the waiting room where this story began.

Clara Dumas, Reverend Dumas's widow, has become a close friend over the years. Clara, her daughter, Pam, and her grandson, Brian, drove from their home in Granite Quarry to Fort Bragg, North Carolina, to take a pan of brownies to my grandson, Sergeant Colin Arden, before his first deployment to Iraq.

Reverend Eric Leake had long ago completed his master's and doctoral degrees, and was now pastor of Martin Temple African Methodist Episcopal Zion Church of Chicago, Illinois.

All the while, Doug and I traveled to every Sacred Harp singing we could manage—from the West Coast to the East Coast, and even to England and Wales.

Genealogical searches to discover family roots have proliferated around the world. One such search that might predictably have led only to a dead end has found resolution with a slave's story that has come full circle. Joseph Opala, the anthropologist in the story of the Gullah melody and now a professor of history at James Madison University in Virginia, helped connect the dots through seven generations.

The winter 2007 issue of *American Legacy, the Magazine of African-American History & Culture* told of a slave named Priscilla, who had been kidnapped in 1756 at the age of ten in her native Sierra Leone, died in 1811 on the Comingtee Plantation in South Carolina, which retained extensive records. In 2006, one of Priscilla's descendants, Thomalind Martin Polite, a speech therapist in Charleston, South Carolina, traveled to Sierra Leone for a bittersweet homecoming "to take [Priscilla's] spirit back to her resting place."

Truth, once assumed lost in time, is being revealed.

As the four hundredth anniversary of Jamestown approached, news of activities relating to the upcoming 2007 observation held my attention. The Jamestown Rediscovery Archaeological Project, which excavated the original colonial fort, brought a major rethinking of the accounts of England's first permanent settlement in North America. The fort itself had been thought to have been washed away by the James River. But the discovery, following a long-held hunch of archaeologist William Kelso, of the true location of James Fort has amazed the world.

Literally inches below the visible surface, beneath a layer of Civil War embattlements and commemorative statues of John Smith and Pocahontas, Kelso and his archaeological team unearthed evidence of the fort that was incredibly built under the hurried and harsh conditions we have not previously appreciated. The fort was then was abandoned and inexplicably lost during Jamestown's first struggling decades.

James Fort still retains much of its original structure, including palisade walls, bulwarks, interior buildings, a well, and a warehouse. The fort is triangular-shaped with circular bulwarks at each corner where the palisades meet—exactly as William Strachey, secretary of the *Sea Venture* voyage, had described it:

> "The fort . . . about half an acre . . . is cast almost into the form of a triangle and so palisaded. The south side next the river . . . contains 140 yards, the west and east sides a hundred only. At every angle or corner, where the lines meet, a bulwark or watchtower is raised and in each bulwark a piece or two well mounted . . . And thus enclosed, as I said, round with a palisade of planks and strong posts, four feet deep in the ground, of young oaks, walnuts, etc. . . ."

Extensive preparations planned for more than a decade by the Association of the Preservation of Virginia Antiquities (APVA) promised a momentous, unforgettable year-long anniversary celebration. Queen Elizabeth II would be present in early May to mark the occasion, as she had done for the 350th observation fifty years earlier. A new facility, the Archaearium, was constructed to exhibit artifacts from the James Fort excavation. The majority of the artifacts, which numbered nearly a million, dated to the times of Queen Elizabeth I and King James.

On November 10, 2007, Richmond would be the site of the James River Sacred Harp Convention for their annual singing and dinner on the ground. The combination was irresistible. Our son Michael gifted us with two weeks at his time-share condominium in nearby Williamsburg.

Because I'd been following reports of new discoveries pictured on the APVA website, I already had an idea of what I hoped to see at the Jamestown archaeological site. At the top of my list were the Delft tiles that had been

The "dig" at Historic James Fort showing circular "palisaded" bulwark, exactly as William Strachey described it in 1610. (2007 photo.)

The dig in November 2007 showing the earliest excavated level to the year of 1608. Here exposed are two fireplaces made of brick on the site. The mostly-intact fireplaces could be the oldest surviving brickwork in English America.

found in the backfill of Civil War earthwork in the vicinity of the governor's residence. The tiles were said to be evidence of the fine quality of the structure from the time that Governor Yeardley and his family had lived there. I wanted to see for myself the charming figures outlined in blue on creamy white tiles. No longer would I have to simply try to imagine objects and scenes in Lady Temperance's life. These were a part of her real world.

Another must-see artifact was William Strachey's signet ring found in the southeast bulwark of the James Fort site. The brass ring was finely engraved with the figure of a large bird with a cross on its breast. This was the official crest that the Strachey family had registered at the College of Arms in London. Strachey had lost the ring at some time in the brief three or four summer months that he was in Virginia in 1610, and it was found there four hundred years later. Because it was found at the southeast bulwark, we might imagine that it was lost as he was meticulously calculating the measurements of the fort to describe for us.

This type of signet ring was used for impressing wax seals on documents. It is such a ring that is listed, along with "all my messauges [home] and lands in Scottow or elsewhere in the county of Norfolk" in the will of Lady Temperance's mother, Martha Stanley Flowerdew Garrett, bearing the date of "3 February, 1625/6." She stated, "I give unto my daughter Temperance Yardlie alias Flowerdewe my seal ring of gold." I wondered if Temperance did in fact receive her mother's seal ring before her own death in 1628, or if it, too, had been unknowingly dropped into the abyss of time. And I wondered about the women's closest-to-the-heart sentiments expressed that should be guarded by such a seal.

A similar seal, in silver, was found inside James Fort near the northern bulwark. The silver seal is an intricate depiction of a skeleton holding an hourglass in one hand and an arrow in the other, representing the passage of time and the brevity of life, which is also a recurring theme in Sacred Harp music.

> *Death, like an overflowing stream, sweeps us away; our life's a dream,*
> *An empty tale, a morning flow'r, cut down and withered in an hour.*

"Exit" #181 in *The Sacred Harp*
Words, Isaac Watts, 1707; music, P. Sherman, 1808

When we arrived in Virginia, I predictably spent considerable time in libraries. After a first visit to the active archaeological digging site, I was so drawn to new daily discoveries that we returned on three additional days. We had not even dreamed that the public would be offered a rare opportunity to share the moment of discovery as archaeologists continued to unearth the remaining unexplored portions of the 1607 James Fort. Only a slender rope separated us from the archaeological team as they sifted the earth on which the colonists actually stood and worked.

Easily-recognizable areas in which the digging was complete had been documented and filled again with shells. The archaeologists had continued to peel away successive layers until they had finally reached the earliest level of colonial times. There they had found an original underground cellar that served as a workshop and laboratory until it eventually became a large basement kitchen. The kitchen possibly served the earliest governor, as well as those who succeeded him, until the early 1620s, which would include the time of Governor George Yeardley.

On our second visit to the active digging site, I recognized from a photograph Dr. William Kelso, the project's Director of Archaeology, and I chatted with him while Doug hurried to the car to retrieve our copy of his book, *Jamestown, the Buried Truth,* for him to autograph. Dr. Kelso said the cellar has been one of the most significant sites yet found inside the palisade lines. The architectural remains and the artifacts discovered read like a history book of life as it was happening at the fort.

At least three successive floor levels have been uncovered. The earliest level, where the team was currently working, contained iron tools and a scattering of metal particles from a blacksmith. High fired clay cups known as crucibles and fragments of ceramic pharmaceutical or chemical pots, along with piles of wood ashes, indicate that the 1608 metallurgical experiments in search of precious metals may have taken place in the building. In another area, there was evidence of copper smelting, which may have been used in attempts to produce brass.

The later kitchen conversion of the cellar included two bake ovens—constructed of brick made on site—and a brick chimney foundation. The mostly-intact fireplaces could be the oldest surviving brickwork in English America.

The walls of the building had collapsed at some point and left behind an open cellar hole that colonists had later used as a trash pit, thus yielding an amazing trove of artifacts. The scattered appearance of specific artifacts of this "occupation" level suggests that the space had mysteriously been abandoned at one violent, slicing instant of time.

A fire once burned beneath a Virginia Indian pot, and nearby was a butchered hip-bone of a pig and a butchered turtle shell, indicating that someone was in the process of preparing a meal when the cook was interrupted without warning. A dagger, still in its sheath, was discovered within arm's reach of the cooking fire, and behind it was a musketeer's bag of gunflints, lead balls, and powder, suggesting that the objects were left behind suddenly and had remained undisturbed for four hundred years.

I could only stand in wonder at the revelations of the time capsule being opened before my very eyes. Ashes that remained behind in the fireplace appeared as fresh as to still be warm. But why was it necessary for a cook to be armed?

Recorded incidents in the lives of Sir George and Lady Temperance replayed in my head, and I again saw them as people who had lived, breathed, and experienced danger on the very soil being exposed as the scraping away continued. I suddenly recalled the alarming moment in 1622 when Yeardley was alerted to the Indian massacres that almost wiped out the colony and which were in progress at that very moment.

Yeardley quickly sent his household to the safety that he was sure would be provided by his good friend, Chief Debedevon, the "Laughing King" of the Accomack tribe on the eastern shore, between Chesapeake Bay and the ocean, while Yeardley himself rushed, too late, to the aid of the colonists on outlying plantations. Elizabeth, the Yeardley's eldest child, would have been no more than three years old, and her brother Argall, still a toddler. Temperance was probably pregnant with the youngest son, Francis.

Sir George Yeardley reportedly personally retrieved the communion silver from the smoldering ruins of the church at Southampton Hundred. The silver, of significance to Christians everywhere as a symbol of the timeless universal church, was a gift of Mistress Mary Robinson of England. It was brought to the colony with the Yeardleys on their 1619 voyage to Jamestown.

After the destruction of Southampton Hundred in the 1622 massacres, the silver was kept at the Yeardley home in Jamestown until it was transferred by Lady Temperance after the death of Sir George to the church at Southampton. Southampton Hundred, the former Smith's Hundred, had been purchased in 1620 by Henry Wriothesley, Earl of Southampton, Shakespeare's patron and political ally of Sir Edwin Sandys, George Yeardley's mentor. George Yeardley was also a stockholder, or *venturer*, with Southampton in the purchase of Smith's Hundred. According to William Robertson Garrett in the January 1896 issue of the *American Historical Magazine,* the liberal political alliance within the Virginia Company of these men angered King James; however, the same alliance made a lasting imprint on our present lives with the influence of the Great Charter on the Constitution of the United States. The same communion silver rescued by Sir George remains to this day at St. John's Episcopal Church in Hampton, Virginia, where it continues to be used on occasion.

In his will, Yeardley spoke first of commending his soul "to the hands of Almighty God, my Creator and Redeemer," before he addressed his temporal estate. He then said, "It is my will and desire that my wife, Temperance, shall have the custody and keeping of . . . the children . . . desiring that great care may be had for the governance, education, and bringing up of the said children in the fear of God, of which I make no doubt."

Sir George and Lady Temperance had seen heart-to-heart. They joined their lives and brought their hopes and dreams into reality, for their generation and for those to come; even when their efforts appeared hopeless, their steadfast faith in God gave them hope.

When Doug and I returned to Texas, I examined my photographs of the cellar fireplace and belatedly recalled the early assignment of George Yeardley, as captain of the military troops under Governor Gates, to lead an expedition to search for precious metals. Perhaps he was in the cellar laboratory when the experiments were in progress. The archaeology team might have discovered proof.

Dr. Kelso later assured me by email that the time of occupation of the cellar began well before the time of Yeardley's residence. The colonists had begun their search for gold and other metals at the earliest possible moment. Their assignment was to make the venture profitable. The Spaniards had discovered great riches, and the English investors expected no less.

When I considered trials and failures, repeated time and again, in a desperate effort for the colony to find a means of self-sufficiency and profit, their sense of urgency was palpable. Given the scope of the task and the extent of knowledge available to him, I had to recognize that George Yeardley's accomplishments were truly noteworthy.

I finally began to see him as I should have from the beginning—a person who lived in his own segment of time. I'd blamed him for slavery in the English-speaking New World. However, Yeardley had been criticized as a protégé of Sir Edwin Sandys, whose voice was raised in opposition to the use of Africans in Virginia. (Philip Alexander Bruce in *History of Virginia, Volume I.*)

There had been more to learn about the circumstances surrounding the unexpected arrival of the Dutch ship in the Jamestown harbor in August of 1619. The ship of Africans was brought *to* Yeardley; he did not seek it. Its crew, as well as its kidnapped cargo, was in dire need of food and supplies. The captives had been pirated in the West Indies from a Spanish vessel that intended to sell them as slaves, and they would have starved or been thrown overboard.

Once they were in the colony, the Africans' status was similar to that of any indentured servant. Slavery as an institution did not yet exist in the colony. In *A Documentary History of Slavery in North America,* Willie Lee Rose tells us that the laws that established slavery in Virginia did not evolve until the mid-seventeenth century. Indeed, at least some of the Africans brought into the colony in 1619 became free within a few years. Some of their seeds were sown on fertile soil.

In my mind's eye, I could see Yeardley's face and read there his undaunted determination to secure the continuance of the ideals so recently planted in America's first elected legislative body. Our country, though imperfect, still treasures the ideals of life, liberty, and happiness, and people the world over still clamor to come here with the hope of making a better life. We continue to be beneficiaries of such political visionaries as Yeardley's mentor, Sir Edwin Sandys, whose thoughts and policies Sir George promoted. The result was the beginning of representative government in our country.

Dr. Kelso reiterated his observation that the significance of Strachey's ring was more than simply a cameo connection of the colony to William Shakespeare. It was an indication of the high intellectual level of the leaders of the colony. Strachey's position as secretary of the voyage had been sought by the famed metaphysical poet and preacher, John Donne. Strachey's letter, aside from inspiring William Shakespeare, is noteworthy in itself: "Truth is the daughter of Time, and men ought not to deny everything which is not subject to their own sense."

The connection with Shakespeare is musically significant. A reference by Sacred Harp historian Warren Steele to Shakespeare's use of fasola solfège in his play, *King Lear,* had caused me to do a syllable-related computer search through the complete works of Shakespeare. I found two additional usages: "ut, re, sol, la, mi, fa," in *Love's Labours Lost,* Act IV, Scene 2, and "You can sol-fa, need sing it," in *The Taming of the Shrew,* Act I, Scene 2. This was evidence that Shakespeare acknowledged fasola music in the context of everyday singing.

Lady Temperance and Sir George knew the music. They would have sung from the Sternhold and Hopkins Psalter that was often distributed with the Geneva Bible in England during Queen Elizabeth's reign. "All people that on earth do dwell, sing to the Lord with cheerful voice." The tune for Psalm 100, the same tune we sing today, was the French tune for Psalm 134. Perhaps they, too, sang the Fa-So-La syllables before the words to sound the tune.

With a chorus of their last words and actions echoing in my mind, I began to realize that one's actions in life *are* our lasting words to those who follow—words from one's sacred harp, our human voice. I had thought these ancestors were forever gone, their bodies nothing more than dust. Yet, their harps' music rises up to guide and comfort us. Their history, all of it, is within the music. They poured the sum of their lives' entirety into the music—*as they lived it.*

Through the years that I have struggled to know them, to understand them, and thought them mute—yes, all this time, my ancestors have been speaking to me through the words and music of their sacred harps.

The music of Sacred Harp enables us to share in the emotions our ancestors experienced. They speak to our souls through its music, ever changing, ever the same. We continue to speak with our sacred harps, composing our own legacy to the generations who follow.

Music is the language of the spirit, a language that needs no words—as in the Gullah melody or the simple syllables of Fa-So-La—to communicate with Him and with each other. We become one vast choir linked across the centuries. The music of the sacred harp gives wings to the soul, lifting it beyond earthly cares to soar for an ecstatic moment in the realm of the spirit.

Burst, ye emerald gates, and bring To my raptured vision
All th'ecstatic joys that spring Round the bright Elysian.

"Elysian" #139 in *The Sacred Harp*
Richard Kemperfelt, 1777

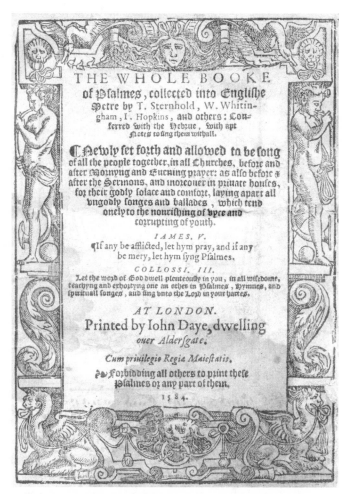

Title page of *The Whole Booke of Psalmes*, collected into Englishe
Metre, published in 1584 in London by "T. Sternhold, W. Whitingham,
I. Hopkins, and others." (Photo courtesy of Bowld Music Library,
Southwestern Baptist Theological Seminary, Fort Worth, Texas.)

170 Pfalme. C.

all honour to him doe:
His footeſtoole woʒſhyp him befoʒe,
foʒ it is holy to.
6 Moyſes, Aaron, and Samuell,
as Prieſtes on him did call:
when they did pʒay he heard them well,
and gaue them aunſwere all.

7 Within the cloud to them he ſpake,
then did they labour ſtill:
To keepe ſuch lawes as he did make,
and pointed them vntill.
8 O Loʒd our God thou didſt them heare,
and aunſweredſt them agayne:
Thy mercy did on them appeare,
their deedes didſt not maintayne.

9 O laud and pʒayſe our God and Loʒd,
within his holy hill:
foʒ why? our God thʒoughout the woʒld,
is holy euer ſtill.

2. Iubilate Deo omnis terra. Pſal. C.

The exhoʒteth all to ſerue the Loʒd, who hath made vs and enter into his
courtes and aſſemblies to pʒayſe his name.

A

All people that on earth doe dwell, ſing

to the Loʒd with chearefull voyce, him ſerue
with

"Psalme C" in the Sternhold, Whitingham, Hopkins Psalter, showing
the first "Psalm 100" in English using the tune for Psalm 134 in the
French 1551 Genevan Psalter. (Photo courtesy of Bowld Music Library,
Southwestern Baptist Theological Seminary, Fort Worth, Texas.)
Photo 22.05 "Psalme C" in the Sternhold, Whitingham, Hopkins

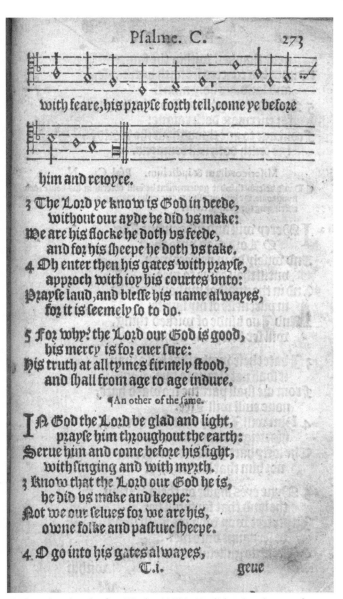

Psalter, showing the first "Psalm 100" in English using the tune for Psalm 134 in the French 1551 Genevan Psalter. (Photo courtesy of Bowld Music Library, Southwestern Baptist Theological Seminary, Fort Worth, Texas.)

APPENDIX

Operated the Tavern and Ferry

MY ANCESTRY
↓

David Dumas I (1730-1803)	Frances Dumas	Sarah Dumas
m. Sarah Moorman	m. Francis Smith	m. Edmund Lilly
↓ (1754-1803)	↓	↓
Andrew Moorman Dumas	Unity Smith	John Lilly
m. Jamima	m. Geo. Hammon	m. _____
(1756-1787)		
Benjamin Dumas III	Sarah Smith	James P. Lilly
m. Susannah Hutchins D. 1805	m. _____ Pemberton	m. Nancy Hendrix
Unity Dumas	Elizabeth Smith	Frances Lilly
m. _____ Spiva	m. _____ Buchanan	m. Joel McLendon
Francis Lucy Dumas	Francis Smith	Robert Lilly
m. Arnold Thomason	m. _____	
Jeremiah Dumas IV B. SEPT. 10, 1767 D. OCT. 4, 1841	David Smith	
m. Nancy Mackersham		
Sarah Dumas	Nathaniel Smith	
m. Frederick Scarborough		
Obadiah Dumas	John Smith	
m. Mary Hutchins		
Zachariah Dumas	Richard Smith	
m. Elizabeth Lucy		

Nehemiah Dumas
(Not married)

Azariah Dumas
m. (1) Mary Harris
   (2) Susannah Hare

Stephen Dumas
m. _____

Mary Dumas
m. John DeBerry

Pastor of Rocky River Baptist organiz... 17... - STILL ITS PAS...

THIS UNCLE MOVED TO GEO... THE THREE SONS OF B... FOLLOWED HIM:
1. DAVID
2. MOSES
3. BENJAMIN

I (1705-1763)

Clark

Operated the Plantation

mas III

Benjamin Dumas II

m. (1) Jamima McLendon	m. (2) Ruth Serdow
Jamima's children	Ruth's children
↓	↓
Eleanor Dumas m. John B. Lilly	Pleasant S. Dumas (Never married)
Penelope Dumas m. Benjamin Tedder	Fanny Dumas m. James W. Wilson
David Dumas II m. Mary________	Elizabeth A. Dumas m. Zadock Sturges
Benjamin Dumas IV m. Sarah Atkins	Anne Dumas m. Lodewick Key
Silus C. Dumas m. Mary ________	Sally Dum
Jeremiah Dumas V m. ________	
Amos Dumas m. Drucilla Agee	
Elhanan Winchester Dumas m. Elizabeth Brashier	
Francis Dumas m. Joel McLendon(?)	
John Lilly Dumas	

DUMAS

NOTE: BASIC CHART IS FROM JOHN WILSON'S DUMAS FAMILY VOL. II 1988

BIBLIOGRAPHY

A Tale of the Huguenots or Memoirs of a French Refugee Family, translated and compiled from the original manuscripts of James Fontaine by one of his descendants. Published 1838 by John S. Taylor. New York: Library of the Huguenot Society of the Founders of Manakin in the Colony of Virginia, Midlothian, Virginia.

Abstracts of Wills, York County, Virginia: White, Henry, 1671 (grandfather of Unity Smith Dumas). Richmond, VA: Virginia State Archives.

Adventures and Discourses of Captain John Smith, 1579-1631. Newport News, Virginia: Mariners Museum Library.

Akrigg, G.P.V. *Shakespeare and the Earl of Southampton.* Cambridge: Harvard University Press, 1968.

Ames, Susie M., ed. *County Court Records of Accomack-Northampton, Virginia, 1640-1645.* Charlottesville: University Press of Virginia, 1973.

Bailey, James Henry. "Shakespeare and the Founders of Virginia." *Virginia Cavalcade* (Winter 1951): pages 9-10.

Baird, Charles W. *Huguenot Emigration to America.* 1885. Reprint, Baltimore, MD: Baltimore Regional Publishing Company, 1966.

Bancroft, Frederick. *Slave Trading in the Old South.* New York: Frederick Ungar Publishing, 1959.

Barbour, Philip L. "Captain Newport meets Opechancanough." *Virginia Cavalcade* (Winter 1968): pages 42-47.

_____. *Jamestown Voyages under the First Charter, 1606-1609, Volume II.* Cambridge, U.K.: Published for the Hakluyt Society at the Cambridge University Press, 1969.

Barka, Norman F. *Archaeology of Flowerdew Hundred.* Williamsburg, VA: Southside Historical Sites, Inc., 1976.

Bayne, Howard R. *The Year 1619 in the Colony of Virginia.* New York: Historical Papers of the Society of Colonial Wars in the State of New York, 1899.

Beer, Mrs. Robert David. "The Huguenot Family of Faure." *The Huguenot*, Volume 7 (1935): pages 191-195, 220-221.

Boyd, Joe Dan. *Judge Jackson and the Colored Sacred Harp.* Birmingham, AL: Alabama Folklife Association, 2002.

_____. "Judge Jackson: Black Giant of White Spirituals." *Journal of American Folklore 83,* Number 330 (October-December 1970).

_____. *Negro Sacred Harp Songsters in Mississippi.* Hattiesburg: University of Southern Mississippi, 1972.

Bradley, Lee. *A Lexical Companion to the Hymns of the Sacred Harp.* Valdosta, GA: SCOLT Publications, 2005.

Bradshaw, Ura Ann and Vincent Watkins. *York County . . . 1000 Marriages (1623-1900).* Privately published, 1957.

Breen, T.H., "Looking Out for Number One: Conflicting Cultural Values in Early

Seventeenth-Century Virginia." *South Atlantic Quarterly* (Summer 1979): pages 342-360.

_____. *Tobacco Culture.* Princeton, NJ: Princeton University Press, 2001.

Breen, T.H. and Stephen Innes. *Myne Owne Ground.* New York and Oxford: Oxford University Press, 2004.

Brewster, C. Ray. *The Cluster of Jesse Mercer.* Macon, GA: Renaissance Press, 1983.

Brock, R. A. *Huguenot Emigration to Virginia.* Richmond, VA: Virginia Historical Society, 1886.

_____. *History of the Virginias.* Richmond, VA: Virginia Historical Society, 1886.

Brodie, Fawn M. *Thomas Jefferson—An Intimate History.* New York: Norton Press, 1998.

Brooks, E.M. *History of the Rocky River Baptist Church.* Charlotte, NC: Heritage Printers, Inc., 1928.

Browning, William S. *A History of the Huguenots.* London: Whitaker and Co., 1840.

Bruce, Philip Alexander. *History of Virginia, Volume I.* New York and London: Putnam, 1910.

Burgwyn, Collinson P. E. *The Huguenot Lovers.* London: Simpkin, Hamilton, Marshall & Kent, 1890.

Buttner, F. O., ed. *The Illuminated Psalter: Studies in Content, Purpose, and Placement of its Images.* Turnhout, Belgium: Brepols Publishers, 2005.

Byrd, William, II, Louis B. Wright, and Marion Tinling, eds. *The Secret Diary of William Byrd of Westover, 1709-1712.* Richmond, Virginia: Dietz Press, 1941.

Cabell, Priscilla Harris. *Turff and Twigg, Volume One—The French Lands.* Richmond, VA: Carter Printing Company, 1988.

Calhoun, Robert M. *Religion and the American Revolution in North Carolina.* Raleigh, NC: North Carolina State University Graphics, 1976.

Cathcart, William. *The Baptist Encyclopedia.* Philadelphia: Louis H. Everts, 1883.

Cathey, Cornelius O. *Agriculture in North Carolina before the Civil War.* Raleigh, NC: North Carolina Historical Publications, 1966.

Chalker, Russell M. *Pioneer Days along the Ocmulgee.* Carrollton, GA: Carrollton Press, 1970.

Chamberlayne, C.G., transcribed and edited. *Vestry Book and Register of St. Peter's Parish, New Kent and James City Counties, 1684-1786.* Richmond: published by the Library board of Richmond, Division of Purchase and Printing, 1937. One of three editions (five copies) located in General Collection of the Virginia Historical Society, Richmond, VA.

Chappell, Absalom H. *Miscellanies of Georgia.* Atlanta: J.F. Meegan, 1874.

Chinard, Gilbert. *A Huguenot Exile in Virginia, or Voyages of a Frenchman exiled for his Religion: The Hague Edition of 1687.* New York: Press of the Pioneers, Inc., 1934.

Collins, Ace. *Stories behind the Hymns that Inspire Americans.* Grand Rapids, MI: Zondervan Press, 2003.

Collins, Winfield H. *The Domestic Slave Trade of the Southern States.* New York: Broadway Publishing, 1904.

Cooper, Wm. Durant, ed. *Foreigners Resident in England, Lists of Foreign Protestants and Aliens, 1618-1688*, 1862.

Cope, Robert S., *Carry Me Back—Slavery and Servitude in 17th Century Virginia.* Pikeville, KY: Pikeville College Press, 1973.

Craighead-Dunlap Chapter of NSDAR, *Genealogical Records of Anson County, North Carolina.* Raleigh, NC: North Carolina State Archives, Volume 2, pages 6-7, 1949.

Currier-Briggs, Noel. *Parentage and Ancestry of Sir George Yeardley and Temperance Flowerdew.* Gloucestershire, England: Phillimore & Co., Ltd., 1985.

Davis, Burke. *A Williamsburg Galaxy.* Williamsburg, VA: Holt, Rinehart and Winston, Inc., 1968.

Davis, David Brion. *The Problem of Slavery in the Age of Revolution, 1770-1823*, Ithaca, NY: Cornell University Press, 1975.

Davis, Jane Eliza. *Round about Jamestown.* Hampton, VA: American Geographical Society, 1907.

Davis, Virginia Lee Hutcheson. *Tidewater Virginia Families.* Baltimore, MD: Genealogical Publishing Co., Inc., 1990.

De la Warr, Thomas West. *The Relation of the Right Honorable the Lord De la Warre, Lord Governor and Captain General of the Colonie.* 1611. Reprint, London: Reprinted by C. Whittingham, 1858. Newport News, VA: The Mariners Museum Library.

Doherty, Kieran. *Sea Venture: Shipwreck, Survival, and the Salvation of the First English Colony in the New World.* New York: St. Martin's Press, 2007.

Doran, Joseph I. *Sir George Yeardley.* Philadelphia: Pennsylvania Society of Colonial Governors, 1914.

Douglas, Donald. *The Huguenot.* New York: Dutton, 1954.

Downey, James Cecil. "Music of the American Revolution." PhD Diss., Tulane University, 1968.

Evans, June B. *Men of Matadequin.* New Orleans, LA: Bryn Ffyliaid Publications, 1984.

Fletcher, John. *Studies on Slavery.* Charleston, New Orleans, and Philadelphia: Jackson Warner, 1852.

Fleet, Beverly, comp. *Virginia Colonial Abstracts, Volume 24, York County, 1633-1646.* Baltimore, MD: Genealogical Publishing Co. 1988. These are recorded court rulings; many involve Joseph Croshaw, son-in-law of Sir George Yeardley and Lady Temperance, illustrating America's early litigious society. Located in the Library of Virginia, Richmond, VA. Now also available in paperback from Amazon.com. Published between 1938 and 1949, the original thirty-four paperback volumes of Virginia Colonial Abstracts were based on the earliest records known to exist in English-speaking America. York County, 1633-1646 (original vol. 24), and York County, 1646-1648 (original vol. 25) are now included in Volume III of the paperback editions.

_____. *Virginia Colonial Abstracts, Volume 25, York County, 1646-1648.* Baltimore, MD: Genealogical Publishing Co. 1988. Located in the Library of Virginia, Richmond, VA. Court cases and filings provide a view of our ancestors' everyday lives. Page 10 pertains to stock of bees belonging to sons of Joseph Croshaw, son-in-law of Sir George Yeardley and Lady Temperance.

Gaines, William H., Jr. "Master John Rolfe, Husbandman." *Virginia Cavalcade* (Summer 1951): pages 28-32.

Gardner, Robert. *History of Georgia Baptist Associations.* Macon, GA: Mercer University Press, 1983.

Garrett, William Robertson. "The Father of Representative Government in America." *American Historical Magazine* (January 1896): pages 2-21.

Genovese, Edward D. *Roll, Jordan, Roll.* New York: Oxford University Press, 1972.

Gilman, B. Malcolm. *The Huguenot Migration in Europe and America, Its Cause and Effect.* Red Bank, NJ: Published by the Arlington Laboratory for Clinical and Historical Research, 1962.

Glazebrook, Eugenia and Preston G. Glazebrook. *Hanover County Migrations, Volume I.* Richmond, VA: Privately published by the authors, 1943.

Goochland County, Virginia, Wills and Deeds, 1728-1736. Richmond, VA: Virginia State Archives, pages 9, 58, 59.

Greenberg, Kenneth S. *Masters and Statesmen, The Political Culture of American Slavery.* Baltimore: Johns Hopkins University Press, 1985.

Grizzard, Frank E., Jr. *The Jamestown Colony: A Political, Social, and Cultural History.* Edited by D. Boyd Smith. Santa Barbara, CA: ABC-CLIO, Inc., 2007.

Gwathmey, John Hastings. *Twelve Virginia Counties where the Western Migration Began.* Petersburg, VA: The Dietz Press, 1937.

Haile, Edward Wright, ed. *Jamestown Narratives, Eyewitness Accounts of the Virginia Colony, The First Decade: 1607-1617.* Brighton and Hove, U.K.: Roundhouse, 1998.

Harris, Malcolm Hart. *History of Louisa County.* Richmond, VA: Dietz Press, 1936.

_____. *Old New Kent County.* Richmond, VA: Virginia Historical Society, privately published, 1977.

Hartz, Fred R. and Emilie K. Hartz, ed. *Genealogical Abstracts from the Georgia Journal, 1809-1818.* Milledgeville, GA: Gwendolyn Press, 1990 and 1995.

Hatch, Charles E., Jr. *The First Seventeen Years in Virginia, 1607-1624.* Charlottesville, VA: University Press of Virginia, 1957.

Henrico County, Virginia, Deeds, 1677-1705. Richmond, VA: Virginia State Archives.

Honeycutt, James E., and Ida C. Honeycutt. *A History of Richmond County.* Raleigh, NC: Edwards & Broughton Co., 1976.

Hopkins, Garland Evans. *York County Source Book.* Winchester, VA: Privately issued, 1942.

Horn, James. *A Land as God Made It.* New York: Basic Books, 2007.

Howe, Henry. *Virginia, Its History and Antiquities.* Charlotte, NC: Wm. R. Babcock, Publisher, 1845.

Huddleston, J. O., and Charles O. Walker. *From Heretics to Heroes: A Study of Religious Groups in Georgia, with Primary Emphasis on the Baptists.* Jasper, GA: Pickens Tech Press, 1976.

Hudson, James Paul. "A Knight's Tombstone" *Antiques Magazine* (June, 1967): pages 760-761.

James, Geo. Payne Rainsford. *The Huguenot.* London: Longman, Orme, Brown,

Green, 1839.

James, James Alton. *The Life of George Rogers Clark.* Chicago: The University of Chicago Press, 1928.

Jameson, J. Franklin, ed. *Narratives of Early Virginia, 1601-1625.* Original narrative edited by Lyon Gardner Tyler. New York, NY: Charles Scribner's Sons, 1907.

Jester, Annie L., and Martha Woodroof Hiden, comp. and ed. *Adventures of Purse and Person, Virginia, 1607-1625,* 2nd edition. Princeton, NJ: Princeton University Press, 1964.

Johnson, Charles A. *The Frontier Camp Meeting.* Dallas: SMU Press, 1955.

Kelso, William M. *Jamestown, the Buried Truth.* Charlottesville, VA: University of Virginia Press, 2006.

Kennerly, Karen. *The Slave Who Bought His Freedom—Equiano's Story.* New York: Dutton, 1971.

Kupperman, Karen Ordahl. *Captain John Smith.* Chapel Hill, NC: University of North Carolina Press, 1988.

Kurth, Peter. *Anastasia, The Riddle of Anna Anderson.* Boston, New York, Toronto, London: Little, Brown and Co., 1983.

Lancaster, Robert Bolling. *Early History of Hanover County Virginia and Its Large and Important Contributions to the American Revolution.* Hanover, VA: Hanover County Historical Society, 1979.

Lassiter. Mable S. *Pattern of Timeless Moments—a History of Montgomery County, North Carolina.* Troy, NC: privately published, 1975.

Leonard, Cynthia Miller, comp. *The General Assembly of Virginia, 1619-1978.* Richmond, VA: Published for the General Assembly of Virginia by the Virginia State Library, 1978. Book is located at the Virginia Historical Society, Richmond, VA.

Littlefield, Daniel C. *Rice and Slaves: Ethnicity and the Slave Trade in Colonial South Carolina.* Champaigne, IL: University of Illinois Press, 1991.

Low, W. Augustus, and Virgil A. Clift, eds. *Encyclopedia of Black America.* New York: McGraw-Hill Book Co., 1981.

Lumpkin, William L. *Baptist Foundations in the South.* Nashville: Broadman Press, 1961.

Manahan, John E. "British Origins of Old Virginia Families" address to Virginia Genealogical Society, August 1, 1966. Charlottesville, VA: privately published, 1966.

_____. "Coats of Arms at Manakintowne." *The Huguenot,* Volume 19 (1961): pages 118-121.

_____. "Cavaliers of the Northern Neck in the 17th Century." *Northern Neck Historical Magazine III,* No. 1, (December 1953).

_____. "The Old Families of Northumberland" *Northumberland County Historical Society Bulletin,* Volume VI (1969).

Mason, George Carrington. "The Colonial History of New Kent." *The Commonwealth Magazine of Virginia* (1954): pages 69-74.

Matthews, Blakely H. *History of Rocky River Church.* Wadesboro, NC: privately published, 1900. Pages 1-12. Housed in Baptist Historical Collection of Wake

Forest University, Winston-Salem, North Carolina.

McBeth, H. Leon. *The Baptist Heritage.* Nashville, TN: Broadman Press, 1987.

McDonald, James J. *Life in Old Virginia.* Norfolk, VA: Old Virginia Publishing Co., 1907.

McIlwaine, H.R. "The Huguenot Settlement at Manakin Towne." *The Huguenot,* Volume 6 (1933): pages 66-77.

Meade, Bishop William. *Old Churches, Ministers, and Families of Virginia.* Philadelphia: J. B. Lippincott Company, 1906. (Orig. published 1857.)

Medley, Mary L., ed. *History of Anson County, North Carolina, (1760-1976).* Charlotte, NC: Heritage Printers, Inc., 1976.

Meltzer, Milton. *The American Revolutionaries, a History in Their Own Words, 1750-1800.* New York: Harper Collins, 1987.

Meyer, Virginia M., revised and ed. *John Frederick Dorman's Adventures of Purse and Person, Virginia 1607-1624/5,* 3rd edition. Richmond, VA: Dietz Press, Inc., 1987.

Miller, John Chester. *The Wolf by the Ears—Thomas Jefferson and Slavery.* New York, NY: New York Free Press, 1977.

Miller, Kiri. *Traveling Home: Sacred Harp Singing and American Pluralism.* Urbana and Chicago: University of Illinois Press, 2008.

_____, ed. *The Chattahoochee Musical Convention, 1852-2002.* Carrollton, GA: The Sacred Harp Museum, 2002.

Mitchell, Mabell White. "Huguenot Musicians." *The Huguenot,* Volume 6 (1933): pages 118-119.

Monroe County Historical Society. *Monroe County, Georgia—a History.* Forsyth, GA: Monroe County Historical Society, 1979.

Morgan, Philip Morgan, ed. *Don't Grieve after Me—the Black Experience in Virginia, 1619-1986.* Hampton, VA: Virginia Foundation for the Humanities and Hampton University, 2006.

Morison, Samuel Eliot. *The Oxford History of the American People, Volume 2.* New York: Oxford University Press, 1965.

Music, David W., and Paul A. Richardson. *I Will Sing the Wondrous Story.* Macon, GA: Mercer University Press, 2008.

Music, David W., ed. *We'll Shout and Sing Hosanna, Essays on Church Music in Honor of William J. Reynolds.* Fort Worth, TX: Southwestern Baptist Theological Seminary, 1998.

Norton, Kay. *Baptist Offspring, Southern Midwife—Jesse Mercer's Cluster of Spiritual Songs (1810).* Sterling Heights, MI: Harmonie Press, 2002.

Orgel, Stephen, ed. *The Oxford Shakespeare.* New York, NY: Oxford University Press, 1987.

Osbeck, Kenneth W. *101 Hymn Stories.* Grand Rapids, MI: Kregel Publications, 1982.

Parent, Anthony S., Jr. "Either a Fool or a Fury: the Emergence of Paternalism in Colonial Virginia Slave Society." PhD diss., University of California, Los Angeles, 1982.

Paschal, George Washington. *History of North Carolina Baptists 1663-1805.* Raleigh, NC: Printed by Edwards and Broughton Company; published by Raleigh

General Board, North Carolina Baptist State Convention, 1930.

Peterson, Harold L. *The Book of the Continental Soldier.* Harrisburg, PA: The Stackpole Company, 1968.

Powell, William S., James K. Huhta, and Thomas J. Farnham, eds. *The Regulators in North Carolina, a Documentary History 1759-1776.* Raleigh, NC: State Department of Archives and History, 1971.

Price, John Milton, intro. *The Civil War Tax in Louisiana, 1865 Direct Tax to States, August, 1861.* Baton Rouge, LA: Provincial Press, Fourth edition, 2003.

Public Record Office, The National Archives (U.K.): Will of Martha Garrett of Scottow, Norfolk, dated 3 February, 1625/6 (mother of "Temperance Yardlie alias <http://www.nationalarchives.gov.uk/documentsonline>. Accessed May 30, 2010.

Purefoy, George W. *A History of the Sandy Creek Baptist Association.* New York: Sheldon & Co., Publishers, 1859.

Quarles, Benjamin. *The Negro in the American Revolution.* Chapel Hill, NC: University of North Carolina Press, 1961.

Ratliff, Dr. W. M. *Biography of Ralph Freeman.* Greenville, SC: Privately published, 1942. Winston-Salem, NC: Baptist Historical Collection of Z. Smith Reynolds Library at Wake Forest University, pages 1-7.

Reamon, G. Elmore. *The Trail of the Huguenots in Europe, U.S., South Africa and Canada.* Toronto, Canada: Thomas Allen Limited, 1963.

Rose, Willie Lee. *A Documentary History of Slavery in North America.* New York, NY: Oxford University Press, 1976.

Rossingham, Edmund. *Interrogatories, 1629/30, March 18—1630, November.* 1 manuscript. Located in Colonial Williamsburg Special Collection of John D. Rockefeller, Jr. Library in Williamsburg, VA. Edmund Rossingham was a nephew to Temperance Flowerdew Yeardley and one of the two burgesses elected from Flowerdew Hundred to the first General Assembly in 1619. The other burgess was James Jefferson, ancestor of Thomas Jefferson, which provides a circumstantial link of families as early neighbors on James River.

Rouse, J. K. *Historical Shadows of Cabarrus County, North Carolina.* Charlotte, NC: Crabtree Press, 1970, pages 1-7.

Siegel, Frederick F. *The Roots of Southern Distinctiveness: Tobacco and Society in Danville, Virginia, 1780-1865.* Chapel Hill: University of North Carolina Press, 1987.

Simmons-Henry, Linda, ed. *The Heritage of Blacks in North Carolina, Volume I.* Charlotte, NC: published by the African-American Heritage Foundation and Delmar Publishing Company, 1990.

Singleton, Theresa A., ed. *The Archaeology of Slavery & Plantation Life.* Orlando, FL: Academic Press, 1985.

Skinner, Elliott P., ed. *Peoples and Cultures of Africa.* New York: Doubleday/Natural History Press, 1973.

Smiles, Samuel. *The Huguenots in France after the Revocation of the Edict of Nantes.* New York: Harper and Brothers, 1874.

Southall, James P. C. "Concerning George Yeardley and Temperance Flowerdew."

Virginia Magazine of History and Biography (1947): pages 259-266.

Spears, John R. *The American Slave Trade, 1900.* Reprint, New York, NY: Kennikut Press, 1967.

State Records of North Carolina, Volume XXI, 1788-1790. Letter of 26 May, 1788, from John Jay in the U.S. Office of Foreign Affairs regarding *Mr. Dumas* located in the collection of Governor's correspondence in North Carolina State Archives, Raleigh, NC.

Staton, John Samuel, ed. *Bicentennial History of Rocky River Missionary Baptist Church.* Burnsville Township, Anson County, NC: Privately published, 1976. 73 pages. Located in the Baptist Historical Collection of Z. Smith Reynolds Library at Wake Forest University, Winston-Salem, NC.

Tadman, Michael. *Speculation and Slaves.* Madison: University of Wisconsin Press, 1996.

"The Story of the Huguenot's Sword." *Harper's Magazine* (April 1857): Chapters I-XII.

Turman, Nora Miller. *George Yeardley, Governor of Virginia.* Richmond, VA: Garrett and Massie, Inc., 1959.

Upshur, Thomas Trackle, "Sir George Yeardley, Governor and Captain-General of Virginia, and Temperance, Lady Yeardley, and some of their Descendants." *American Historical Magazine* (October 1896): pages 1-6.

Vestry Book of King William Parish, Virginia, 1707-1750. Midlothian, VA: Huguenot Society of the Founders of Manakin in the Colony of Virginia, 1966; reprinted 1988. Book is accessed online through the Virginia Historical Society and is available for purchase through the Huguenot Society of the Founders of Manakin in the Colony of Virginia at Manakin Episcopal Church in Midlothian, Virginia.

Waldman, Milton, 1952. *Queen Elizabeth I.* London: Collins, St. James's Place, 1952.

Walvin, James. *Slavery and the Slave Trade.* Jackson, MS: University Press of Mississippi, 1983.

Waters, Henry Fitz-Gilbert. *Genealogical Gleanings in England.* Boston, MA: New England Genealogical Society, 1901.

Watkins, Vincent, comp. *York County, Virginia—Deeds, Orders, Wills, Book Three, 1657-1662.* Poquoson, VA: Poquoson, 1989. Includes Croshaw litigation, family property; pages 75, 84, 86, 88, 90, 93. Earliest known extant parish register of the Colony of Virginia; now on microfilm in the Library of Virginia, Richmond, VA; see www.lva.virginia.gov.

Weisiger, Benjamin B., III. *York County, Virginia, Records, 1659-1662.* Athens, GA: New Papyrus Publishing, Company, 1989. Transcriptions of recorded wills, deeds, orders, depositions, etc.; includes legal recordings of Joseph Croshaw and his son-in-law, Henry White, grandfather of Unity Smith Dumas.

Weiss, M. Charles. *History of the French Protestant Refugees.* Translated by William Herbert. New York: Stringer and Townsend, 1854.

Whitelaw, Ralph T. *Virginia's Eastern Shore, Volume I.* Camden, ME: Picton Press, 1951; reprinted 1989, pages 286-287.

Williams, Carolyn White. *History of Jones County, Georgia, 1807-1907*. Fernandina Beach, FL: Wolfe Publishing Co., 1951.

Williams, Lorraine Malone. "Education in Redbone Community." *History of Lamar County, Georgia*. Barnesville, GA: Privately published reprint, 2003.

Wilson, John H. *The Dumas Families, Volume I* and *Volume II*. Fort Worth, TX: privately published, 1986.

Wilson, John H., Carine Dumas Nolan, and Lorena Craighead Dumas. *Dumas Families of Union Parish, Louisiana: The Dumas Reunion*. Fort Worth, TX: Privately published, 1979.

Wise, Jennings C. *The Early History of the Eastern Shore of Virginia*. Baltimore, MD: Regional Publishing Co., 1967.

Woolman, John. *Some Considerations on the Keeping of Negroes*. Originally published 1753. Irvine, CA: Reprint Services, Corp., 1999.

Wright-Smith, Annie Laurie, compiled and alphabetized. *The Quit Rent Rolls of Virginia, 1704*. Richmond, VA: Expert Letter Writing Company, 1957.

Wright, Louis B., ed. *The Prose Works of William Byrd of Westover*. Cambridge: Belknap Press of Harvard University Press, 1966.

Yardley, Capt. J. H. R. *Before the Mayflower*. New York: Doubleday Doran & Co., Inc., 1931.

INDEX

Carwell, John, 65
Chambless, Z., 174, 180
Chancellorsville, Battle of, 140
Charente River, 186
Charleston, 156, 226
Charlottesville, 176, 194
Chattahoochee Musical Convention, 45
Chattanooga, 133
Cherry Ridge, 74, 76
Chesapeake Bay, 212, 231
Chetham, John, 200
Civil War, 18, 30, 55, 70, 73, 137, 227
Clark, Don, 13
Clark, Frances, 92, 103
Clark, John, 103–104, 117, 143, 177
Clark, William, 103
Clark's Creek, 104
College of Arms, 229
College of William and Mary, 205
Collier, Winifred, 33, 48, 62
Collier, Nancy, 49, 62
Collier, Randolph H., 49
Colony of Virginia, 175, 182, 190, 194, 205
Columbus, 204
Colwell, Betty Rose, 160–163
Comingtee Plantation, 226
Confederacy, 140
Congress, 154, 156
Corinth, 19
County of Hanover, 194–195
Covington, B. H., 127
Creek Indians, 104
Crenshaw, Douglas, 125
Crenshaw, Mabel Dumas, 95, 103, 125–128
Croshaw, Captain Raleigh, 190, 203
Croshaw, Elizabeth Yeardley, 190
Croshaw, Joseph, 190, 203–204
Culpepper, John, 153–159
Culpepper, Martha McClendon, 143

D
Dacus, Margaret, 2
Dahlonega, 70
Dallas, 5, 13
Dames, Colonial, 9, 218
Davisson, Ananias, 129
de la Fontaine, Jacques, 177–179, 183–184
de Medici, Catherine, 169–170
Debedevon, Chief, 212, 231
DeBerry, John, 137
Declaration of Independence, 200
Delaware, 210

Demons, Isles of, 209
Denson, Paine, 35
Denson, "Uncle" Tom, 5
Department of Transportation, 105
Depression, 9, 13, 21
Desert Storm, 132
Doddridge, Philip, 102
Donne, John, 233
Dudley, Robert, 206
Dumas, Aaron David, 29, 33, 48, 50–51
Dumas, Alexandre, 34, 83, 112
Dumas, Annie Lee, 115
Dumas, Asia, 110–112, 116, 118, 134, 137–138, 159
Dumas, Sarah, 97–98, 100
Dumas, Benjamin
I, 1–2, 26, 28–29, 31, 33, 36, 39–40, 49–53, 57–58, 62, 64, 66–67, 70–71, 73, 79, 96, 99, 102,103–105, 137–138, 143, 145–148, 153, 154,160, 163, 166, 168, 176, 195, 198, 201–202
II, 137
III, 92, 100–102, 121, 123, 126–127, 129–130, 137–138, 145, 153–154, 163
Dumas, Charles, 30, 35
Dumas, Charlotte, 62
Dumas, Clara, 132–141, 226
Dumas, David, 29, 32–34, 48, 50–51, 62, 64, 92, 99–101, 106–107, 123–124, 126, 137–138, 146–147, 152, 195
Dumas, Davie, 27, 30, 32, 34, 36, 48, 51, 62, 64, 83
Dumas, Edmund, 1, 3, 8, 13, 28, 32, 36–38, 40–45, 48, 58, 62, 94–95, 98, 100, 122–123, 128, 134, 163, 202, 217, 220
Dumas, Isabel, 40, 62, 94, 98
Dumas, James Franklin, 2, 87
Dumas, Jean, 164, 186
Dumas, Jeremiah, 2, 15, 18, 26, 41, 52, 66–67, 70, 72, 76, 79, 187, 220
Dumas, Jeremie, 184–187, 220
Dumas, Jerome, 104, 143, 160, 168, 172–173, 175–177, 179, 194–198, 201–203
Dumas, Margaret, 16
Dumas, Martha, 50, 62, 98–99, 127
Dumas, Martha Urcery, 39
Dumas, Martha Ussery, 29, 50, 109, 127
Dumas, Mathen, 168
Dumas, Terry, 4
Dumas, Phillip, 34
Dumas, Obadiah, 138
Dumas, Obediah, 92

Mercer University, 154
Michaux, Abraham, 188
Midlothian (Virginia), 167
Mississippi, 19, 60, 67–68
Mississippi River, 67
Missouri, 44
Monroe, Dumas, 33, 51
Monroe Advertiser, 27–28, 30, 32–35, 51
Monroe County, 1, 9, 27–29, 32–34, 37,
    49–51, 77
Montgomery County, 96, 115, 138, 154
Monticello, 195, 201
Montpelier, 188
Moore, William, 117, 150
Moorman, Sarah, 92
Mount Gilead, 103, 105, 107, 109–111, 115–
    116, 118, 135, 137–138, 159, 220
Moyers, Bill, 6
Mulberry Island, 210
Murphreesboro, 140
Music, David W., 151
Musical Arts Conservatory, 14

N
National Huguenot Society, 169
Navarre, Henry of, 170
Nehemiah, 92
Nelly (Aunt), 58
Netherlands, 124, 171, 204–205
New Britain, 6–7
New Orleans, 32, 132–133
New World, 176–177, 201, 204–205, 212–
    214, 219, 232
Newport News, 208
Newton, Jane, 52
Newton, John, 47, 83, 114
Nicholson, Lieutenant Governor Francis,
    177
Nixon, Richard, 136
Nolan, Burch, 4
Nolan, Carine Dumas, 9, 14–15
Nolan, David Burch, 10, 73
Nolan, Dumas, 9, 14
Norfolk, 190, 208, 229
Norfolk County, 190, 208, 229
North America, 213, 227, 233
North Carolina, 94, 103–104, 109, 111, 123,
    127, 135, 137–138, 159, 198, 202
North Carolina Legislature, 96, 158
North Carolina State Library, 105, 125, 144
North Cobb County, 94

O
Oakhurst Baptist Church, 143
Old Hundred, 94–95, 134, 200
Olympics, 25
O'Neal, W.S., 43
Opala, Joe, 87
Opechancanough, 204

P
Parish of Saint Paul, 194–195, 198
Parish of Saint Peter, 198
Parish of Union, 14, 75, 160
Parker, Battle of, 140
Parker Crossroads, Battle of, 140
Parliament, 169, 178
Peachtree Street, 24
Peedee River, 105, 108–109, 118, 123, 126
Pemberton Mall, 67
Philadelphia, 106, 123
Philip III, 204
Phoenix, 140
Pike County, 49
Pleasant Grove Academy, 38
Plunkett, John, 45
Pocahontas, 227
Poitou Province, 186
Polite, Thomalind Martin, 226
Ponce de Leon Baptist Church, 143
Pope Alexander VI, 204
Pope Leo X., 171
Potomac, 204
Powhatan, 204
Purefoy, George W., 151

R
Raleigh, 103, 105, 116, 148
Raleigh, Sir Walter, 213
Raleigh Tavern, 108
Ramah Church, 58
Randolph, William, 195
Read, David, 23
Rees, J. P., 46
Reese, H. S., 122
Reese, J. P., 44
Revere, Paul, 171
Revolutionary War, 126–127, 138, 145, 152
Richardson, Paul A., 151
Richmond, 96, 128, 144, 174–175, 192–194,
    197, 208, 215, 220, 227
Richmond County, 96, 128, 144, 151
Riviore, Apollos, 170
Robinson, Mistress Mary, 231